God Still Matters

Continuum Icons

Great books never go out of style, but they can go out of print. The Icons series is an attractively packaged collection of the greatest works of well-known authors. Enjoy them for the first time, or take some time to reacquaint yourself with these wonderful writers.

Books in the series include:

God Still Matters

Herbert McCabe OP

Edited by
Brian Davies OP

continuum
LONDON • NEW YORK

CONTINUUM
The Tower Building, 11 York Road, London SE1 7NX
15 East 26th Street, New York NY 10010

www.continuumbooks.com

First published 2002
This edition published 2005

British Library Cataloguing-in-Publication Data
A catalogue record for this book is available from the British
Library.

ISBN: 0-8264-7669-4 (paperback)

Typeset by Kenneth Burnley, Wirral, Cheshire
Printed and bound in Great Britain by MPG Books Ltd, Bodmin,
Cornwall

Contents

Contents

Foreword

It is not easy to be a Thomist. Partly this is because of the complexity of Aquinas's work. What makes that work an exemplar for Catholic thinking is Aquinas's insistence on making theology answerable to the questioning of natural reason, by taking philosophical enquiry as far as it can be taken, yet doing so in order that natural reasoning should recognize its limits and that at those limits it points beyond itself to and needs to be instructed by God's self-revelation. And partly it is because so many generations of commentary have interposed themselves between us and the texts. So that instead of learning from Aquinas how to do again for our own time what he did for his, we are all too apt to become mere expositors and, even worse, when we read Aquinas through the eyes of commentators, expositors of expositors.

It was Herbert McCabe's remarkable achievement to understand Aquinas both in his own terms and in ours and so to overcome these difficulties. The result was a theology that was characteristically Thomist and yet distinctively McCabe. Herbert's ability to make Aquinas's questions his own he owed to his Dominican teachers. But his earlier education had prepared him well. At St Mary's College in Middlesbrough he had received that solid grounding of a conventional kind that is indispensable for those who are going to be able to break out into genuine originality. At Manchester University he had been taught by Dorothy Emmet, whose fate it was to provoke her most gifted pupils into sharp, but constructive disagreement of a dialectically skilful kind, so that when, as a Dominican student brother, his teacher was Victor White, he had learned how to learn what Aquinas has to teach. It was Victor White's gift not to interpose himself between the student and the text, but to teach his students how to be open to what the text discloses. And this is what Herbert learned.

Victor White and the other Dominicans who became Herbert's teachers belonged to a remarkable generation in the history of the English Province. In the nineteen thirties when English society was economically and culturally divided and embittered, they had engaged with it by providing a model of critical integrity, insisting on holding together – within a Thomistic theological framework – what others took to be disparate and opposed truths. I think here of such friars as Thomas Gilby and Gervase Mathew. It was the latter who identified the source of that integrity in the primacy accorded by Dominicans to the contemplative appropriation of truth: 'action was never to be the purpose of contemplation, but always its natural result'.

What these Dominican teachers communicated to Herbert and his contemporaries was a certain temper of mind and heart, defined by this understanding of contemplation and action. What they did not provide, and could not have provided, was a set of directions for the Dominican mission in England to take in the decades after the Second World War, and this for several reasons. First, English society underwent extraordinary changes from 1945 onwards, a history of patched over disruptions and discontinuities, and part of that history was the transformation of universities, institutions for which Dominicans have always recognized a peculiar pastoral and intellectual responsibility. So Herbert's Dominican generation had to learn how to speak to the condition of a new kind of student, something that Herbert achieved with varying, but sometimes dazzling, success.

Secondly, the philosophical landscape had changed. It had become impossible to avoid reckoning with Wittgenstein, and Wittgenstein's philosophy too was a mode of questioning and requestioning. So good work in philosophy required Herbert to learn how to address both Thomas's questions and Wittgenstein's within a single enquiry. And, thirdly, the politics of England and Ireland from the sixties onwards called for a new kind of radical vocation, one that involved rethinking our relationship to Marx. No one could have made these three tasks his own, as Herbert did, without becoming involved in tension and conflict. But he was able throughout to draw on the resources of long-standing friendships: with Eric John who brought the resources of an historian to the same questions, with Anthony Kenny to whose understanding of Wittgenstein Herbert was greatly in debt, with Terry Eagleton whose Marxist insights took on a new theological life in Herbert's thought. Herbert also learned, perhaps more often than he recognized, from those with whom he disputed. I think here of Cornelius Ernst.

One aspect of Herbert's theology is particularly worth noting: its Wittgensteinian and Thomistic understanding of human beings as embodied minds and of the human body as expressive in its deeds and its words, an understanding which is a prologue to reflection on God's self-revelation through His Word made flesh and through His sacramental presence. A human body is never a mere physical object and a human being is not a physical object plus a mind. Both physicalism and dualism obscure what it is to be human. And a central task for theology, understood as Herbert understood it, is to enable human beings to understand what they are *qua* human beings.

Much of Herbert's best writing took the form of homilies, essays, and lectures. They were often intended to be occasional pieces, but they were always more than that. Through them he still speaks to us and argues with us, both in the collection that he himself made, *God Matters* (1987) and in this new collection. Some of those who wrote about Herbert immediately after his death tended, quite understandably, to dwell on what seemed to them colourful and eccentric. Yet the effect of reading what he wrote, like that of listening to what he said, is to be continually recalled to what is truly central to our lives and with it to recognize that, if Herbert sometimes seemed to be at odds with what made for intellectual and social acceptability in late twentieth-century England, it was not so much because he was eccentric, but because it was.

ALASDAIR MACINTYRE
April 2002

Introduction

Herbert McCabe, who died in 2001, was one of the most intelligent Roman Catholic thinkers of the twentieth century. An influence on philosophers such as Anthony Kenny and Alasdair MacIntyre, he also befriended poets and literary critics such as Seamus Heaney and Terry Eagleton. Equally at home in theology and philosophy, he despised jargon and intellectual posturing as a substitute for reason and argument. He was a notable advocate of the teachings of St Thomas Aquinas, but he was also prepared to ask questions that Aquinas did not ask. He was a faithful Catholic priest, but his view of the Catholic Church was thoroughly unsentimental. And he was an extraordinary preacher.

In 1987 McCabe published a collection of lectures, papers, and sermons under the title *God Matters*. The present volume reflects the structure of that book (hence its title) and gives readers a further chance to hear McCabe speak on the topics which chiefly interested him: philosophy of God, Christology, Fundamental theology, Sacramental theology, and ethics. Like *God Matters*, the present volume also includes some of McCabe's sermons. In due course, I hope to be able to edit for publication one or more volumes of these, for he left many behind at the time of his death.

McCabe was born on 2 August 1926 in Middlesbrough and was baptized John Ignatius. In 1944 he went to study chemistry at Manchester University, but he graduated in philosophy. He was well known in the then small and intimate wartime university and was active in its Catholic student circles. In 1949 he joined the Dominican Order (the Order of Preachers, founded by St Dominic). As a Dominican student he was taught by several notable English Dominicans including Victor White, Daniel Callus, Gervase Mathew, and Columba Ryan. He took solemn vows as a Dominican in 1953 and was ordained to the Roman Catholic priesthood in 1955. He then worked at an inner city parish in Newcastle upon Tyne. Later he was sent to Manchester to find a suitable house near the university to replace the Dominican parish house in Salford. From there he travelled to lecture on theology and philosophy to student societies in most of the universities of Britain.

In 1965 McCabe was sent to Cambridge to become Editor of *New Blackfriars*, a journal published by the English Dominicans and devoted to theology, philosophy, and literature. In its February 1967 issue he wrote an editorial prompted by the departure from the Church of Fr Charles Davis, then commonly regarded as the most distinguished of English Roman Catholic theologians. The editorial argued that the manifest corruption of the Church was no good reason for leaving her. It led to McCabe's dismissal as Editor of *New Blackfriars*. It also led to his suspension from the priesthood – a move that was rescinded after five days. The whole sorry story of McCabe's editorial and its aftermath was later documented by Simon Clements and Monica Lawlor in *The McCabe Affair* (1967).

The 1970 Provincial Chapter of the English Dominicans reappointed McCabe as Editor of *New Blackfriars*. During years that followed he was active as a preacher throughout the United Kingdom. He also worked as a visiting lecturer in the Department of Theology and Religious Studies at Bristol University. He paid regular teaching visits to the United States and to the University of Malta, but, for most of his teaching life, his home was Blackfriars, Oxford, from which he continued to edit *New Blackfriars*, and where he lectured for twenty-five years. The Novitiate of the English Dominicans was at Blackfriars for a long time, and McCabe was Novice Master there from 1981 to 1988. He did not relish being in charge of friars in formation (he was always uncomfortable as an authority figure), but he turned to his Oxford teaching with vigour and enthusiasm and was a brilliant lecturer.

His great love was the thought of Thomas Aquinas, an author whom he approached in a truly original way (in acknowledgement of which the Dominican Order fittingly conferred on him its highest intellectual honour, the degree of Master of Theology). McCabe was unsympathetic to the project of treating Aquinas as an authority on all things whose ideas should be uncritically accepted with no reference to developments in philosophy and theology since the thirteenth century. He had a horror of being referred to as a 'Thomist'. He aimed to approach Aquinas as a contributor to contemporary discussions. In doing so he was particularly sensitive to the work of philosophers in the analytical tradition, especially Ludwig Wittgenstein, whose thought he believed to be in many ways close to that of Aquinas. McCabe was well aware of the fact that Wittgenstein and Aquinas speak in very different voices, but he was able to tease out similarities between them and to use them to good effect, especially with respect to topics in philosophical psychology and philosophy of language or meaning. Some of his thinking on these subjects can be found in *God Matters*. Also of significance is Volume 3 of the Blackfriars edition of Aquinas's *Summa Theologiae* (1964) in which McCabe translated and commented on Aquinas's teaching on the way in which we can know and talk about God. On McCabe's reading, Aquinas clearly emerges as a negative theologian – as someone concerned to stress what we do not know about God.

Central to McCabe's thinking was the idea that God can be no inhabitant of the world, no conceivable object alongside anything we can imagine. God, as he once put it, is 'the unknown beyond and behind the whole universe' who 'does not come within the scope of our interpretation of the world or our language'. In his Commentary on Aristotle's *Peri Hermeneias*, Aquinas maintains that God exists 'outside the realm of existents, as a cause from which pours forth everything that exists in all its variant forms'. And this was very much McCabe's position, one that he employed to notable effect in, for example, his discussions of the problem of evil. Theists frequently argue that God's moral goodness can be defended since much evil is due to human free choice and not to God. But this way of thinking found no place in McCabe's teachings. He took it as idolatrous to conceive of God as a moral agent, whether well or badly behaved. And, while anxious to deny that God directly causes sin, his view of God as the source of all created reality led him frequently to insist that God is at work even in human free choices. 'Whatever my freedom means', he argued, 'it cannot mean not depending (in the creative sense) on God.' For him, 'God brings about all my free actions and . . . this does not make them any the less free.' As he put it in one place: 'The creative causal power of God does not operate on me from outside, as an alternative to me; it is the creative causal power of God that makes me *me*.'

Wittgenstein held that philosophy leaves everything as it is. McCabe held that there is a sense in which the philosophy of God leaves everything as it is since God makes no difference to anything: not because God is impotent, but because God is the reason why there is anything at all. Yet McCabe was very much concerned with the difference that people can make. So he always had strong interests in moral philosophy. Some of his ideas on this subject came to print in *Law, Love and Language* (1968), in which he lucidly presents a complex view of the human being as embodied communicator. Drawing on Aquinas and Wittgenstein, the book provides a clearheaded philosophical context for all ethical enquiry, including theological enquiry. Later in his life McCabe displayed the same gifts of economy, lucidity, and insight in *The Teaching of the Catholic Church* (1985). This book was designed as a catechism, but it is as remarkable for its questions as for its answers. It includes not only the questions that we ought to ask yet may not have asked, but also, to an extent that is unusual in catechisms, the questions that many of us do actually ask.

One of McCabe's great gifts was the ability to ask pointed questions. Readers of what follows will quickly get a sense of how that was so. They will also get a sense of how good a communicator McCabe was. Clarity and conciseness were notably present in almost everything he wrote, as the present collection bears witness. Most of its contents are previously unpublished. For permission to include 'God', 'Aquinas on the Trinity', and 'Aquinas on Good Sense', I am grateful to the Editor of *New Blackfriars*. For permission to include 'The Logic of Mysticism', 'Prayer', 'Christ and Politics', and 'Sense and Sensibility', I am grateful to Cambridge University Press, the Editor of *Doctrine and Life*, the Editor of *The Month*, and the Editor of *International Philosophical Quarterly*. Some of the material in this Introduction originally appeared in *The Times*, London, 11 July 2001, and is published here with permission. For help with the copy editing and reading of proofs for this book I am very grateful to Michael Moreland and Fr David J. White.

BRIAN DAVIES OP

Part One

God

One

God

'God', 'Theos', 'Deus' is of course a name borrowed from paganism; we take it out of its proper context, where it is used for talking about the gods, and use it for our own purposes. This is quite a legitimate piece of borrowing and quite safe so long as it does not mislead us into thinking that the God we worship (or don't) is a god. We always do have to speak of our God with borrowed words; it is one of the special things about our God that there are no peculiarly appropriate words that belong to him, as with the language of carpentry or computer-speak. He is always dressed verbally in second-hand clothes that don't fit him very well. We always have to be on our guard against taking these clothes as revealing who and what he is.

For this reason it is sometimes safer to use clothes that are quite obviously second-hand, words that have been quite scandalously ripped from their proper context and stretched and bent and distorted to suit our purposes. That is one reason for preferring 'The Father' to 'God' as a name for our God. 'The Father' is manifestly being used in a metaphorical or extended sense and so is unlikely to mislead us. It is also the word that Jesus prefers to use.

For Christians any talk about God has to take account of and perhaps start from the radical change that Jesus made in our understanding of the divine. It has to start, in fact, from what we have come to call the Trinity. Jesus did two things – well, he did a whole lot of things, but two that interest me at the moment – first, he introduced us to a new and shocking concept of love. I don't mean he simply gave us a new idea, he actually gave us the love which is the foundation of the Christian movement, an understanding of love developed from the Jewish Old Testament prophets that we have gradually become familiar with over the centuries, the love we have called *agape* or *charity* and which we at least profess to value above all other things. Putting such a high value on this kind of love is a characteristic of Christians – I mean, Jews of Old Testament times did, of course, discover this, but it was Jews of New Testament times who made it central to their lives. I don't think Buddhists or Muslims are quite so obsessed with love – so that John could say, 'He who does not love does not know God; for God is love.' So first of all Jesus is the source of this love, he gave a new and specially deep sense to the word; and secondly he said unequivocally that the Father loved *him*, and this was the most remarkable claim he made.

This is because Christian love implies equality; it is distinct from philanthropy, it is different from being kindly, affectionate, caring. There can be a perfectly good and honourable and life-enhancing relationship between unequals, between, even let us say, master and slave. A master sometimes can be kindly and considerate to his slave, the slave can be loyal and affectionate towards his master: all this within the terms of his slavery. The master's kindness does not make him any less a master, the slave's affection does not make him any less a slave. There are all sorts of humane and good human relationships that can grow up within and be sustained by hierarchical structures. Within the relationship of superior and inferior there can be communications which are in no way dehumanizing – or at least which do not *have* to be dehumanizing. Consider the relationship of parents and children, of schoolteachers and pupils, consider – by association of ideas – the relationship between owners and pet animals. These relations need not be harsh, they need not involve bullying. There can be authority and obedience which is not domination and subservience. All these can be very good relationships, but they are not in themselves love.

They are not love because love begins and ends in equality. In a sense to love just is to see the equality of another. Love can coexist for a while within structures of hierarchy, of superiors and inferiors, but in the end it corrodes and subverts them precisely because its drive is always towards equality. Now obviously I am using 'equality' here in a very special sense: people who love each other do not have to be exactly equal in height, or in IQ, but they have discovered an equality which makes all such differences irrelevant. And because the differences are irrelevant, they will, if they are man-made, finally disappear. That is why love is slowly corrosive of hierarchy, and vice versa.

Hierarchy is something very ancient and deep among human beings. It belonged to millions upon millions of years of our *pre*linguistic ancestors. It is to be found pretty well everywhere amongst the developed mammals and other animals. It is ingrained in our bones. But with us it is slowly subverted by love. Christianity, amongst other things, is the movement of humankind away from hierarchy and in the direction of love. Let me say it again; hierarchical structures are not evil or even necessarily unloving, and they are much better than individualist anarchy, but they are not love. We will shed them as we have already shed our tails.

The turning point of human history, the moment when we realized what we were about, the moment when we saw that the meaning of being human was love, was the crucifixion of Jesus. This marks a break comparable with, but even more radical than, the breakthrough to language, the emergence of the linguistic animal. With the gospel it becomes definitive that what we are about is loving, not kindliness and caring (not *just* kindliness and caring) but the special relationship of equality, of recognizing the otherness and independence of others. And so all structures of hierarchy, whether overtly benign or exploitative and unjust, become relativized and temporary and irrelevant.

Let me put it this way: we *grow up* into loving. It is not something we begin with. It is something that, if we are lucky, we learn. To be able to love, to recognize the equality of another, to recognize another person for who she or he is in herself or himself and not just as object to me, as recipient of my favour or subservient to my command – all this is something that comes with maturity; indeed it *is* maturity. The infantile world is an hierarchical one and we stay in it for most of our lives.

I am inclined to think that the discovery of adult love between equals is rather a chancy thing, and most of the time we settle for something less than love. If I may say so in passing, it seems to me that the structures of the Church are for the most part hierarchical structures of authority and obedience rather than of love. I don't mean by this that they are necessarily loveless, still less that they are consciously opposed to or inhibiting of love. But they function at a different level, they evade the adventure of love, the risk of love, they can very easily remain fixated at an immature, even infantile, level.

We learn to love when we grow up and discover an equal. Now the problem is that it seems God the creator of heaven and earth simply cannot discover an equal; he can it seems never therefore discover what it is to love creatures. Of course he can be kind and forbearing and take care of his creatures, he can be in this sense loving – as indeed he is said to love Israel in Hosea and Deuteronomy and elsewhere. But this does not have to be love in the sense that since Jesus we have come to understand it. Can this be the real abandonment to an equal that adult love implies? It is plainly impossible for God to have this kind of love for creatures precisely because they are creatures and totally dependent on him for everything they are and everything they have, including their human freedom. He may be immensely kindly and good to them but he cannot be in love with them, any more than you can literally be in love with a pet dog. A prisoner in solitary confinement can develop a perfectly genuine relationship with a pet spider, which keeps him sane. The prisoner can have real affection and concern for the spider. But if he thinks he is in love with the spider then pathology has taken over.

Now it is even more absurd for God to be in love with a creature than it is for the prisoner to be in love with the spider. The gulf is absolute; there is, it seems, no way in which a creature can be equal to God, no way therefore in which a creature can be loved by God in the full sense, in the adult sense in which we fleetingly achieve love, a love between equals. God therefore seems confined to an infantile relationship of authority to his creatures, he is not capable of the self-abandonment that love involves, there is no one to whom he could abandon himself. In this sense surely we are more adult, more mature than God. And this is what Nietzsche saw and that is why, since Nietzsche, bourgeois Europe has been atheist; its religion, it seems, has lingered on only as a form of infantilism. Religion, like childhood, is charming, perhaps more suitable for women, anyway for unliberated women, but has to be regretfully put aside when we enter the adult world – or thankfully put aside, depending on the kind of childhood we envisage.

For God, the creator and manipulator of the world, cannot himself, it seems, be other than a vast omnipotent baby, unable to grow up, unable to abandon himself in love. Nietzsche, and, from a different starting point, Karl Marx, saw that to accept this God was to accept a kind of slavery. However kind and good God might be, we were ultimately his servants; perhaps well-treated servants or slaves, perhaps slaves compassionately forgiven and rewarded with the life of heaven, but still fundamentally slaves. If you believe that the essence of the human is freedom then you cannot accept this benign slave-master of a God. The heart of modern atheism, certainly the heart of Marxist atheism, lies in the rejection of this master-slave relationship. God is not rejected because he is evil or cruel but because he is alienating and paternalist; he is rejected not in the name of human happiness but in the name of human freedom.

Now to a Christian the interesting thing is that this God who is rejected by the modern atheist is in fact pre-christian. It is just this God that is abandoned first by the Ten Commandments and then by Jesus. The central thing that Jesus says is something he says about himself; it is that the Father loves him. His primary announcement is that the Father *is*, after all, capable of love, that after all God has grown up. God is capable of love and he, Jesus, is the object of that love. Of course God cannot love the creature as such, there could be no foundation of equality there. But Jesus announces himself as the beloved of the Father and this reveals a depth in him that is beyond creaturehood. To say that Jesus is divine and to say that God is capable of love is to proclaim one and the same doctrine. Any unitarian view of God, or Arian view of Christ, immediately destroys the possibility of divine love – I mean divine love in the serious adult sense. We are left with a benign dictator, what Bishop John Robinson in *Honest to God* called a 'Top Person'. It is only the doctrine of the divinity of Christ (and thus the doctrine of the Trinity) that makes possible the astounding and daring idea that God can after all genuinely love. He is in love with the Son, and the exchange of divine love between them is the Holy Spirit.

Of course it remains that God cannot love his creatures as such – he can merely be kind to them. The adult love of God belongs within the Trinitarian life of the Godhead, the Father can only love what is divine. But as Jesus announces that God is grown up, that he can love, he does so by announcing that he is loved by the Father and simultaneously announces that we are taken up into this love. (There is no gap between God in himself and God-for-me.) God cannot, of course, love us as creatures, but 'in Christ' we are taken up into the exchange of love between the Father and the incarnate and human Son, we are filled with the Holy Spirit, we become part of the divine life. We call this 'grace'. By grace we ourselves share in the divine and that is how God can love us.

As creatures, as having our human nature, we cannot be loved by God, only kindly treated. But because we are given a share in the life of Christ, because we are filled with the Spirit, because we have grace, we are divine, and, like Christ, we are the beloved of God. Well, not just like Christ; the Father loves us in the very love that he has for Christ, in the Holy Spirit.

Notice that, so far, we have not said anything about sin. It is not precisely because we are sinners that God cannot love us. It is because we are creatures. We need not only to be forgiven from sin but to be divinized from simple creaturehood. Though of course sin is nothing but our deliberate settling for simple creaturehood, settling for what we are, for what we can achieve, closing ourselves off and rejecting the gift of God's love, the adventure of transcendence, the risks of divinity.

So with Christianity God ceases to be primarily the creator God, Lord of the universe. The gospel is that he is primarily the lover of Jesus Christ. With Christianity the ultimate activity is not making or doing, creating, but love. The primary reality, the reality that lies at the very depth of humanity, the divine reality, is not even creativity, but love.

So the gospel announces that our fundamental relationship to God is not that of creature to creator – a relationship which cannot but be one of servant to master. For the gospel, our fundamental relationship is that of lovers, of lovers in equality. We have this equality to the Father because we are given a share in the life of Christ.

In Jesus we have one who, of course, owes his being to the Father, but one who is not created but loved into existence; for, of course, it is not that the Son first exists and then is loved by the Father, his divine existence is for him eternally to be loved by the Father. This is what Jesus announces to us: that the very centre and heart of his being is his being loved by the Father, he exists only in this relationship to the Father. When he searches into his own identity, when he asks himself 'Who am I?' he finds that the ultimate thing about him is the Father's love. And by grace, by our receiving the Holy Spirit, by our sharing in the death and life of Christ, this becomes the ultimate thing about us too. Not that we are created, but that we are loved. We are not objects of the Godhead, but, by being in Christ, we are within the Godhead. The difference between our divinity, our divinization through grace, and the divinity of Christ himself is just that our divinity is a gift from the Father through Christ, the gift we call the Holy Spirit. This is the precise meaning of the statement that it is grace that makes us free. This does not mean that without grace we are incapable of free decisions; it means that without grace we are stuck in a servant/master relationship to God (and an unfaithful servant at that) instead of participating in the divine life itself. Our freedom in this sense is precisely the 'glorious freedom of the children of God' – where 'children' is contrasted not with adults but with 'servants of the household.' Without this divine life we are, as Paul puts it, 'under the law' – he means the moral law of God. Without this divine life we would have to live according to rules laid down by our master, our creator. Excellent rules, of course; none other than the way of life that would lead to human flourishing and fulfilment and happiness, liberated from idolatry and all the gods, but nonetheless rules laid down by our master and maker. To live ultimately under law in this sense, even a good law, is in the end to be a slave. There is of course nothing wrong with laws; they are a necessary part of social life. But to be obedient to a law is not, for the gospel, the essence of man, the deepest thing about him. The essence of man is freedom. It is a mysterious fact about human beings that even to conform to the law of our own being is to be restricted. We naturally tend beyond ourselves.

Without grace we are subject to law, slaves to the lawmaker; but more than that: since as a matter of history we cannot be without grace except by rejecting it, since we cannot in fact be without grace except through sin, we are not only slaves but guilty slaves. The illusory God that we envisage when we depart from grace is the God of righteous wrath, the punitive avenging God – the projection of our guilt into the skies. It makes little or no difference whether we think of this God as real or unreal, whether we are in this sense atheists or not (for, as I say, modern atheism is precisely the rejection of this supreme boss). Faith in the Christian sense springs only from our being in grace, from our own sharing in the divine life. The man who has rejected grace can only envisage God in a distorted punitive form. What we call the forgiveness of sin is nothing other than our being given the gift of shifting from the punitive image of God to a true vision of the God who is totally in love with us, who is absolutely and unconditionally loving, who loves us whether we are sinners or not. But to realize this, to believe this, is to be freed from sin.

So with the gospel we move from seeing God primarily as creator, as author of the world and hence of the natural and moral order of the world, to seeing the Trinitarian life of God which we are called to share. We see God as primarily engaged in loving and only secondarily concerned with creating.

But we must not lose sight of the creative side of God, for on this hangs the autonomy of our own nature. We are not just divine; we are divinized human beings and human nature has its own reality and autonomy. We may be saved, in one sense, by faith alone, but we certainly do not live by faith alone; we live also by human communication, human society, by language and intelligence, by human affection, by human contrivance. It is, I suppose, a specially Catholic and, I think, Jewish thing to defend the autonomy and rights of the nature in which we were created, to reject any view that exalts the importance of grace at the expense of seeing nothing in nature, of seeing nature as totally corrupt.

To acknowledge the Trinitarian Godhead then is not to deny God as creator, it is simply to refuse to settle for God as creator, it is to refuse to be content with a creature/creator, slave/master relationship with God. This sets us the task of accommodating the creator God within the context of the Trinitarian God of love. From the standpoint of our shared divinity we can see the act of creation in the perspective of the redemption, in the perspective of our call to divine life. We can see the act of creation as itself an act of love.

For this purpose it may be more helpful to picture God as space rather than as an object. Think for a moment about space. In the material world space is, of course, a relative concept, relative in fact to the size of our bodies and the range of our senses. We are accustomed, quite rightly, to contrast the solid matter of the earth with the vacant interstellar spaces. But, apart from the fact that, after a few miles down, the earth is mainly liquid anyway, we are all familiar with the idea that, molecularly speaking, solids are mostly empty space and, conversely, there is presumably a macroscopic view from which our galaxies constitute the particles of a solid. Space then is a merely relative concept referring to the obviousness or relative unobviousness of the contact between things. Absolutely speaking all things are in contact, over a greater or less distance. I am interested here in a metaphor, you will understand. So far as our impersonal context is concerned we are hemmed in by things. What provides us with space, real free space, is other people, the love we receive from others.

To love others is: we can put it two ways: we can say it is to give them themselves or we can say it is to give them nothing – the priceless gift of nothing, which means space in which to move freely, to grow and become themselves. Every gift we give to others (apart from the gift of ourselves) imposes something upon them – they have about them something of ours, if it is only a new tie or a drink. But love, which is the gift of ourselves, does not *add* anything to them from outside, it is the gift of the space in which they can be themselves. You can see this quite clearly in the love of parents for children, especially if we contrast it with counterfeit love and possessiveness. Children with genuinely loving parents are able to be free, they are secure enough to be spontaneous, to be really themselves. Without this love they are left to the impersonal world which hems them in and ties them down. They haven't got room to breathe. Nothing, empty space, is not what we start from, we cannot take it for granted as though it would be there anyway. Nothing is very precious and is created by persons for each other, it is the pre-requisite of freedom. God in this sense is the great primordial source of nothing. I should say, I suppose, that we should 'take it for granted' because it always has to be granted. And only if it is granted can we grow into ourselves. We receive ourselves at each other's hands. Not because we make and mould each other, but because we let each other be. Nature will not let you be. Only persons can let you be.

Love of course is very similar to indifference, even though it is as different as anything could be. Indifference is the caricature of love. Indifference says: 'I don't *care* what he does.' Love says: 'I don't care *what* he does.' The picture I drew earlier of the absolutely unconditionally loving God who loves us whether we are sinners or not, could be caricatured as a God of indifference, for whom sin does not matter. But this God of indifference would in fact be merely the other side of the punitive God, it would not be far from the atheism which rejects the punitive God and yet has never come across the loving Trinitarian Godhead.

How to discern the immense abyss between love and indifference, I won't go into now. It's a gap that is a millimetre wide and a thousand miles deep. It is just that indifference is a way of protecting yourself, while love is a way of risking yourself so that another can be.

Once we have seen how the gift of love, the gift of yourself, can, by giving space, by giving nothing, enhance the life and freedom of others, we can see how love is a source of life, and we can at least pretend to ourselves that we can see what might be meant by 'being loved into being', the procession of the Son from the Father.

But creation too is an act of love, it is the giving of a world in which things and ourselves can be. Creation too, as we saw, is not an interference with things. Any other kind of making, any making within the world changes things, but creation obviously does not change anything, or add anything to things; it makes things to be what they are, it does not make them any different. It should be clear that if we take the notion of creation seriously we cannot think that creation leaves any vestiges in things. Creation unlike other causal actions does not just make things to be like this instead of like that; it makes them to be rather than not to be at all.

Creation, then, does not make any difference to things. If you like, it makes *all* the difference, but you cannot expect to find a 'created look' about things. The effect of creation is just that things are there, being themselves, instead of nothing. Creation is, of course, an unintelligible notion. I mean it is unintelligible in the sense that God is unintelligible. It is a mystery. Not that the notion is self-contradictory, but it involves extrapolating from what we can understand to what we are only trying to understand. To be created is to exist instead of nothing; but the notion of 'nothing' is itself a mystery unintelligible to us.

Unless we grasp the truth that creation means leaving the world to be itself, to run itself by its own scientific laws so that things behave in accordance with their own natures and not at the arbitrary behest of some god, we shall never begin to understand that the Lord we worship is not a god but the unknown reason why there is anything instead of nothing. We know of God not by understanding him but by recognizing that there are questions which impose themselves on us to which we reach out to answer but cannot yet. In this phase of grace, in this life so far, we cannot see an answer to our question – only that it is a genuine question demanding an answer – in this era we can have no concept of God. As Aquinas said, 'We cannot know God in himself, we know him only from his effects.' We live only in faith and not in seeing for ourselves. Even the revelation of God's Son as a human being is just the greatest of the effects of God among his creatures. Through him we have faith that all these effects are the works of God's love for us. We will see God when we no longer have faith but clear knowledge, when we have died with Christ and so shared in his resurrection, to share in the eternal life of the Trinity of knowledge and love, the life of Father, Son and Holy Spirit.

Two

The Logic of Mysticism

This title represents, I suppose, a kind of challenge; for there seems at first sight some incompatibility between the practice of logic and mysticism, a contrast between the rational and the intuitive, the tough-minded and the tender-minded. In taking up this challenge, I propose to argue with the help of two thinkers commonly admired for their attention to logic and its rights. I shall refer for the most part to St Thomas Aquinas but with occasional reference to Wittgenstein. Whatever may be said of the latter, it seems to me quite clear that St Thomas was a mystical thinker in that he was centrally concerned with the unknown and, in one sense, ineffable mystery of God and that he devoted a great deal of thought and writing to the problems associated with speaking of what is, in this sense, ineffable. I want to argue that in what is sometimes misunderstood as his dryly rational approach, even in his arguments for the existence of God, he is in fact engaged in, and inviting the reader to be engaged in, a mystical exploration, which is not at all the same thing as a mystical experience. Here the key notion is that of what he refers to as *esse*.

Perhaps I should say right away that for St Thomas we come to see the need for the particular use he has for the word *esse* (which is, after all, only the Latin infinitive of the verb to be) as the result of an argument, not as the result of an experience – not even the experience of being convinced by an argument. It is a central thesis of his that we grasp the use of this word not as we grasp other meanings – by what he calls simplex *apprehensio*, the having of a concept or the understanding of a meaning, such as having learnt and not forgotten the meaning of, say, '*fatwah*' – but as we deploy such concepts in the making of true or false judgements which issue not in meanings but in statements. It is not simply in our capacity to use signs, our ability, for example, to understand words, but in our actual use of them to say what is the case that we have need of and lay hold on the *esse* of things. It is only by analogy that we can speak of the 'concept' of *esse*, we do not have a concept of existence as we have a concept of greenness or prevarication or polar bears.

In order to make sense of this use of *esse* I shall need to begin with our familiar understanding of things existing and not existing. It is generally believed that there are no dodos any more. If, however, the rumour arose that some had survived in the remote interior of Mauritius, an expedition might set forth for these parts to inquire into the matter. Whatever else these explorers brought with them, an essential piece of equipment would be some understanding of what distinguishes dodos from parrots and ptarmigans. They would have to grasp the meaning of the word 'dodo' sufficiently to be able, in that geographical context, to pick out dodos from other things. They would then hope to discover something that fitted their formula: some x, such that x was a dodo. It is in just such a context that the conventional account of what it is to say that something exists is at home. Philosophers have been anxious to point out that when we want to know whether dodos exist we do not go and look at dodos to see whether they have existence or not; we go to see whether there is anything at all that would count as a dodo. It was a point familiar to Aristotle and to medieval thinkers: to ask *an sit* (whether it is) you have to start with at least some meaning for a word.

Suppose, then, to everyone's surprise, we are successful and we find some dodos. We shall then have answered the question *an sit*. Having done so we shall be able to settle down with them in their proper habitat, and by living amongst them over the years we may come slowly to some *scientia*, some scientific understanding of what is essential to being a dodo, what it takes for it to exist at all, and what is merely adventitious, as, for example, living exclusively in Mauritius or looking slightly ridiculous to slightly ridiculous European observers. This will ordinarily involve the elaboration of a new section of language or a jargon. What first struck people about dodos was their apparent foolishness and clumsiness, hence the original Portuguese name *'doudo'*, meaning awkward, and the international term *'didus ineptus'*. As we came to understand more clearly the nature of the dodo, its essence or substance, we should have probably devised some quite new name to signify this nature. In this way chemists devised the sign H_2O, the meaning of which (that is, its relationship to such other signs as $HC1$, CO_2, etc.) expresses, on the one hand, the essential structure common to such apparently quite diverse objects as those called 'ice', 'water' and 'steam', and, on the other hand, the natural physical relationships of such substances to what used to be called 'muriatic acid' and 'carbonic acid gas'. We should, in fact, try to devise a jargon with a structure of meanings reflecting the actual structures of the physical, chemical, biological world. Thus we should get closer to what an Aristotelian would call a definition expressing the essence of the thing, we would be closer to answering the new question: *quid sit?* – what does it take for such a thing to exist? If, as Aristotle remarked, there is nothing corresponding to our definition, nothing with this essence, then what looks like a definition of the essence is, in fact, nothing more than an explanation of the meaning of a word.

Understanding of what a dodo is would come ordinarily from a lengthy process of observation and experiment, a process I have called 'living with' the object of our study, and for this to take place there obviously have to be such objects. So, to repeat, we start with the common meaning of the name, sufficient for picking out the object in a particular context; we can then answer the question *an sit*, and if we answer that in the affirmative we can go on by investigation to get clearer about *quid sit*. Despite what nominalist philosophers may say, this is what ordinary working scientists such as chemists and botanists think they are sometimes engaged in. Our conventional account of what it is to say that tame tigers exist or that yetis do not exist is at home in just this context. Of course not all, in fact rather little, of our rational discourse is like doing chemistry – not even for chemists. One way of understanding our rational discourse concerning God is to see how radically it differs from this.

In seeking to show that we can prove the existence of God, that God's existence is *demonstrabile*, St Thomas faces a technical objection. In a true demonstration, as for example in the theorems of Euclid, we show not merely that something is the case but that it has to be the case. To demonstrate is to produce *scientia*, an understanding of how and why the world is as it is. Anyone may know that sugar, unlike marble, dissolves in water; it takes a physical chemist to show how this has to be the case given the molecular structure of the materials involved. His aim is to demonstrate that because of the nature of sugar, because of his definition of its essence, of course it dissolves.

The objector begins by stating that '*medium demonstrationis est quod quid est*', that the central link of demonstration is the defined nature (*Summa Theologiae*, Ia,2,2). Then, he argues, to demonstrate that God exists must be to show that, given the definition of his nature, he has to exist; but since we do not know the definition of his nature, but only what he is not, we cannot have a demonstration that he exists. The objector is arguing that the only demonstration that God exists would have to be something like the Anselmian ontological argument in which the existence of God is thought to follow logically from something about God's nature. St Thomas in reply does not deny that we are ignorant of God's nature, but he points out that answering the question *an sit* is quite other than the kind of demonstration in which you show how some operation or effect has to flow from a thing the definition of whose nature you already know. Trying to find if there are any yetis is quite different from trying to show that sugar has to dissolve in water. We go looking for footprints in the snow and if we find them we argue that, given this evidence, it has to be the case that yetis exist; we do not seek to show that yetis have to exist, just that they do. We are arguing that an opponent necessarily has to accept the proposition, not that the proposition is a necessary one.

In such an argument, then, we start not by knowing what God would be but only from features of the world we do know and which seem to be effects of God. It is our knowledge of these effects and not any knowledge of God's nature that gives us our rules for the use of the word 'God'. So you start by claiming that certain phenomena are effects, that they must have a cause. Not everything that is the case does have a cause: the stars in the night sky are arranged, it is alleged, in patterns reminiscent of various Greek gods and heroes, but it would be very odd to look for some power whose characteristic activity was the cause of this. But St Thomas, as is well-known, thought that certain phenomena such as real change from mere potentiality to actuality, and the power of certain things to effect such change, did demand causal explanation. So he answers his objector here: 'When we argue from effect to cause, the effect will take the place of the definition of the cause in the proof that the cause exists; and this is especially so if the cause is God. For when proving anything to exist the central link is not what that thing is (we cannot even ask what it is (*quid est*) until we know that it exists (*an est*)) but rather what we are using the name of the thing to mean. Now when demonstrating from effects that God exists, we are able to use as link what the word 'God' means, for, as we shall see, the names of God are derived from these effects' (*Summa Theologiae* Ia,2 ad 2).

In this reply, as it seems to me, St Thomas is, as so often, simply saying enough to answer an objection; not, as it were, showing his whole hand. We should in fact be misled if we took it that his arguments for the existence of

God start from a 'nominal definition' of God, as though he said: 'This is what people use the word "God" to mean, this is how we can at least pick out God from other things, now let us see if there is one.' It is, to my mind, of the greatest importance that his arguments end with, but certainly do not begin with: 'and this is what people call "God"'. The arguments do not presuppose any view of the nature of God, they simply begin with philosophical puzzles arising from features of the world that we understand and take us to what we do not understand. They start with questions we can answer and lead us to a question we cannot answer. St Thomas would accept Wittgenstein's statement: 'A question [can exist] only where there is an answer' (*Tractatus*: 6.51), but in this case we know that we cannot give the answer, for that would be to know God's nature, which is beyond the margins of our ways of grasping meanings. But of this more in a moment.

We need to take a brief look now at the kind of argument St Thomas has in mind. We may begin by noticing that there is some parallel between dependence in causality and dependence in information; indeed the latter is a particular case of the former. Some of the things I know I know because I am a witness to them, but most of what I know (and nearly all the interesting things) I do not know in that way but by hearsay. If I am to know by hearsay it is not, of course, sufficient merely to have been told. I must have been told by one who is reliable, and her reliability must be due either to her being herself a witness or else to her having had, in her turn, a reliable informant, and so on. Unless hearsay is finally anchored, as it were, in what is not hearsay but witness, there can be no reliable hearsay, only baseless rumour. I can really know what I am told only if there is or was someone who knows or knew without being told. Faith, which 'comes by hearing', has to depend on somebody's knowing.

This argument you will perhaps recognize as having the same logical structure as the one St Thomas sketches as the second of his Five Ways. If there are things that have to be brought from potentiality to existence by the power of another thing, there must be one or more things that are not under this condition, things that exist actively and are not brought into existence and activity by another. Just as what I am told is only as reliable as the witness who did not need to be told, just as the truth I think I know on hearsay depends totally on the truth of what that witness says, so the existence of anything that has to be brought into existence by another depends totally on the existence and activity of one that does not have to be so brought into existence. Note that in each case the conclusion of the argument is to something that is known negatively, to something that does NOT have a dependency of some sort. There is no suggestion of what, positively, such a being might be. All the arguments lead to a power which is not of a kind we understand: to an unknown God. When I repeat what I know by reliable hearsay I am ultimately being the mouthpiece of the original reliable witness. In the same way every creature that exercises its power to bring things or features of things into being is ultimately the instrument of the power which is not the instrument of anything.

It seems (though I shall want to qualify this later in the case of God) that nothing exists except by being something, some kind of thing. What exists does so by having a particular form. 'No entity without identity' as Quine used to say; *'forma dat esse'* as St Thomas used to say. When a cause brings an effect into being it does so by providing the form by which this effect is and has its particular essence – though in the case of caused features of things (which, as St Thomas says, rather *insunt* than *sunt*) we should perhaps speak of an 'inessence'. A cause in nature does this by giving a new form to what previously existed by another form but was capable of losing this (perishing or changing) and being given a new one. When I was brought into existence by my parents they trans-formed material things of various kinds – the food they had eaten, the genes they had inherited, into a material thing of a new kind, existing by a new *human* form we call a human *life*. Before I existed there was already a natural world of material things that were potentially of my kind – not in the sense that they themselves had the power to become human, but simply in the sense that they could be made into, trans-formed into, a human being; and there were other material things with the power to effect this trans-formation. Before I existed there was already a natural world with a me-shaped hole in it waiting to be filled by the active power of a cause. Now natural causality is like hearsay: trans-formation is a genuine source of existence, as hearsay is a genuine source of truth. The possibility of receiving existence from a merely trans-forming cause (like the possibility of receiving truth from mere hearsay) depends on anchorage in a being which is more than a trans-forming cause, a being which is the source of existence as the original witness is the source of a truth. Such a being would not make by the trans-forming of what already has another form, a making 'out of' what already exists. Its bringing into existence must take place without the attendance of a background world, without any background at all, not even empty space.

Natural causes, operating as trans-formers, provide the answer to the question: Why did these things come to exist instead of those others that used to exist or instead of those others that might have existed? Answer: Because they were brought about by this cause that operates in this particular way because of its own particular form. (Explanation by appeal to the specific causal powers of things within the world – things with their own special natures – is the characteristically Aristotelian alternative to the Platonic appeal to participation in the eternal forms.) God, on the other hand, would provide the answer to the question: Why is there anything at all rather than nothing? The object of natural trans-forming causes is the existence of something that has this or that particular form. The object of the divine creative cause is the existence of everything that has existence. I say that God *would* provide the answer to that question (Why is there anything instead of nothing?) because, since we do not know what God is, we do not have an answer to our question.

Natural agents can only have the power to bring things into existence by transformation because they are instruments of God's causality – just as hearsay can only convey truth because it is from the mouthpiece of the original witness. We can certainly say that it is the fire that brings into being the boiling of the water (because that is its nature and natural power); we also say, in a different tone of voice, that God, using the instrumentality of the fire, boils the kettle. Everything that is brought about by natural causes is brought about by God; and there are some things, like human free decisions, that are not brought about by any natural causes but *only* by God.

The artist's colours are arranged in blobs on his palette and his brush moves them and puts them in a new arrangement on the canvas so that a painting is made. In this way the power of the brush to move the paint makes a work of art. But that it makes a work of art is because it is wielded by the artist. In this illustration we can for the artist read *God*, for the paint-brush read *the natural trans-forming cause*; for the new arrangement of the paint read the new form, and for the work of art, *the new thing* that exists by this form.

We refer to natural trans-forming causes when, given the world, we want to ask scientific questions: Was it the fire that boiled the water or was it the microwave? We refer to God when we are asking a more radical question: Why do explanations explain what they do? Why do trans-forming causes bring things into existence? – as we might ask: Why is this hearsay reliable?

Given the natural world, we understand the natures of things by contrast with what they are not. Given the world, we understand what it is for this to exist through its particular form by contrast with what exists by another form. The structuralist is surely right here to insist that meanings consist in oppositions of contraries. This at least seems right when we are allowed to take the world for granted. But suppose we try to understand not simply what it is to exist by this particular form – to see it as the expectable product of this power in the world and not that – but the existence of the world itself. This would be trying to understand the power upon which particular powers depend for their efficacy. If it be true that there has to be such a power, then the world we take for granted must be *granted* in a much richer and more mysterious sense.

It is this gratuitousness of things that St Thomas calls their *esse*: their existence not just over-against the possibility that they might not have been a part of the world (if natural causes had operated differently – which is why the dodos do not exist), but their existence over-against the possibility that there might not have been any world at all. In thinking of the *esse* of things we are trying to think of them not just in relation to their natural causes but in their relation to a creator. If we can simply take the world for granted, then within this world to exist is just to be this kind of thing (there is an x such that x is a dodo), for things in the world that come into existence and perish (contingent things) there is a polarity of potential matter and actualizing form, but there is no demand for a polarity of essence and existence. It is only when we consider the world as created that we see that even non-contingent, 'necessary beings' (which would not, indeed, depend for their existence and meaning on other natural causes) would have a dependent existence in relation to God. So in all created things beyond the polarity belonging to contingency (based on the distinction of matter and form) there is the polarity of createdness (based on a distinction of essence and existence) which would belong to even 'necessary beings'. Only in the Uncreated is there no potentiality in any sense at all, not even a distinction of essence and existence; only the Uncreated exists without *having* existence. This distinction between contingency with respect to form and dependency with respect to existence is clearly spelled out in St Thomas's Third Way.

Put it this way: you may at some time have a very strong feeling of the gratuity of things, a quasi-religious experience as in nature-mysticism, which seems to contain or lead into a sense of gratitude for there being a world. In the Romantic tradition this was associated with the wilder countryside, especially Cumbria. The sense that we are here understanding some great truth is, however, vulnerable to recognizing the naturalness of nature, a scientific recognition of the complex causes by which the world just had to become the way it is. You may remember the story of the man expatiating on the wonders of Niagara Falls – all those thousands of tons of water cascading down every minute – and his friend who remarked: 'But, after all, what is there to stop it?' It is understandable that Victorian scientific rationalists should have sought to replace such Romantic nature-mysticism with the 'wonders of science' which seemed less likely to threaten them with metaphysics. 'Wonder' is, however, not part of the vocabulary of science, any more than is 'existence' or 'God' or, indeed, 'science'.

But there remains the wonder that there is science at all, that there is a world of powers and action and new existents. This is not itself one of the wonders of science, and however fascinating the work of physicists investigating the Big Bang it is not relevant to this mystery of gratuitousness, the createdness, the *esse* of things.

When I speak of science I am not restricting the term to the mathematically governed 'physical sciences'; I mean any and every account of how what happens in the world 'has to happen' (necessarily or naturally or of course). What characterizes science in this sense is not necessarily an appeal to mathematics but an appeal to an order of nature, to the essence and character of things such that they act in expectable ways. David Hume, for whose empiricist epistemology knowing was essentially a matter of having mental images, denied that things really have powers and tendencies and expectable behaviour, for while you may be able to make a picture of me balancing a billiard cue on my nose, you cannot in the same way make a picture of me being able or likely to perform this feat. However, knowing what things are capable of and likely to do is a large part of understanding what they are; a man who showed no surprise at all at seeing a rabbit chasing a wolf would show that he knew very little about the nature of rabbits and wolves. Our scientific understanding of what goes on around us is rooted in such expectations. But talk of *esse*, the gratuitousness of things, has no place, and ought to have no place, in such natural science.

When Wittgenstein in the *Tractatus* says, 'Not *how* the world is, is the mystical, but *that* it is' (6.44), it seems to me that he is engaged with the same question as St Thomas is when he speaks of *esse*. As St Thomas distinguishes between the creative act of God (which we do not understand) and natural causality (which we do), between creation and trans-formation, Wittgenstein distinguishes the mystical from 'what can be said' (6.53). Positivist interpretations of the *Tractatus* took this as a cheerful dismissal of all such metaphysical talk, but it now seems to be the general view that this was far from his intention and the unease which is shown (but cannot be said) at the end of the work is an unease with the sharp dichotomy of *either* scientific language *or* silence, an unease which perhaps subsequently bore fruit in his later stress on the multiplicity of language-games.

For St Thomas, then, the *esse* of things turns out to be their createdness, their gratuity; so that all talk of God has its foundation in the *esse* of creatures. This is not a reductionist view of God-talk (as though we were saying that all talk of God is 'really' about features of the world). It is not reductionist just because what is in question is their *esse* and this is not a feature of things that, for example, distinguishes them from other things: clearly we cannot set the class of existents over against a class of non-existents – not even an empty class of non-existents. We can however, as St Thomas points out, distinguish between nouns and noun-phrases such as 'the power of seeing' which refer to something that is, and terms such as 'blindness' which refer to an absence of what might have been expected to be. In that sense we can say that blindness is a non-being. We can also distinguish the sense in which a dog is, and the irreducibly distinct sense in which his barking is or in which he is upside-down or is in Germany. We can distinguish, in fact, different categories of being. What we cannot do is set a class of existent things, activities or relations over-against a shadowy class of non-existent things, activities, and relations. In a trivial sense you could say that what is common to absolutely everything is existence; but in saying this you would be conveying nothing at all: this Highest Common Factor is purchased at the cost of having no height at all. It is not in this way that *esse* is common to all – not, that is, as the asymptotic point at which specificity or determinateness vanishes altogether. No, *esse* is, in St Thomas's phrase, 'the actuality of every form', the determinately distinct actuality of every form.

For an Aristotelian, matter is what is relatively indeterminate and unstructured, waiting to be determined by some form or structure, the wood that may be made into the table, the table that may become part of the dining room suite. Matter in one form, one actualization, is said to be potential with respect to being actualized by some other form. You never catch matter without some form or other. Form is the relatively determining factor giving being and intelligibility to a thing. With this in mind we can see that in a definition which is made by differentiating a genus (as the specific difference, rational, determines the genus, animal, in the classical definition of the human), the meaning of the genus word 'animal' is, in a sense, material, potential, open, waiting to be determined by the differentia word 'rational' which determines *in what sense* this is an animal. So to say that a human being is a rational animal is logically quite different from saying that a milkman is a man employed to deliver the milk; for men employed to deliver the milk and men not so employed are men in exactly the same sense; whereas rational and irrational animals are not animals in the same sense. Being rational is not an adventitious accidental feature of a general-purposes animal, it is having a certain (specific) kind of animality; whereas being employed to deliver the milk is an adventitious accidental feature of a general-purposes human being and does not signify a special kind of humanity. You never catch anything that is simply generically an animal without being differentiated as this or that species, just as you never catch matter which is not actualized and determined by some form. So, to repeat, genus words are 'open' (material) words that need to have their meaning 'closed' (formally) by a specific difference.

Now it is an Aristotelian thesis that *esse*, being, is not simply the widest, most all-embracing, most 'open' or material of genus words; it is not a genus at all. Cornelius Ernst puts it well:

> The community of the indefinite variety of all that is in *esse* is not only trans-generic in the sense that ens is found in all the genera (substance, quality, quantity and so on); it is trans-generic in the more fundamental sense that it is quite unlike the community of genus at all. For while the community of genus is subordinate and quasi-material, awaiting the formal determination of specific difference, the community of *esse* is superordinate and quasi-formal, the community of whatever has already achieved its appropriate differentiation as this or that discriminate individual: as [St Thomas] puts it in the Summa Theologiae (1a.4,1*ad*3): *ipsum esse est actualitas omnium rerum, et etiam ipsarum formarum* [*esse* is the actuality of all things including forms themselves]. Or again (1a.8,1) corp.): *Esse autem est illud quod est magis intimum cuilibet, et quod profundius omnibus inest, cum sit formale respectu omnium quae in re sunt* [*esse* is that which is most intimate to each thing and what is in them most profoundly, for it is formative (*formale*) with respect to all that is in them]. (Ernst, 1972, pp. xx–xxi)

To go back to the painter with his brush and his (and its) achievement: this achievement, that of being a work of art, is the ultimate actuality (cf.

esse) which is the work of the painter in being the actuality of the paint-arranging (cf. trans-forming) achievement of the brush. The various works of Picasso may or may not have certain characteristic features in common, but when we say they are all Picasso's works we are not referring to these features or to any common feature, we are speaking simply of their common dependence on his action. The community of all things in *esse*, therefore, is their community as creatures of God, and it is this that is *das Mystische*.

The characteristic work of the paint-brush is to re-arrange paint, and simultaneously, in the same operation, the characteristic work of the artist wielding the brush is to make a painting: the work of the brush counts as painting because it is the work of the artist. It is thus the *esse* of things that leads us to speak of God – which for Wittgenstein in the *Tractatus* cannot be done. For him, we approach the mystical simply by recognizing the limits of what can be said. 'We feel that even if *all possible* scientific questions be answered, the problems of life have still not been touched at all. Of course there is then no question left, and just this is the answer' (6.52).

St Thomas does not give up so easily. He sets himself to understand how language is used in the biblical tradition to which he belonged. He whole-heartedly agrees that we cannot say what God is, and he sets himself the task of understanding how we could speak of what, being the source of *esse* itself, is outside the scope of the world of existents, of what could not be an inhabitant of any world or subject to any of the intelligible limitations implied in being such an inhabitant, of what could not be one kind of thing rather than another, nor of course subject to the special limitations of material spatio-temporal beings, of what could not be *here* and *then*. We construct and learn the meanings of our language, and thus acquire our concepts, in coping with our world characterized by all these limitations, and intelligible precisely in terms of these limitations, in terms of forms which have their meanings as opposed to and distinct from other forms. No such concepts could possibly express what it means to be God.

Nevertheless, St Thomas concludes that there are two considerations which make it possible to give sense to the traditional biblical God-talk: first that we can understand what God is not, and second that we can use words not only to say what they mean but also to point beyond what we understand them to mean.

In listing just now the reasons for finding God unintelligible, I was pointing to just the negative knowledge which can form a basis not only for the negative statements I was making but for positive statements as well.

Knowing what God is not can be a basis for saying (though not for understanding) what God is, or at least certain things about God. Let me give an example: God is intelligent (I think this may be what some people mean by saying that God is 'personal').

St Thomas regards both intelligence and intelligibility as a transcendence of material limitation. Sensation is necessarily subjective, rooted in this individual body with all its unique peculiarities. Because sensation is a kind of knowing, sensations are meanings. A meaning is always the role or function of some part in an organized structure – as, for instance, the meaning of a word is the part it plays in the language. The meaning which is a sensation is a bodily role, a meaning within the structure of my nervous system and brain. It is just in this way that sensing provides me with an interpretation of my world. Thus, for example, we determine whether a certain kind of animal has the sense of sight or not, not by looking to see if it has any eyes but by observing whether or not its behaviour (and hence its interpretation of the world) is any different when it is in the light or in the dark. It is because of this subjectivity of sensation that nobody else can have my sensation though, being the same kind of animal, they are likely to have similar ones. But with the advent of language we create a structure of meanings which is nobody's private domain. In principle nobody could have my sensation; but in principle everybody could have my thought. For the meanings of words are their roles not within the structure of any individual body but within the structure of language, which is in principle (in order to be language at all) shared by all. Because of the essential historicity of human language and human thought, it may be impossibly difficult in practice to think the thoughts of Homer or Moses, but at least we would here be failing in a task; there is no such task as having the sensations of Homer or Moses or of the man next door. For St Thomas, what is bodily and material about me constitutes my privacy, my individuality; whereas my intellectual capacities liberate me from the prison of my subjectivity. My thought can never be just mine as my sensations are mine (there could scarcely be a greater contrast with the world of René Descartes). St Thomas did, however, think (and brilliantly argued in a little book called *De Unitate Intellectus*, which we may translate as *Is there only a single mind?*) that the act of thinking my thought is my own – because my capacity to think it is a capacity of my soul which is individuated as being the form of this individual material body: in this sense my thinking is mine just as my walking or digesting is mine. My thinking is my capacity to transcend my individuality; it is my thinking of meanings which are not just mine.

The point of that excursus was to make the connection between immateriality and understanding. For St Thomas's way of thinking, whatever is not subject to material limitation is intelligent. He thought rationality, our form of intelligence, was the lowest kind, being the activity of a being whose existence was as a material bodily being, though having a capacity to transcend purely bodily action. It is, however, the only kind of intelligence we are able partially to understand. Because intelligence belongs to the immaterial, if we deny materiality to God we must say he is intelligent. Because of a piece of negative knowledge, we can make this positive statement. But of course we are not saying that God has our kind of intelligence, that he is limited to rationality. We do not, in fact, understand the intelligence we are attributing to God. We can confidently assert that God is intelligent (or 'personal') while cheerfully admitting that we do not know what intelligence would be in God.

By similar processes of argument we can attribute to him goodness, justice, power, and will without claiming to understand what these attributes would be in God. St Thomas, indeed, argues that having a multiplicity of attributes is itself a limitation that has to be denied of God. As they are in us, justice, mercy, intelligence, and happiness are distinct characteristics: no such divisions could have place in God. God, indeed, could not have any characteristics as he does not have existence. The mystery of his intelligence and the mystery of his mercy and of his justice must be just the one mystery which is God. It cannot be one thing for him to exist and another for him to be wise and another for him to be good. The predicates we attach to the word 'God' have, indeed, different meanings in that their meaning is derived from our understanding of these things as properties in our world, but what they refer to in God is a single mystery which is quite unknown to us. We have some understanding of the wisdom that God creates in us, but when we say that God is wise we mean neither that he is the creator of wisdom in us, nor simply that he is not foolish; we mean that the quality we call wisdom in us exists in God in some higher and utterly mysterious way (cf. *Summa Theologiae*, Ia,13,5).

If we are surprised that we should use the same words to refer in God to something quite different from what we use them to refer to in our world, St Thomas refers us to the common phenomenon of the analogous use of words. I may say that I love wine, my mistress, my country and my God, but nobody supposes that the word 'love' here signifies the same thing in each case. Nor does anyone suppose that I am merely making puns. It is common enough for a word to be used in different contexts with systematically different senses, with what St Thomas would call a different *modus significandi*. St Thomas argues that this is just what happens with a great deal of our language about God, especially when we are doing theology: with, however, this special feature that in the case of God we do not (yet) understand the *modus significandi* of the words we use. That will have to wait for the beatific vision when we shall know God by sharing in his self-knowledge. St Thomas did also think that even in this life we may share, through faith, in that divine self-knowledge, but faith seems to us rather a darkness, an awareness of ignorance, than an intellectual clarity.

So for St Thomas, when we speak of God we do not know what we are talking about. We are simply taking language from the familiar context in which we understand it and using it to point beyond what we understand into the mystery that surrounds and sustains the world we do partially understand.

St Thomas, however, also insists that the greater part of our religious language is not, and should not be, understood in this way: most of the language we use in speaking of or to God is not even used analogically but metaphorically, by an appeal to images. What he calls *Sacra Doctrina* – meaning God's activity in teaching us in and through Scripture – requires, he says, such imaginative language. We need a great many images, preferably incompatible images (God is a mighty fortress, a still small voice, a vine-dresser, a mother eagle, he is wrathful and he is compassionate, he is faithful to his word but he repents of what he has done, and so on); moreover, it is better to have many grotesque and base images (*sub figuris vilium corporum*), for all this preserves us from idolatry, from mistaking the image for God, from thinking of God as subject to the limitations of our imagery.

St Thomas distinguishes words like 'hearing', 'courageous', 'seeing', and 'wrathful', all of which have as part of their meaning a reference to what is material (you cannot be wrathful without the bodily emotions associated with aggression; you cannot see without eyes occupying a definite position in space) from words which, although we learn how to use them in bodily experience, do not have this physical reference as part of their meaning: as 'justice', for example, 'love' or 'goodness'. The former can only be used metaphorically, to provide images of the unknown God; the latter can be used to speak of him literally though only analogically, so leaving him still utterly mysterious to us.

For St Thomas, metaphor is the heart of religious language but it cannot be sufficient of itself. It needs to be underpinned by such non-metaphorical but analogical assertions as that God exists, that God is good, that God is the creative cause and sustainer of our world, that he is loving. It is these literal assertions that are subject to the caveat of analogy. Although we do not understand what they refer to in God, they are our way of asserting that the riches of religious imagery are more than the art-form of a particular culture (though, of course, they are that) but are part of our access to a mystery beyond our understanding which we do not create, but which rather creates us and our understanding and our whole world.

Three

The God of Truth

'God of truth, you hate those who serve false gods' – as it says in one of the psalms.

A lot of people have pointed out that pictures of hell are so much more interesting than pictures of heaven, and some people have argued that stories of wickedness are more fun than stories of virtue – though I think this depends on whether the stories are true or not. I am inclined to think that in real life, wickedness is mostly banal and boring; if only because the protagonists are so wrapped up in themselves that there is not enough variety.

Anyway, it occurred to me that one way of starting to talk about the God of truth would be to say just a little about the gods of falsehood. It is characteristic of false gods that they are nothing but *objects of worship*. They have no other reality. The God of truth has to exist in his own right whether we worship her or not; talk about the gods has to be talk about human belief and cultures.

For Jews and Christians and Muslims this thought, that false gods have no existence of their own, is not just a matter of opinion. Nor is it just a matter of rational consideration. It is a point of faith, very close to the foundation of our faith. We are commanded not to believe in the gods and, of course, not to worship them. The Ten Commandments, you may remember, begin: 'I am Yahweh, your God, who brought you out of slavery . . . you shall have no gods.'

Many in our Western society, which rather cheekily calls itself 'post-Christian', are of the opinion that there are no gods. But very rarely is this a matter of rational consideration. In any case they are mistaken; they have rather a lot of gods. Mostly they haven't given the matter much thought. So little thought that they vaguely imagine that the God of the Bible and the

Koran (neither of which they have read) is meant to be one of the gods. The price they pay for not bothering to think about all this is the tedium of listening to enthusiastic people who have rediscovered paganism and druids and witches and what not, the cult of which is thought to be somehow more 'ecological' than the faith of those who refuse to worship anything except the creator of the whole of nature, who loves it and finds it, or rather makes it, 'very good'. The price they pay for not being interested in God the Creator is that, if they do avoid the inanities of neo-paganism, they still make to themselves ridiculous gods and do not even know that they are doing so. And they worship these gods without even knowing that this is what they are doing.

Since I said that the gods are nothing but objects of worship, I had better say what I mean by worship: It is 'reverence or veneration paid to a being or power regarded as supernatural' (that's from the Oxford English Dictionary). The supernatural must mean what is above or beyond what fits into our natural or expectable order of things. Presumably there cannot be a physics of the supernatural or a technology for coping with the it. Nevertheless worship of the gods often does contain an element of what you might call quasi-technology. If the forms and rites of worship are performed correctly in the traditional way, then certain results will ensue. The god will be propitiated and stop doing whatever nasty things it may be engaged in, like blighting the crops or withholding the rain, or whatever. If it doesn't you have got the ritual wrong. The gods are more powerful than we are but they can be manipulated by presenting gifts of a kind they are known to like, or by flattering their vanity and so on. For the gods, powerful as they are, are still fellow members of the universe.

This, indeed, is the fundamental reason for *not* including the Creator (source of all being, truth, and goodness) among the gods. For whatever else the creator might be he, she or it, cannot be a part of what it creates. It would have to exist before it exists; which is a contradiction. Moreover since as creator it must bring about whatever exists or occurs in the universe, it cannot be influenced by, or manipulated by, or change its mind because of, anything in the universe.

But back to the gods. Many of the gods that we know about are thought to be generally malevolent towards humans. So propitiation is a big part of dealing with them. But there are others that quite like the human race, and there are gods with their own favourites (like Athena with Odysseus). It is clear that worship of any kind must always be directly related to *belief* rather than knowledge. Of course scientific knowledge itself presupposes a number of beliefs – some of them not quite so confidently held as they used to be (the belief, for example, in the general integrity and honesty of your fellow-workers in the field). Nevertheless scientific conclusions are more or less publicly checkable in a way that beliefs about the gods are not.

So, the worship of one of the gods is directly dependent on the belief that the object of the worship is part of the world order but nonetheless supernatural, not subject, or not altogether subject to the natural laws of physics or other sciences. A god has a mystique about it.

As an example of worshipping a familiar minor god let me take the British National Lottery. Since the time at least of Pascal there has existed a scientific account of the laws of probability. I don't want to go into details (mainly because I am incompetent) but it seems clear that if you want to increase the amount of spare cash you have without actually doing any work, your chances of doing so successfully by investing it in what look like reliable stock, or even just putting it on a deposit account in the bank, are, by a large factor, greater than if you buy a ticket or scratch card in the lottery. Yet a large number of people choose the lottery. The conclusion can only be that they regard it (probably without thinking of this) as supernatural, to some extent outside the order of nature. There is a mystique about the National Lottery and it has become part of the national religion, and also a lot of fun (but only for those with money to spare, as many who play the lottery have not).

Let us look at another much more important god, though nowadays one losing a little of its popularity: nuclear weapons. Nuclear weapons, people tell themselves, are to be used for deterrence. This means that according to the doctrine of Mutually Assured Destruction (MAD for short) we threaten to use them against an enemy if we detect him starting to use them against us – and with modern techniques we can detect them as they leave their silos on their way to destroy us. So for the faithful of this cult these weapons of mass destruction are really to preserve the peace. What this belief proposes is something like this: if a large part of our territory is reduced to a nuclear wasteland and most of the population is either starving or dying of radiation sicknesses, the best thing for us is to destroy or cripple the only source of medical help and food supplies that could rescue us, which is the enemy country. It is surely only by being efficiently invaded that at least some of us could be rescued. It is plain that no sane person could be taken in by the idea that if a lot of people are killed, the best thing is to kill a lot more, just as no sane person could think of the lottery as an efficient way to increase one's wealth without working for it. And so there is a mystique about nuclear weapons, they are gods, they are to be trusted irrationally although they are perfectly worthless and, indeed dangerous (for some lunatic might in an access of religious fervour, actually use them).

It will not have escaped your notice that while one reason for the existence of the lottery and nuclear weapons is that people need to cultivate illusions of sudden great wealth without working, or security and peace, again without working for it, another much more straightforward reason is that certain groups of people make a lot of money out of them in both cases – not, of course, by playing the lottery, but by running it, or, in the other case, by manufacturing the weapons.

So the gods have three characteristics: they perpetuate a false irrational account of the way things are; and secondly, they serve to legitimate the power of some group to dominate the rest. I do not mean to suggest that there is a conspiracy, that someone does this consciously and deliberately. The people whose power over others or relative wealth is consolidated by the worship of the gods will most likely be quite sincere and are perhaps as bamboozled as their victims. The third characteristic of the gods is that they cause suffering, in various degrees to their worshippers.

It would be tedious to list the well-known gods of this exceptionally superstitious twentieth century. Quite apart from surviving old ones like astrology, there are a lot of new ones like racism, nationalism, The Market, the Leader . . . you name it. It is quite easy to see why, as I was saying, that great atheist manifesto, the Ten Commandments, begins 'I am Yahweh your God who brought you out of slavery.' And it is easy to see why St John has Jesus proclaiming that 'the truth will set you free'.

So let us leave the gods temporarily behind and consider the God who is not a god, the God of truth. I would like to do this in two parts, each beginning very properly with a little quote from Scripture. First, Genesis saying: 'In the beginning God created the heavens and the earth'; and second, St Paul saying 'We preach Christ crucified' – the first being about what *God* is not, the second being about what *we* are not.

Around about the time of the prophet Ezekiel, the people who came to call themselves Jews began to understand rather clearly that Yahweh, their God, was not just their God, but the God of the whole universe. They were shortly to be encouraged in this view by the fact that Yahweh did not rescue them from exile by enabling them to defeat their enemies but rather by enabling Cyrus king of Persia to defeat their enemies. They quickly came to see that

Yahweh does not just preside over the destiny of the Jews but of all the peoples of the earth. From there it was a relatively short step to seeing God as creator of *all* the earth and the stars and whatnot. These Jews were convinced that it was unworthy of human beings to worship anything less than the creator of all things. To do so was an insult to the majesty of the creator and an insult to the dignity of human beings.

Once you have had the thought that God, Yahweh, is not a god but Creator, then you will see him as at work in all things and bringing to pass all events. You will see him as maker of my thoughts and decisions and of everything that happens – including my prayers. You might say that if there were any gods they too would be creatures of God.

Now if to tell the truth is to tell it like it is, then, since the Creator makes everything to be like it is, the creator is source of all truth. And moreover, if you have got rid of the gods who serve, amongst other things, as an explanation of why blights and earthquakes and good harvests happen, then the way lies open for you to seek the causes of what happens not outside the world, in the gods, but within the world itself.

The fifth-century Greeks got to somewhat the same point simply by being sceptical of their own gods. They did not have a notion of a creator, who makes it that the whole shebang should be there and that every event should occur. But at least they were inquisitive about the immediate causes of particular kinds of events and were able to give explanations, sometimes even accurate explanations, of what more barbarous people were content to refer to as the whim of the gods. In fact they got a great deal further than the pre-Christian Jews in such explanations. What they lacked, strangely enough, was the philosophical underpinning for such science by which such particular explanations are related back to the primal question: 'Yes, but why anything at all?' And this question was just the one that interested the Jews. They had the question, but of course they were well aware that they did not have, and could not have, an answer. They recognized that the creator was a mystery beyond human language and thought; they insisted that they could not name God. They could give names to (you might say: scientifically understand) all the beasts of the earth, but not to God.

In the Jewish/Christian/Islamic tradition we do not ask 'Does God make the kettle boil or is it the gas underneath?' We say the gas boils the kettle and God makes the gas to be such that it boils the kettle; because God makes everything that really happens. So the one God we can worship, who is the cause of *all* that is, allows us to speak of causes or particular things at another level, at the level we examine scientifically. There is no quarrel between the scientific project and worship of the creator; there is only sometimes a quarrel between science and the religion of the gods. What is curiously called Christian 'Creationism' is in fact a denial of the doctrine of creation, and makes God a mere god, a substitute for science.

So our God, the only God we worship and the only God that exists, liberates us to explore his world, to find order and truth and meaning in it. This God is the God of truth. But by our faith we also realize that God has revealed to us the truth about human life as well. The gods invariably claim to empower us in this way or that. There is nothing wrong with power so long as you do not worship it, so long as it is relativized and given its proper limited place in human life. At the heart of God's revelation to us is Christ without power, Christ crucified. This is the gospel, the good news: that the weakness of God, the suffering of God in the suffering of his people, is what really determines our destiny. 'Blessed are the victims, the poor, for theirs is the kingdom of God.'

That is why, whatever temporary political options we may make, whatever way we vote next time (and this, of course, is an extremely serious matter) we can never put our whole heart, our whole loyalty, our worship, in any government, in any group who want the power to solve our human problems. When we are confronted by promises of a new world, with new solutions to the obvious dreadfulness of our society, we may respect all this, we may vote for it, but we have learned to ask: who are the victims? Who is going to suffer? For it is there that we shall find Christ crucified. Christ our kind of king. It is there, not in the people of power, the people who manage, but in the people who suffer, that we will find our king. 'For I was hungry and you gave me food . . .' That magnificent passage from the Letter to the Colossians sums it all up: 'He has delivered us from the dominion of darkness and transferred us to the kingdom of his beloved Son, in whom we have redemption, the forgiveness of sins . . . For in him all the fullness of God was pleased to dwell, and through him to reconcile to himself all things, whether on earth or in heaven, making peace by the blood of his cross.' It is Christ's blood, God's blood, shed in agony and weakness and failure, that liberates us from darkness into light. It liberates us because it is the sign, the sacrament, of God's vulnerability: the weakness and vulnerability that belongs to human love.

For the cross is about the triumph of human love; that strange triumph that comes not through asserting yourself, nor even defending yourself, but by losing yourself in giving yourself to another. The truth about being human is in the love that God has, the love that God *is*, the triumph that God has by taking our humanity and losing himself in giving himself for us. The triumph of the love of God incarnate, the truth about humanity, was revealed when God was spat on and beaten and hanged from a cross – because that is what in truth we do to one of us who is really loving. God was made flesh and dwelt amongst us, and we killed him because we fear to admit love, and because he loved us too much to resist us. But simultaneously the truth about humanity is triumphant because in Christ it refuses to be defeated by us, by our scorn and contempt, our cynicism in the face of God's appeal to us. God will be among us, united with us, will share with us, at any cost, even at the cost of being totally rejected and killed.

Jesus, God the Son incarnate, lived out his life and death in obedience to the mission given him by his Father. He was sent to be among us, *to be human*. He was not sent with a secret message from God, some information to be confided to his disciples. He was simply sent to be human amongst frightened humans, distorted and twisted by sin; and all that Jesus did, and most especially all that was done to him, springs from this fact: that in obedience to his Father he was the first really *human* being, the first to live wholly by love, which is what being human is about. And so, of course, he was too dangerous to us to let him live. We got rid of him lest we should have to be human too. The truth revealed about us is complex and paradoxical. It is the blood of the cross that shows us the humanity of God, this Godfulness of a man. For humanity is not in truth just the shoddy thing that we have made of it. Humanity is about love and the suffering of love, and the triumph in this suffering.

This is what the God of truth reveals to us about ourselves: that it is not in the relative, limited, transient, and ambiguous power of technology, still less in the delusive power of the gods, that we come to and constitute the kingdom of heaven, but in the weakness and vulnerability of human love, made possible for us by our sharing in his divinity who shared in our humanity.

Four

Aquinas on the Trinity

That God is one and three is, of course, for Aquinas a profound mystery which we could not hope to know apart from divine revelation. But we can only begin to understand what he has to say about it if we recognize that for him God is a profound mystery anyway. There are people who think that the notion of God is a relatively clear one; you know where you are when you are simply talking about God whereas when it comes to the Trinity we move into the incomprehensible where our reason breaks down. To understand Aquinas it is essential to see that for him our reason has already broken down when we talk of God at all – at least it has broken down in the sense of recognizing what is beyond it. Dealing with God is trying to talk of what we cannot talk of, trying to think of what we cannot think, which is not to say that it involves nonsense or contradiction.

This similarity is sometimes obscured for us by the fact that Aquinas thinks we can prove the existence of God by natural reason whereas such unaided natural reason could tell us nothing of the Trinity. This, however, does not, for him, make the latter a mystery where the former is not, for he thought that to prove the existence of God was not to understand God but simply to prove the existence of a mystery. His arguments for the existence of God are arguments to show that there are real questions to which we do not and cannot know the answer. He seeks to show that it is proper to ask: 'Why is there anything at all instead of nothing at all?'; he seeks, that is, to show that it is not an idle question like 'How thick is the equator?' or 'What is the weight of Thursday week?' It is a question with an answer but one that we cannot know, and this answer all people, he says, call 'God'. He is never tired of repeating that we do not know what God is, we know only *that* God is and what he is *not* and everything we come to say of him, whether expressed in positive or negative statements, is based on this.

After his arguments for the existence of God, for the validity of our unanswerable question, he says,

> When we know that something is, it remains to inquire in what *way* it is so that we may know *what* it is. But since concerning God we cannot know what he is but only what he is not, we cannot consider in what way God is but only in what way he is not. So first we must ask in what way he is not, secondly how he may be known to us and thirdly how we may speak of him.

This, at the opening of Q.3, is his programme for the next ten questions and beyond. And none of the hundreds of questions that follow in the four volumes of the *Summa* marks a conscious departure from this austere principle. Indeed Aquinas constantly comes back to it explicitly or implicitly.

God must be incomprehensible to us precisely because he is creator of all that is and, as Aquinas puts it, outside the order of all beings. God therefore cannot be classified as any kind of being. God cannot be compared or contrasted with other things in respect of what they are like as dogs can be compared and contrasted with cats and both of them with stones or stars. God is not an inhabitant of the universe; he is the reason why there is a universe at all. God is in everything holding it constantly in existence but he is not located anywhere, nor is what it is to be God located anywhere in logical space. When you have finished classifying and counting all the things in the universe you cannot add: 'And also there is God.' When you have finished classifying and counting everything in the universe you have finished, period. There is no God in the world.

Given this extreme view of the mysteriousness and incomprehensibility of God we may well ask Aquinas how he thinks we have any meaning at all for the word 'God'. Surely if we do not know what God is, we do not know what 'God' means and theology must be a whole lot of codology. To know what a daisy is and to know the meaning of the word 'daisy' come to much the same thing. Aquinas replies that even among ordinary things we can sometimes know how to use a name without knowing anything much about the nature of the thing named. Thus the businessman may quite rationally order a computer system to deal with his office work without having the faintest idea of how a computer works. His meaning for the word 'computer' is not derived precisely from knowing what a computer is, it is derived from the effect that it has on his business. Now Aquinas says that with God it is like this but more so. We have our meaning for the word 'God', we know how to use it, not because of anything at all that we know about God, but simply from the effects of God, creatures. Principally that they *are* instead of there being nothing. But the businessman is better off because knowing what a computer is for is a very large part of knowing what it is. Whereas God does not exist in order to make creatures. So the meaning of 'God' is not the same as the meaning of 'the existence of things instead of there not being anything'; we have the word 'God' because the existence of things instead of there not being anything is mysterious to us (and, Aquinas argues in the five ways, ought to be mysterious to us).

What we say of the word 'God' has also to be said of every other word we use of God; if we speak of God as good or wise it is not because we understand what it is for God to be good or wise – we are wholly in the dark about this – we use these and similar words because of certain things we know about creatures. When we do this we take words which have at least a fairly clear sense in a context of creatures and seek to use them in a different context. This, in Aquinas's terminology, is to use them *analogically*. Certain words, of course, simply cannot be taken out of their creaturely context because this context is part of their meaning. Thus we could not, even speaking analogically, say that a mighty fortress is our God, because mighty fortresses are essentially material things and God could not be a material thing. We could only say that metaphorically not analogically.

Thus when we say that God is maker or cause of the world we are using 'maker' and 'cause' outside their familiar contexts in senses which we do not understand.

So it should be clear that for Aquinas the existence of God at all is as mysterious as you can get. The Trinity for him is no less and no more mysterious. To say that there is Father, Son, and Holy Spirit who are God is for him no more mysterious than to say there is God at all. In neither case do we know what we are saying, but in neither case are we talking nonsense by contradicting ourselves. This latter is, of course, the next point to consider.

Aquinas holds that although we do not know what it is for God to be maker of the world it is not nonsense to say this of God in the way that it would be nonsense to say literally that God is a mighty fortress or a cup of tea. It is frequently the case that we find we have to apply several predicates to God, and because we do not understand them in this context we cannot see *how* they can be compatible with each other; but this is very different from saying that they are *in*compatible. It is one thing not to know how something makes sense and quite another to know that it does *not* make sense. Aquinas's task is to show that while we do not see *how* there can be Father, Son and Spirit who are all one God, we can show that it is not nonsense.

The thought may (at least at first) appear to be simpler if we look at the mystery of the incarnation. Here Aquinas holds that we do not understand how anyone could be simultaneously divine and human in the way that, for example, we can understand how someone could be simultaneously Russian and human. But he holds that we can understand that for someone to be both divine and human does not involve a contradiction in the sense that for something to be both a square and a circle would involve a contradiction.

Now similarly he holds that we cannot understand how God could be both Father, Son, and Spirit as well as utterly one and simple, but we do understand that this does not involve the kind of contradiction that would be involved in saying, say, that God is three Fathers as well as being one Father, or three Gods as well as being one God.

What we have to do in this case is to see how we are compelled to say each of the things but not to try to imagine them being simultaneously true or even try to conceive of them being simultaneously true; we should not expect to form a concept of the triune God, or indeed of God at all; we must rest content with establishing that we are not breaking any rules of logic, in other words that we are not being intellectually dishonest.

There is nothing especially odd or irrational about this. It only seems shocking to those who expect the study of God to be easy and obvious, a less demanding discipline than, say, the study of nuclear physics. In physics we are quite accustomed to the idea that there are two ways of talking about the ultimate constituents of matter, both of them necessary and both of them internally coherent, and yet we do not know how to reconcile them: one in terms of waves and the other in terms of particles. It is not a question of choosing between them; we have to accept them both. We do not, however, need to conceive of how anything could be both wave and particle; we simply accept that, at least for the moment, we have these two languages and that the use of them does not involve a contradiction although we cannot see how it avoids contradiction. It is true that most physicists would look forward to some future theoretical development in which we will devise a single language for expressing these matters, but they do not see themselves as talking nonsense in the meantime. This too is rather similar to Aquinas's position, for he also looks forward to a theoretical development by which we will come to see, to understand, how God is both one and three, but this he thinks can only come by sharing God's own self-understanding in the beatific vision. But meanwhile we are not talking nonsense.

To take another parallel: the square root of a number is that which when multiplied by itself yields that number. Since any number, whether positive or negative, when multiplied by itself yields a positive number, what could be made of a notion like the square root of a negative number, the square root of minus 2 for example? There is plainly no way in which we could conceive of the square root of minus 2 but this does not faze mathematicians; they are content to use it in a rule-governed way and find it a very useful device.

Aquinas, then, is faced with a situation similar to the physicist's. We have on the grounds of revelation to say two quite different kinds of things about God, that God is altogether one and that there are three who are God. We cannot see how they can both be true but that need not faze us; what we have to do is to show that there are no good grounds for saying that they are incompatible. We have to show in fact that the conditions which would make them incompatible in other cases do not and cannot apply to God – remember that all we know of God is what he is not, what he cannot be if he is to be God, the reason why there is anything instead of nothing.

One of the basic principles which Aquinas employs in considering the Trinity is the principle quoted, I think, from Augustine that *everything that is in God is God*. This is again something we cannot understand, we cannot see how it could be true but we are forced to assert that it is true. It follows, in Aquinas's view, from the fact that there can be no passive potentiality in God. This means that there is nothing in God which might not have been in him; there is never anything which he might be but is not or that he is but might not have been.

This in its turn follows from the fact that God cannot be changed by anything. If God were the patient or subject or victim of some other agent he could not be the source of the existence, the reality of everything that is. Rather, there would be something (this other agent) who would be a source of something in God. If God were not the source of the existence of all that is he would not be what we use the word 'God' for. Now Aquinas holds, surely reasonably, that it makes no sense to speak of what does not exist as acting or doing anything or bringing anything about. Hence what is merely potential – what might exist but does not – cannot act to bring itself about nor can it bring anything else about. What is potential can only be brought into existence by something that is actual. We must not confuse potentiality in this sense with power, an active capacity to do something; we mean simply what might be but isn't. Thus if there were any potentiality in God in this passive sense, he would need to be acted on by some other agent and thus, as we have seen, would not be God. God is thus, in Aquinas's phrase, *actus purus*, sheer actuality. He does not become, he just is. He cannot become because then there would be something he might be but is not. It is for these reasons that Aquinas says that God is totally unchanging and timeless.

Because of this, Aquinas argues that there can be no 'accidents' in God. Let me explain that. It is accidental to me that I am giving a lecture. This means that I would still be me if I were not giving it. Similarly it is accidental to me that I am wearing the clothes I am in and that I am six feet high. I am still me in other clothes and I was the same me when I was four feet high. What is accidental is opposed to what is essential. Thus it is not accidental but essential to me that I am an animal or that I am a human being. If I ceased to be an animal I would cease to exist, I would turn into something else – a corpse. By what is essential to a thing we mean what it takes for it to exist. What it takes for me to be is my being human, what it takes for Fido to be is being a dog, but both Fido and I have many other things about us which are not essential in this sense, many things which we could lose or gain without ceasing to be. This is what 'accidents' means.

Now it is clear that if giving a lecture is accidental to me I might not have been giving it – I mean I would still have been me if I had gone down with flu or simply been too scared. To have accidental features then is to be potential in some respect. Fido is eating a bone but he might not have been. He is not barking but he might be. To have accidental features as distinct from essential ones is to have some potentiality. Hence a being, God, with no potentiality can have no accidents. Every feature of God must be of his essence, essential to him.

Now please notice that all this argument is based not on any knowledge or understanding that we have of God; it is simply what we are compelled to say if we are to use the word 'God' correctly, that is to mean whatever unknown mystery is the source of the being of all that is (whatever would answer the question: 'Why is there anything rather than nothing at all?'). Whatever 'God' refers to, it could not be anything with potentiality and hence it could not be anything with accidental features.

This means that whatever is in God *is* God. My giving a lecture is not my being me, it is accidental to me, whereas my being human *is* my being me. Now with God *everything* he is is just his being God.

So if we say that God is wise or omnipotent we cannot be referring to two different features that God happens to have over and above being God. The wisdom of God just is his being God; so are his omnipotence and his goodness and whatever else we attribute to him. Now of course we cannot understand what it would be like for something to be its own wisdom. The wisdom we understand is always an accidental feature of persons, and so is power or goodness. When we use such words of God we must be using them analogically, outside the context of their first use, and we do not understand what we mean by them. We have no concept of the wisdom of God; for that matter we have no concept of God.

So every feature we attribute to God just is God, it is the divine essence or nature. But now we come to a complication because not everything we say of God attributes in this sense a feature to him. I mean not every sentence beginning 'God is . . .' or 'God has . . .' is intended to attribute some real feature to him. This is because some of the things we say about God are relational. Let me explain that.

Suppose that next week I shall become a great-uncle. At the moment it is, we shall say, not true that I am a great-uncle; next week it will become true. Are we then to say that a potentiality in me to become a great-uncle has been fulfilled? Not so, because my becoming a great-uncle involves no change in me at all; it is entirely a matter of a change in my niece Kate and what is in her womb. So although a sentence like 'Herbert is becoming a great-uncle' sounds just like 'Herbert is becoming wise' or 'Herbert is becoming a Dominican', we should not be misled by the grammar into thinking we are talking about a change in what is named by the subject term. The fact that there really is a new thing to say of me does not have to mean to say there is a new reality in me. Relational expressions are quite often like this. For example: 'You are on my left but you used to be on my right' doesn't have to imply any change in you; I may simply have turned round. You have not fulfilled any potentiality in yourself to become on my left. There would be only a *verbal* change – something new to *say* about you. Similarly 'you are farther away' or 'you have become richer than I' may or may not be true because of changes in you; they may be, for you, merely verbal changes.

Now consider the profoundly mysterious truth that God sustains Lady Thatcher in existence. This was not true of God in, say, 1920 because in those far off happy times Lady Thatcher did not exist and so God could not have been sustaining her in existence. So God began to sustain her, he *became* the sustainer of Lady Thatcher. But, Aquinas says, this does not entail any change in God any more than becoming a great-uncle entails any change in me. Thus becoming the sustainer of Lady Thatcher is not a real happening to God, in our sense, although it becomes true of him. It is true of him not because of some new reality in him but because of some reality in Lady Thatcher – that she began to be alive. Of course that she is alive is due to a reality in God: his profoundly mysterious eternal will that she should come to exist at a certain date. But this eternal will is not something that comes about at a date, so this does not imply any real change in God.

So when Lady Thatcher was conceived there was something going on in her, but on God's side the change is merely verbal; we have a new thing to say about God, but it is not a new thing about God that we are saying.

So there is a great deal of logical difference between saying that God is wise and saying that God is the sustainer of Lady Thatcher, or in general saying that he is creator. In the first case we attribute a real feature to God, wisdom, which (because there can be no accidents in God) must therefore be identical with being God. In the second case the reality is in the creature and there is merely a verbal change in God – a change in what has to be said of him. For this reason we are rescued from the appalling fate of suggesting that being creator and sustainer of Lady Thatcher is essential to God, that he would not be God had he not created Lady Thatcher.

So being creator of the world is not part of what it is to be God. God did not become God when in, say, 4005 BC he created the world. Indeed he did not change at all. Although saying he became creator sounds like attributing an accident to God it is not in fact attributing any new feature to him at all; we say it in order to say something new about the world. (Strictly speaking of course even the world itself did not change when it was created because until it was created it wasn't there to change. But that is another question.) We should remember, of course, that when we say God does not change, we do not mean God stays the same all the time. God is not 'all the time'. God is eternal. To attribute *stasis* to God is as mistaken as to attribute change to him.

The main point is this: that what we say of God because of his creative relationship to creatures does not attribute any new reality to God and thus does not speak of God's essence.

James Mackey in his interesting book *The Christian Experience of God as Trinity* (1983) (the title ought to be enough to warn you) has a generally hostile account of Aquinas's treatment of the Trinity, and he finds the notion I am trying to explain especially unlovable. He says,

> (Aquinas) is quite clear in his insistence that the Trinity cannot be known from creation – the principle *opera ad extra sunt indivisa* is by now sacrosanct and he further distances from our world all discussion of real divine relation by stating quite baldly 'there is no real relation in God to the creature'. Creatures, that is, may experience a real relationship of dependence upon and need of God, but God experiences no such real relationship to creatures.

I'm afraid this is a dreadful muddle. Whether a relationship in me is real or merely verbal has nothing whatever to do with experience. The fact that the relationship of being a great-uncle is not a real one in me in no way makes it something I do not experience; it in no way makes me less aware of my great-niece nor less concerned about her.

God, of course, for Aquinas does not experience anything in the world. He has no need to. He does not, as I do, have to learn about the world from outside. He is at the heart of absolutely everything in the world, holding it in existence and bringing about everything it does.

The principle that whatever is in God is God, then, does not apply to such relational predicates as being creator or being sustainer of Lady Thatcher. It *does* apply to non-relational predicates like 'is wise' and 'is good' and 'is merciful'. God's wisdom, goodness and mercy are all identical with his essence and there is no real distinction in God between his goodness and his wisdom. On the other hand there *is* a real distinction between God sustaining Lady Thatcher and God sustaining me, though it is not a real distinction in God but a very fundamental one between myself and Lady Thatcher, one for which I thank God every day.

It is indeed a great mystery that the wisdom of God is God, and the power of God is God, and the goodness of God is God, and all three are the same God – we cannot understand how this can be, but it is not like the mystery of the Trinity because we cheerfully admit that (in some way we do not understand) all three are in fact identical; there is no distinction between the goodness and the power and the wisdom of God.

In the case of the Trinity, however, we want to say that the Father is God and the Son is God and the Spirit is God and all three are the same God but nevertheless they are *not* identical. There *is* distinction between Father, Son and Spirit.

What we have got to so far is that when we are speaking of what is real in God we are speaking of what is God's essence and all our predicates refer to one and the same identical essence of divinity, not to a number of accidents; our different predicates do not mark real distinctions in God. When, however, we are speaking of God's relationship to creatures, our different predicates do mark real distinctions but not in God because they entail no reality in God.

Aquinas's next move is to speak not of God's activity with regard to creatures, his creative act, but of God's activity within himself. And here we have to notice a difference between transitive and intransitive verbs. Aquinas points out that not all our acts are actions upon something else, acts which make a difference to something else. Carving and writing and teaching are all acts whose reality consists in what happens to some subject, and so is creating. Carving can only be going on if some stuff is being carved, writing can only be going on if some words are being written; but what about the act of, say, growing? You can of course grow in a transitive sense as when a gardener grows begonias, but growing in the intransitive sense is not an activity that does something to something else, nor is boiling or collapsing. To use Aquinas's phrase, it remains within the agent. Still more clearly, the act of understanding is not an act which does anything or makes any difference to anything else. It is a kind of growing or development of the mind itself; not an operation on what is understood or on anything else. Of course there are philosophers who, partly for this reason, think it a mistake to talk of understanding as an *act*, but we cannot pause here to argue with them. For Aquinas, at any rate, it was an act performed by the agent but not passing outside the agent to alter or influence or change anything else. Aquinas occasionally calls such actions 'immanent' acts as opposed to 'transient' ones.

Now can we speak of God's act of understanding? It would take much too long to give an account of Aquinas's general theory of understanding. You will just have to take it from me that for him both understanding and being intelligible have to do with not being *material*. To understand a nature is just to possess that nature immaterially. To possess the nature of a dog materially is to be a dog; to possess the nature of a dog immaterially (to have it in mind) is to understand a dog, to know what a dog is, or what the word 'dog' means.

For Aquinas, you might say, the norm for being is that it should be intelligent, understanding, immaterial being; the exceptional ones are those whose being is curbed and restricted by matter; matter not thought of as some special kind of stuff but as the limitedness and potentiality of things. For Aquinas we can understand because we are just about able to transcend our materiality. While almost all our vital operations are operations of the body, circumscribed by matter, in the act of understanding we have an act which, although it is heavily involved with bodily activity and cannot ordinarily take place without concomitant bodily working, is not of itself an act of the body, a bodily process. Beings which are not material at all, quite unlimited by matter, angels for example, would understand much better than we do, without the tedious need for bodily experience, for what he calls the sense power of the *imaginatio* or *phantasmata* and for the use of material symbols and words.

For Aquinas, then, it follows simply from the fact that God cannot be material that he cannot be non-intellectual, he cannot fail to be understanding. This is part of our negative knowledge of God, our knowledge of what God is not.

We should, however, be quite clear that in saying that we know that God is not impersonal, not lacking in understanding and knowledge, we are laying no claim to knowing what it means for God to understand. Aquinas will go on to speak of God having an understanding of himself or forming a concept of himself but it is clear that we have so far no warrant for saying this. There is no reason to suppose that God's act of understanding is so much like ours. But on the other hand we have equally no warrant for saying that it isn't. I mean we do have warrant for saying that God does not hear or see anything just as he does not chop down trees, for all these are operations of a material body; the idea of God forming a concept of himself is not excluded in that way. It is simply that other things being equal we would have no reason to assert it. Aquinas, however, thinks other things are not equal for he interprets the Logos theology of John as suggesting just this.

When we understand a nature – say, what an apple is – we form a concept of what an apple is and this concept is the meaning we have for the word 'apple'. (When I speak of understanding the nature of an apple I do not mean some profound grasp of the essence of apples; I just mean the situation of someone who knows what apples are as distinct from someone who has never come across them or heard of them.) The concept is not precisely what we understand; what we understand is what apples are, the nature of apples, but the concept is what we have in mind in understanding this nature. It is the meaning for us of apples, the meaning expressed in the word 'apple'. So when you learn, say, what peevishness is, you do so by forming a concept which is the meaning of the word 'peevish' or 'peevishness'. It is not exactly that you learn the word itself, for you may not know that useful word and you may express the meaning you understand by some complicated circumlocution, and again a Frenchman who comes to the same understanding of what peevishness is will form the same concept which for him will be the meaning of the word '*maussaderie*'. The concept, then, is what is conceived in the mind in the act of understanding and because it is the meaning of a word it was called by the medievals the *verbum mentis*, the word of the mind. This does not commit them to any doctrine that we can have concepts before we have any words in which we express them; indeed Aquinas clearly thought we could not, but it is plain that many different words or signs may express the same concept: that is what we mean when we say that this word or phrase means the same as that one.

Now let us return to the understanding of God. God's understanding of me or of any of his creatures is not something other than his creating and sustaining of them. God, you may say, knows what he is doing and what he is doing is keeping these things in their being and everything about them. God's knowledge of me, then, like his creating of me, is a relational predicate true of God because of a reality in me. Just as I will be a great-uncle because of the reality of my great-niece. God knows me not by having a concept of me distinct from a concept he has of you. He knows me by knowing himself and thus knowing himself as creator of me and you. Thus that God knows me and also knows you does not imply that there are two different concepts, two different realities in God, any more than when I become a great-uncle three times over there will be three different realities in me.

But what, asks Aquinas, about God's understanding of himself? Here he will form a concept of himself. The concept, remember, is not *what* is understood but *how* something is understood, what is produced, brought forth, conceived, in the understanding of something. What God understands is himself, identical with himself, but in understanding he conceives the concept, the *verbum mentis*, and this because produced, brought forth by him, is not him.

Let us remind ourselves again that there is no 'must' about it. Aquinas is not trying to deduce the Trinity from God's intellectuality. We do not understand God's understanding, and apart from the revelation about God's Word we should not be talking about God forming a concept. However, given this revelation, it seems reasonable to interpret it this way.

Notice the importance of the switch from looking at God's activity that *passes outside him* to creatures to looking at his *immanent* activity of self-understanding. In the former case there is no reality in God on which the relationship of being created or being understood is based; it is a reality in the creature and a merely verbal thing in God, a change in what is to be said of him. In the latter case, however, there is a reality, a concept, in God himself. A reality distinct from God in God.

And now comes the hammer-blow of that principle we established at the beginning: everything that is real in God is God. We cannot see the concept in God (as we can see our own concepts) as an accident distinct from the essence. In us our concept is a reality distinct from us in us. It is an accident. Our concepts come and go, and we remain what we are; this cannot be true of God. If God has formed a concept it is not an accident of God, it is God. This is quite beyond our understanding, we are merely forced to it by our reasoning. We are not, of course, forced by our reasoning to say that God forms a concept of himself, but we are forced to say that *if* he does so it cannot be merely accidental, it must be God.

The act of creating brings about a relationship between God and his creature. They are *distinct* but *related* to each other as creator and creature. But the basis of this relation is real only in the creature, just as the basis of the relationship of being a great-uncle is real only on one side. The act of God's self-understanding which involves the bringing forth of a concept, a *verbum mentis*, also brings about a relationship between God and the concept. They are distinct but related to each other as conceiver and what is conceived, meaner and meaning. But the basis of this relationship, unlike the relationship of creation, is real at *both* ends. The mind and the *verbum* it produces are really distinct as the opposite ends of a relationship. And whatever is real in God is God.

St Thomas shifts, as does St John himself, from Logos language ('In the beginning was the word and the word was with God and the word was God') to the language of Father and Son. He argues that these come to the same thing: there are two essential requirements for the act of generation – first that A should have been *brought forth* by B and secondly that it should have the *same nature* as B. I did not generate you because although you have the same nature as I have, I did not bring you forth. On the other hand, I did not generate my nail clippings or my thoughts, although I brought them forth, because they are not themselves human beings. I would generate only my children which are both brought forth and of the same nature. The *verbum mentis* of God, however, is both brought forth by him, conceived by him, and also is of the same nature, for, being real in God, it is God. Thus the language of generation, of Son and Father, is here applicable.

It does not in any case seem fortuitous that the language of mental activity parallels that of sexual generation. The word 'concept' itself belongs primarily to the context of generation. Of course all this fits much more easily into an Aristotelian and biblical biology according to which fathers generate their sons merely in the environment of women. Nothing was then known of the splitting of chromosomes and sharing of genes; women were not thought to contribute actively to the generative process. From our more knowledgeable point of view it would make more sense to speak of God the Parents rather than God the Father. (The plural 'parents' would be no more misleading than is the sexual connotation of 'Father'.) However, that of course is not in Aquinas.

So for Aquinas, as indeed for the Catholic faith, Father and Son do not differ in any way (*homo-ousion*). In each case what they are is God and they are nothing except that they are God. The Father has no features or properties which the Son has not. The only thing that distinguishes them is that they are at opposite ends of a relationship. The Father *generates* the Son, the Son is *generated by* the Father. Being the Father just is standing in that relationship to the Son; being the Son just is standing in that relationship to the Father. The Father *is a relation*. It is not that he *has* a relation. Just as in creatures wisdom is always an accident, wisdom of some subject, so in creatures 'a relation to . . .' is always an accident supervening on some already existing subject. It is the lectern that is shorter than I am, that *has* the relation of 'shorter than' to me; relations supervene upon what is already something in its own right. But of course, as we have seen, nothing supervenes on God. In him there are no accidents. Whatever really is in God is the essence of God. So the Father does not *have* a relationship of Fatherhood to the Son; he *is* that relationship subsisting as God. And the Son is the relation of being generated by the Father, subsisting as God.

Need I say that the notion of a subsisting relation is mysterious to us; we do not know what it would mean or what it would be like, but (to repeat) we do not know what subsisting wisdom would mean or what God would mean or what God would be like.

We see then that the only distinction in God is that of being at opposite ends of a relationship due to an act or 'process' within the Godhead. Nothing that is said non-relationally about God makes any distinction between Father and Son, and nothing that is said even relationally about God in virtue of his dealings with creatures refers to any real distinction in God at all. God turns to creatures, as his creatures, the single unified face of the one God, the unchanging, the eternal, the single source of all that is. It is only with God's own interior life, his own self-understanding, that there is a basis for distinction. And of course that interior life is of vast interest to us because we are called on to share it. God does not look upon us human creatures simply as creatures; he has invited us by our unity in Christ to share in Christ's divine life within the Trinity, to share in his Sonship. And this of course brings us, perhaps a little belatedly, to the Holy Spirit, for it is by receiving the Spirit through faith in baptism that we share in the interior life of the Godhead.

The main principles for Aquinas's treatment of the Spirit are already laid down in his discussion of the Father and the Son. This indeed is one of the major difficulties with his treatment. He is, however, quite conscious and explicit about what he is doing. He says that it is necessary to consider the Holy Spirit on the same lines as we consider the Son. His reason for this is that the only possible distinction in the Godhead is the distinction of two opposite ends of a relationship and the only possible basis for relationship in the Godhead is the relation of origin to what is originated, a relation set up by some procession such as the conception of the Word, the generation of the Son.

So the Holy Spirit too must be distinct in its relation to its origin and its origin, says St Thomas, lies in that other immanent operation of the intellectual being, the operation of the will, the operation of love.

This, however, is where the difficulties begin. It is not too difficult to see how in understanding himself the Father forms a concept of himself which being real in God is itself God; it is much less easy to see how anything is formed in the operation of the will. This is especially so if we remember Aquinas's own often-repeated doctrine that while truth is in the mind, goodness is in things. The act of understanding is a taking into the mind of the form or nature of things and this is the formation of a concept; but the act of loving is a going out towards the thing, a being attracted to it or an enjoyment of it. It is not at all clear what it is that is originated in this act of the will. Remember that the Holy Spirit is not what is loved, any more than the concept or word or Son is what is known; what is known and loved is the divine nature itself, it is a question of self-knowledge and self-love; the Word is what is formed in this self-knowledge and the Holy Spirit is what is formed in this self-love.

Well, says Aquinas, we ought not to think of the Holy Spirit as a likeness of what is loved in the way that the concept is a likeness (in this case a perfect likeness) of what is known; rather it is tendency towards a *nisus* or impulsion towards even a kind of excitement – an enjoyment. This, Aquinas thinks, is formed in the act of loving. This is the term of the act of what he calls '*spiratio*', breathing forth. It becomes, then, difficult to speak of the Holy Spirit as a 'thing' that is formed, and I remember Victor White always used to regard this as one of the great strengths and glories of Aquinas's teaching on the Trinity. With the Holy Spirit, at least, we are in no danger of seeing God as a 'person' in the modern sense. Here God is a movement, an impulse, a love, a delight.

It is essential to Aquinas's doctrine that the Holy Spirit proceeds from *both* the Father and the Son, and not merely from the Father. The reason for this is that the only distinction admissible in the Trinity is that of being at opposite ends of a relation based on a procession of origination. If the Holy Spirit does not proceed from the Son there is no such relation between them and therefore no distinction between Son and Holy Spirit.

Thus in Aquinas's account there are two processions in God, one of the intellect, God's knowing himself, which is generation, and one of the will, God's enjoying himself, which is spiration. Each of these gives rise to a relationship with two (opposite) ends, the origin and the originated. There are thus four of these relations. This does not, however, result in four distinct persons, for in order to be distinct a person must be at the opposite end of a relation from both other persons. The Father is opposed to the Son by generating and to the Spirit by spiration. The Son is opposed to the Father by being generated and to the Spirit by spiration. The Spirit is opposed to both the Father and the Son by being spirated, or '*processio*' (in a new sense).

This does not commit Aquinas to the '*filioque*' in the sense in which it is found objectionable by the Eastern Churches. The root of their complaint, as I understand it, is that the *filioque* seems to take away from the Father as unique source or principle of the Godhead. However, the Greek Orthodox theologians who in 1875 came to an agreement with the Old Catholics (Mackey, 1983, p. 186) expressed their faith by saying, 'We do call the Holy Spirit the Spirit of the Son and so it is proper to say that the Holy Spirit proceeds from the Father *through* the Son.' But that last clause is an exact quotation from Aquinas:

*Quia igitur Filius habet a Patre quod ab eo procedat Spiritus Sanctus, potest dici quod Pater **per** Filium spirat Spiritum Sanctum; vel quod Spiritus Sanctus procedat a Patre **per** Filium, quod idem est.*

Because the Son owes it to the Father that the Holy Spirit should proceed from him, it can be said that the Father through the Son breathes forth the Holy Spirit, or that the Holy Spirit proceeds from the Father through the Son, which is to say the same thing.

I think it will be clear that Aquinas's doctrine gives us no warrant for saying that there are three persons in God; for 'person' in English undoubtedly means an individual subject, a distinct centre of consciousness. Now the consciousness of the Son is the consciousness of the Father and of the Holy Spirit; it is simply God's consciousness. There are not three knowledges or three lovings in God. The Word simply is the way in which God is self-conscious, knows what he is, as the Spirit simply is the delight God takes in what he is when he is knowing it. If we say there are three persons in God, in the ordinary sense of person, we are tritheists.

For Aquinas the key to the Trinity is not the notion of person but of relation, and in fact in my account of his teaching I have not found it necessary to use the word 'person' at all. Aquinas quotes with ostensible approval Boethius's definition of a person as 'an individual substance of rational nature'. But, as speedily emerges, the 'persons' of the Trinity are not individuals, not substances, not rational and do not *have* natures. What Aquinas labours to show is that in this unique case 'person' can mean relation. This he does out of characteristic *pietas* towards the traditional language of the Church. But of course even in Aquinas's time *persona* did not mean relation and most emphatically in our time 'person' does not. For our culture the 'person' is almost the opposite of the relational; it is the isolated bastion of individuality set over against the collective. Even if we criticize this individualism, even if we try to put the human being back into a social context as a part of various communities, the notion of person does not become relational enough to use in an account of the Trinity. Aquinas could have made better use of the original sense of *prosopon* or *persona* as the player's mask; and his doctrine of the Trinity might be more easily grasped if we spoke of three *roles* in the strict sense of three roles in a theatrical cast – though we have to forget that in the theatre there are people *with* the roles. We should have to think just of the roles as such and notice how they each have meaning only in relation to and distinction from each other. We could speak of the role of parenthood, the role of childhood and the role of love or delight. This is not to speak of the Trinity as a matter simply of three aspects of God, three ways in which God appears *to us*, as Sabellius is alleged to have taught, for essential to this whole teaching is that God turns only one aspect to us, *opera ad extra sunt indivisa*; it is in his immanent activity of self-understanding and self-love, delight, that the roles are generated.

These roles, firmly established in the life of the Godhead, are then reflected (I prefer the word 'projected' – as on a cinema screen) in our history in the external missions of the Son and the Spirit by which we are taken up into that life of the Godhead. In this way the obedience of Jesus is the projection of his eternal sonship, and the outpouring of the Spirit is the projection of his eternal procession from the Father through the Son. It is because of these missions in time that the life of the Trinity becomes available to us: I mean both in the sense that we know of it, believe in it, and in the sense that we belong to it. These are of course the same thing. It is because we share in the Holy Spirit through faith and charity and the other infused virtues that we are able to speak of the Trinity at all. It is not therefore adequate to speak of God's redemptive act as an *opus ad extra*. It is precisely the act by which we cease to be *extra* to God and come within his own life.

Five

The Trinity and Prayer

I think people must get terribly tired of other people talking about prayer. So just by way of a change I thought I might go in straight off the deep end and begin with God. And that means beginning with the Trinity. I hope that if we begin by thinking about the Trinity we may end up understanding something about prayer.

Of course the proper way, the respectable way, to talk about the Trinity is to begin with Jesus Christ, who is always the real starting-point for any understanding of the Christian life, and then, in view of what we find in the New Testament, to talk of *his* Father and of *their* Spirit. Jesus is sent by the *Father*; the *Spirit* is sent by the Father in and through Jesus. This is surely, as a matter of history, the order in which the Church came eventually to formulate the doctrine of the Trinity, perhaps starting from the original fact that they had received the Spirit through Jesus. We had to ask: How shall we make sense of what we are told of Jesus and his Father and their Spirit? As usual with such formulations by the Church, which are all, in a way, attempts to say who *She* is, and which come out of long-drawn-out arguments and discussions about the identity of the Church ('What is it that makes Christians Christians?', etc.), they are better at shutting off blind alleys than explaining the true way, better at excluding ways of talking than at giving an account of the best way of talking. And this is just as well because there is no best way of talking. I don't think any Council of the Church has ever said 'This is the only way to express the fundamental truths of the gospel.' They have frequently said 'These other ways have turned out to be no good, dead ends.' The pronouncements of Councils normally say 'No Through Road Here' rather than acting as signposts or guidelines or maps.

What I would like to begin with is one very traditional way of looking at the T⋯   ⸱ll not trace its history through the

⸱ Augustine and St Thomas Aquinas).

⸱1 see what light it throws on the New

⸱yer of Jesus. I do this because this may

⸱ body of Christ, his Church, and that

⸱rsonal prayer – not primarily on how to

⸱vhat it is, it may be that we shall find we

⸱t God is. We do not know what we are

⸱d 'God'. We never came across anything

⸱ "god", that is the sort of thing that "god"

⸱of thing with horses and sodium chloride

we have a rough idea of what all these

⸱dea how to use the words we have for sig-

⸱vay with the word 'God'. We do not have

⸱Vhen Jews and Christians came to use the

⸱ound meaning something else – I mean it

⸱ly *could not be*, a god. Whatever we are

referring to w⋯   ⸱d 'God' it can no more be a god than it can

be a model aeroplane or half-past eleven.

Although we have no notion of what God is, we can, I think, be pretty confident about the kind of thing God is *not* because she *could not* be. This is because we use the word 'God' as a label for something we do not know, for the answer to a question we can ask but cannot answer. We use the word God to point us towards a darkness, a mystery that is revealed by our question, revealed by our inability to answer the question. The question takes a fair number of forms, but as a sample it can be 'What is it all for?', 'What is the meaning of the whole shebang?', 'How come there is anything at all instead of there not being anything at all?'. Douglas Adams's novel *The Hitchhiker's Guide to the Galaxy* suggests that the answer is 42, and I take it that the point of this is that there is no answer. Ask a silly question and you deserve a silly answer. But it is *not* a silly question so there *is* an answer, although certainly any answer of ours you might give would be a silly answer. To decide whether it is a silly question or not would need more philosophy than is available in the *Hitchhiker's Guide*. But let us agree that it is not a silly question, that our experience, or our world, or ourselves, or whatever, insist on us asking some form of this question and recognizing that we face a mystery which we cannot understand. To say it is not a silly question but a real one is to say there is an answer although we do not know what it is. This is to say God exists.

But we are not helpless, we are not just ignorant, we do know some things, in fact quite a lot. We know what God could not possibly be: for example he could not be a god. Why? Because gods are bits of the world or anyway bits of the universe. They stand alongside heroes and human beings and teacups, none of which are gods. Gods are different; they are a superior kind of being. The universe is divided into gods and non-gods as it is divided into sheep and non-sheep; the gods are items in the universe. Top items maybe, but still items. It is immediately apparent that whether the gods exist or not they cannot be the answer to why there is a universe at all, for they are part of the universe. Whatever is the answer to our question as put in the form 'Why is there anything?', it could not be one kind of thing in the universe or anything in the universe. In whatever way we understand the phrase 'all of it', God cannot be part of it. God cannot exist in the way that parts of the universe exist. He could not be an item in the universe.

God has to be why there is a universe at all. She has to be *Creator*. And the worship of this Creator is the only worship worthy of a human being. The Creator is the reason why there is a universe with or without gods in it. But if there *are* gods in it, it would be degrading for a human being to worship them. This, you might say, was the great Hebrew discovery: human beings are such that they worship *only* the mystery by which there is anything at all instead of nothing. To worship anything *in* the universe is to be dehumanized. People in the Hebrew tradition were a little unsure whether the gods were simply sticks and stones or demonic forces represented by these images, or both; but in any case they were to be treated with contempt and satire. I suppose this ought to be called a Jewish rather than simply a Hebrew discovery since it only becomes clear with Second Isaiah and post-exilic Judaism. And this Jewish discovery was surely a turning-point in the history of humankind. It implied, of course, a piece of self-discovery about humankind: the human being is now defined, if you like, as the Creator-worshipper, the atheist with no gods to worship, no gods to petition, no gods to pray to, no gods worth praying to. Whatever prayer is going to mean to people in the Jewish tradition, such as Christians, it cannot mean petitioning a god. It cannot mean cajoling and persuading a god to be on your side.

But if it doesn't mean cajoling and persuading a god, what does it mean? And moreover if it doesn't mean cajoling and persuading a god, why are the

Jewish scriptures full of people cajoling and persuading God – not only in the psalms but all over the place?

Maybe the answer to that second question isn't too difficult. We simply don't have to take the cajoling *literally*. God is no more literally persuaded by our prayers than he is literally a mighty fortress or a small voice or a mother hen – all of which the Bible says he is at various times. But if we say that all the words of prayers are, and have to be, a making of images (and good luck to them, so long as we can smash the images afterwards) it becomes that much more urgent to find another way of saying what prayer literally is. And this involves saying what God literally is.

But didn't I say that we have no idea what God is? How then can we *say* what She is? We can use language to say what God is so long as we always realize that we do not know what our words mean. We can say that God is love, so long as we recognize that this love is incomprehensible. We can say God is wise and good and happy, just so long as we are not trying to classify God amongst the wise and good and happy things we are familiar with, so long as we recognize that when used of God these words have a meaning beyond anything we can understand of wisdom or happiness or goodness. But we mean these statements quite literally.

It is quite the opposite with images and metaphors. If I say 'A mighty fortress is our God' I must imagine a fortress I can understand and envisage, towering up with turrets and battlements, looking out enormously and impregnably over the forces of the enemy. If I do not see clearly and concretely what the fortress is, the metaphor dies and loses its impact, its meaning for me. The caveat I have to make with images and with metaphorical statements is that they *can be denied as well as asserted*. I must be able to add 'But of course God is not a mighty fortress.' I must realize that there are a thousand other images quite incompatible with this one. God is a mother, God is a king, God is an eagle hovering over her young, God is breath.

The literal use of language about God is the very opposite of the metaphorical use of language. In literal use we are sure that this must be asserted and not denied, but we do not understand what it is that is being asserted. In metaphorical usage we understand quite well what is being asserted, but we know it could just as well be denied. Now it is metaphorical language and the making of images that is most characteristic of our religious speech and our religious life. The Bible teems with images and with metaphorical statements. 'God repented him of what he had done.' 'The wrath of the Lord was kindled against the people.' 'The mighty hand and the outstretched arm by which the Lord your God brought you out.' 'The Lord became jealous for his land and had pity on his people.' Where would we be without this language? It is the natural language of prayer and prophecy and worship. It was the great Jewish discovery that such language *must* be metaphorical because God is not a god, not a member of the universe who could literally be said to be kindled to anger by what takes place in creation, who could be said to be moved by pity. God is not a god who could be said literally to be moved by our prayers. This was a great Jewish discovery: that nearly all pure language about God must be metaphorical. It was very different from the slightly later Greek discovery that stories about the gods could be treated as philosophical allegories about man; you could re-interpret the myths of the gods into statements about human morality or the human unconscious. You *could* if you wanted to be boring enough. The Jews had a different perspective. They wanted to talk of God all right, not just humanity; if what they said had a profound impact on human morality it was because their talk of God eliminated the gods, and this atheism had devastating effects on political and personal morality. It was a huge human liberation compared to which the Athenian democracy was a game for rich boys played while their armies of slaves kept the real world going.

Nearly all of our language about God is metaphorical, nearly all but not quite all. If it is *all* metaphorical you do not realize that it *is* metaphorical and you are back enslaved to the gods; you are back in the kind of society that is validated by the gods. You are back in the god-bothered society envisaged and warned against in the Ten Commandments, where the only social reality is dominative power, where might is right.

You need a literal critique of your metaphors, you need to be able to say God is not a god, God is not a top person in the universe dwelling in the heavens. On the contrary, in the beginning God *made* the heavens and the earth; and you have to mean *that* literally and not simply as the sort of story of the gods that you get in the Babylonian 'creation' myths where the world containing the gods is already there and they act within it – or, for that matter, the second creation story in Genesis which begins 'when no plant of the field was yet in the earth and no herb of the field had yet sprung up'.

If, as the Jews did, you take literally 'God made the heavens and the earth', you have to recognize that you do not know what 'makes' means. The meaning is no doubt analogous with other uses of the verb 'to make', but it is not a meaning you understand. You may know what it is to make a novel and how different it is from making a statue or making a mistake or making a baby. You see all these as quite intelligible meanings which are quite distinct but related. When it comes to making the heavens and the earth, the meaning is no doubt related but it is not intelligible to us.

The Jewish discovery that God is not a god but Creator is the discovery of absolute *Mystery* behind and underpinning reality. Those who share it (either in its Judaic or its Christian form) are not monotheists who have reduced the number of gods to one. They, we, have abolished the gods; there is only the Mystery sustaining all that is. The Mystery is unfathomable, but it is not *remote* as the gods are remote. The gods live somewhere else, on Olympus or above the starry sky. The Mystery is everywhere and always, in every grain of sand and every flash of colour, every hint of flavour in a wine, keeping all these things in existence every microsecond. We could not literally approach God or get nearer to God for God is already nearer to us than we are to ourselves. God is at the ultimate depth of our beings making us to be ourselves.

How then can we all call upon God, beseech Her, gain His attention, when our very cry for attention is made by God, more due to God than it is to ourselves, for it must be God that brings it about that I pray as it is God that brings it about that I draw my next breath? Jesus stands, of course, solidly in the Jewish tradition. His God is the non-god, the Mystery, and part of his talk of God as our Father is a campaign against the endemic human tendency to treat God as a god, as another kind of being: God is with us with the intimacy and concern of a father or mother, not like some Olympian judge or policeman.

But of course (and I am not going to go into all this) already in Paul, and developing in the synoptic gospels to its consummation in the gospel of John, is the Christian understanding of Jesus as Son of God in a way even more mysterious than creation itself, in a way that itself belongs to the Mystery. In John the sonship or the 'being sent' of Jesus by the Father has become itself the Mystery, the object of our faith, as has the 'being sent', the breathing forth of the Spirit from-the-Father-because-of-Jesus, also become the Mystery itself. I do not think that John's gospel *tells* this; I think it is what John can take for granted, the background of beliefs already there in his Church, the 'Community of the Beloved Disciple', against which John can give his account of the life and death and resurrection of Jesus. The *doctrine* of the Trinity is no more than the Church's attempts to defend this background of beliefs within the Church so that the Gospels can still be read and still be understood.

To go back to the beginning: we know only that God is. There is an answer to our most radical question of all. We do not know this answer, but we know what God is not. We know, for example, that God cannot be less than understanding, that God cannot be subject to the limitations of material things that only act when they are acted on. If even some of God's *creatures* in some feeble way transcend this passive existence, and are to some degree spontaneous and have freedom and understanding, then God surely is not less than they. We do not know, of course, what it is for God to be understanding and to enjoy what he understands. But it seems clear that whatever God is it cannot be less than this. God could not be inanimate and blind.

The particular tradition to which I referred, which is associated with Augustine and Aquinas, says something like this: if we are to have a model of God's understanding, let us think of God as first of all understanding being God, understanding divinity itself, which is God. Let us think of God as forming a concept of being God. Of course we must be careful and not imagine God's concept of being God as something separate from God, in the way that our concepts are separate from us. If *you* think of what it is like to be you, what it is like to be human, whatever concept you form of this is something separate from you, it could come and go, it could change radically without you going out of existence, it is just something that you have, that belongs to you, it is not a human being. We must be careful not to foist all this on God. Whatever God is could not have concepts that come and go, concepts that are other than himself. As Augustine says 'Everything in God is God.' If we are to think of God as having a concept of being God, then this concept itself, this word in which God understands the meaning of God, must itself be God. And if we are to understand God as enjoying the Godhead expressed in this concept, this enjoyment too must simply be God. So God's concept of Herself, if He had such a thing, and God's enjoyment of Herself in this concept, if He had such enjoyment, would not be things other than God but simply divine, simply God.

We have, of course, absolutely no philosophical warrant for constructing this model; we are not neo-platonists who imagine that God, being God, must necessarily produce emanations and whatnot. It is simply that if we *do* have such a model it can function as one framework in which to understand the teaching of the New Testament – certainly a better framework than the model of God as one of the gods. And with this model we can see God not only as Originator but as Originated. We can speak of God the child as well as God the parent, and we can see God not as a person at all but as sheer joy and delight. We can get a hint of what John means when he says God is love.*

We should not, by the way, be distracted by the formula that there are three *persons* in God. It was an excellent, if non-committal, formula in its time. But since then 'person' has taken on a new and much 'thicker' meaning. For us, a person is at least a separate centre of consciousness with its own separate mind, its own will, its own distinct personality. For *us* to say that there are three persons who are God would be like saying there are three people who are God; it would be tritheism. In the traditional model, obviously the Word of God and the Spirit of God do not each have their own separate distinct minds and wills; they do not converse together, exchanging their views and preferences, not even identical views and preferences. There is but one mind and will in God. The traditional model I have been sketching is a model for the working of this one mind and will, not for the existence of three minds and wills of three consciousnesses.

Now in the tradition of which I speak the whole story of Jesus of Nazareth (which is the whole of Scripture) can be seen as the projection on to the history of the world that we have made of the Mystery of God, God's own Word and the Spirit that comes from God because of the Word. By projection I mean something like the projection of a film on a screen. What you see in a projection depends not only on the film itself but on the state of the screen. In our case, the screen is human history and it is as though you projected the film not on a plain silver sheet but on a rubbish dump. If the film which is God's self-understanding and his delight in this understanding appears in our history as a story of misunderstanding, oppression, misery, torture, and murder, this says something important about the screen, about our history. It reveals sin. That the cross should be how God's eternal life and happiness look when projected into our time tells us about sin as well as God's love. It also tells us about prayer. Because for the Christian there is primordially just one prayer: the cross. The cross is the *unity* of God and his Word (expressed as God's enjoyment of his divinity in his Word, what we call the Holy Spirit)

---

* I should say that by models I do not mean images (you can have as many images of God as you like, and the more the better). Models however are to be taken literally (though when we have models for *God* we do not understand the terms we use). The difference between a model we take literally and a literal statement like 'God is wise' is that we are *compelled* to say God is wise by what we know of what God is not, whereas we are not compelled to construct *any* particular model.

projected in our time as the prayer of the man Jesus to God his Father, His prayer for the salvation of His fellow human beings, the prayer that is answered in the resurrection. We preach, says Paul, Christ crucified; for the good and sensible reason that it is here that we find God (Father, Son and Holy Spirit); it is here we find the Mystery, the mystery hidden from all ages.

In Jesus, says John, the Word, God's self-understanding, God's concept of God which was in the beginning with God and was God, became flesh. From now on, the eternal coming forth of the Word from the Father is represented, projected, as the mission of Jesus, his being sent by the Father and his loving acceptance of this mission which is his obedience. From the moment when, as John says, the Word became flesh, it becomes a person, a person in our sense, a human person, and is henceforth referred to as *Son* of the Father. In Jesus, God as Word, God as being originated, as coming forth, God the child, becomes a human being with his own human mind and will which are not the divine mind and will but which are obedient to the divine mind and will. The obedience of Jesus (within which his prayer is encompassed) is the unity of Word and God, of Son and Father in eternity.

So the first thing to say about our prayer, Christian prayer, the prayer of the Church, is that it is just the life of God, the life of the Trinity lived out in us. We, though human creatures and not God, are able to be one with God, as God is one with God, because we are in Christ and Christ is a human being who is one with God as God is one with God.

Let me explain what I meant by all this cryptic stuff about the cross as prayer and obedience of Christ as encompassing his prayer. As I see it, we are saved because of the sanctity, the grace, of the man Jesus of Nazareth. I follow Thomas Aquinas in thinking that it is not precisely because Jesus is divine that we are saved but because he was a saint. It was because he was full of grace, a human being who was utterly obedient to the will of the Father, that he earned, merited, our redemption. He was obedient to what he saw as his mission, and his mission, as I see it, was simply the mission to be human. He was not sent by his Father to suffer and die because the Father wanted to see some suffering. He was sent to be human. That this meant suffering and being murdered is entirely due to *us*. This is the world that human beings have made, this is the screen on which the life of God is to be projected. In the world we have made it is fatal to be human, to be really human, to be open and vulnerable to others, to be loving. This our world perceives as a threat and reacts accordingly. Jesus however was obedient to his Father's command, he was obedient unto this death. And therefore God has raised him up. This is the theology of the letter to the Philippians.

On the cross Jesus left himself completely in the hands of his Father. He himself had manifestly failed. The project of being human and loving in our loveless and inhuman world is doomed to failure; only prayer to, recourse to, and union with the Father can turn such failure to success. The cross was Jesus's acceptance of death and failure, not just resignation to fate but a loving and obedient acceptance that he was capable of no more, that the hope for his fellow human beings lay only with his Father who sent him. This was prayer; the first prayer; in one sense the only prayer; and it was answered: the resurrection is the answer to the prayer which is the cross. There was never any doubt about the answer, for this was not a plea to some remote god who might or might not hear or answer. This uniting of human person with God represented in history the eternal unity of God with God. There is nothing closer than the eternal unity of Son and Father and the human prayer of Jesus was the manifestation of that unity.

And the Church is the sacrament, the proclamation throughout history of that unity between humankind and God. And for that reason it is the sacrament of the unity of mankind itself. In the centre of the Church's prayer, the sacrament of the cross, the Eucharist, the sign of the cross that we use, the sacramental symbol, is the unity of humankind, the common meal that symbolizes our unity in love and makes present Christ in his prayer in his sacrifice of the cross, which is the mystery of our unity with God and the mystery of God's unity with God which we call the Trinity. That essentially is what prayer is.

But what is prayer *like* though? What is it like to pray? There are a thousand answers, but the central one is that it is to ask for what we want and ask in the name of Christ so that our asking is one with his asking, his prayer of the cross. And to do that we have to want. If you want to learn to pray learn how to want.

Six

Prayer

I want to talk about the theological problems associated with the idea of prayer, that is to say I am going to talk about prayer at, at least, one remove and this will inevitably be unsatisfactory. I am wholly in agreement in the end with the view that prayer (like loving) is something you only begin to understand, something you only see as justified, if you do it. So in one way the answer to someone who asks: 'What is the point of prayer?' is: pray and you'll see. But it isn't a satisfactory answer because there are a whole lot of people who do pray and do not see clearly. I, for one, and probably a whole lot of you. Praying may be a necessary condition for seeing the point of praying but it certainly is not sufficient. 'Pray and you'll see the point of praying' is not anything like as simple as 'Taste lychees and you'll see why people eat them' because the whole point of eating lychees is that they taste nice, whereas the whole point of praying is not in the satisfactory experience of praying – at least I cannot believe that it is. I usually do not find praying a deeply satisfying experience.

Though you have to be careful here: there are satisfying experiences that are immediately satisfying like drinking good Irish whiskey, but there are other satisfactions that occur only over long periods of time, like having a decently-furnished room. A well-furnished room is not breathtakingly beautiful (like the Irish whiskey) but it is very satisfying to live with, and if you get rid of it simply because it doesn't give you an immediate kick, you will notice the lack of it only maybe a long time later. So I have to be careful about saying that I usually don't find praying a deeply satisfying experience. It is true I hardly ever get a kick out of it, it almost never takes my breath away, but if you are deprived of, say, a decent liturgy for a fairly long period of time you discover an important gap in your emotional life. I might as well say at this point that I think there is a mistaken tendency, more especially in the United States but to some extent in the United Kingdom, to design the liturgy for too immediate a satisfaction. I have been with the 'underground' groups in the American Church who do not really feel they have celebrated a Eucharist unless they get some kind of immediate experience of personal warmth and enhanced sensitivity. I think the liturgies designed by these people are very frequently in bad taste. I agree with those critics who find the *Missa Normativa* a little dull, except that I do not think it is altogether a criticism. A room furnished in good taste is a little dull compared to one covered in psychedelic posters saying 'Love is Love' and 'Mary, the ripest tomato of them all.'

The Mass a prayer?

But I must not let myself be carried away by passionate conservatism. In one way the reforms of the liturgy have made us at least more urgently and explicitly aware of the problem of prayer. So long as the liturgy was in the nature of an abstract painting it could be regarded as more or less callow to ask what it represents, what it means. Our fathers just told us: 'Go to Mass every week and you will find it somehow a meaningful and supporting experience.' For children this was sometimes rationalized in terms of meeting and having little chats with Jesus, but the basic teaching was: here is a mystery; something like a great work of art that has significance that can be expressed in no other way: never mind what it 'means', just enter into it. And lots of Catholics of a past generation who had almost no aesthetic sophistication, who had a crudely rationalist and utilitarian approach to any painting or literature, were in fact able to appreciate the Mass precisely in this abstract way. These Catholics had in fact the usual problems about prayer but they were not very worried about them because prayer was not central to their lives. What was central was the mystery of the Eucharist.

And now we have these people coming along and saying that Mass is itself a prayer. This is explosive because of course the Mass is immediately devalued. The enormously complex mystery of the Mass has become a mere prayer. It is like saying that Chartres Cathedral is really just an advertisement for the Roman Catholic Church.

I am quite sure that what I am saying here must be quite unintelligible to many of you who were brought up in other Christian traditions; traditions in which prayer is quite central; for you, to say that the Mass is a prayer is to make it meaningfully religious for the first time. But I am speaking from the

English Catholic or perhaps the Irish English Catholic standpoint. If to people like me you say that the Mass is a prayer then you really do have to restate what you mean by prayer – that is if you want me to take you seriously. The Mass is the terrible mystery of our union with Christ – compared with this, 'saying your prayers' is almost a triviality. That is one reason why the problem of saying what we mean by prayer has become urgent for Catholics.

Prayer of petition

There is a special problem too now about prayers of petition. These have for a long time been less than respectable. For many years now people have been a bit furtive about actually praying that they will pass an exam or that their wives recover from a dangerous illness. They did it, of course, but they were rather embarrassed to have to mention it in public. It was rather a disreputable weakness, not exactly a secret vice, but certainly not something to talk about.

And now, for heaven's sake, we have these 'Prayers of the Faithful', all out in the public church. We have people openly acknowledging that they want something and apparently expect God to get it for them. We get over this a bit by asking for large scale things like world peace – indeed with any luck the whole episode can be turned into a political credo to follow the theological one, but you cannot altogether get away from the fact that here are these adults asking God for the things they want.

Since all true progressives are expected to favour this liturgical reform and at the same time all true progressives think the prayer of petition is probably a lot of silly superstition, they have a problem here. Haven't they?

Well, what I think I want to say about all this – and I don't know whether I can say it convincingly – is that if you are going to make serious sense of the idea that the Mass is a prayer you have to interpret prayer in terms of the Mass. All prayer is going to have to take its meaning and point from the sacrifice of Christ. We shall simply have to scrap all the metaphors about the all-powerful kindly father up there whom we can sometimes get through to and draw his attention to what we happen to need. We shall really have to get back to the traditional view that all providence is in Christ, that predestination is the predestination of Christ – that no one comes to the Father except through Christ.

As to petitionary prayer I can only contribute what I find to be the immensely illuminating insight of Thomas Aquinas, which, as is so often the way with insights (especially St Thomas's), turns the whole problem upside down very neatly.

Prayer, God, Christ

But first of all, is the problem of prayer not the problem of God? People feel that if only they could be a bit clearer about who or what God is they would see more sense in praying to him. Now I am afraid it is going to have to be the other way round. The problem of God is the problem of prayer. I am not saying this in a pietistic tone of voice: all these intellectual problems would just go away if you all got down on your knees and prayed a bit more. I am saying that maybe the way we understand God is as 'whatever makes sense of prayer'. I would say: we understand God as the other end of the personal relationship which is prayer, except that this might take us back into seeing prayer as a 'personal relationship' with a god, which would bypass the passion of Christ. In the end I suppose I want to say that God is what makes sense of prayer because God is what makes sense of Christ.

Love and be killed

What do I mean by saying that God is what makes sense of Christ? The Gospels insist upon two antithetical truths which express the tragedy of the human condition: the first is that if you do not love you will not be alive; the second is that if you do love you will be killed. If you cannot love you remain self-enclosed and sterile, unable to create a future for yourself or others, unable to live. If, however, you do effectively love you will be a threat to the structures of domination upon which our human society rests and you will be killed.

This point is well put by Rosemary Haughton in her book *Love* that I have just been reading. She is casting doubt on the idea that correct instruction and orthodox teaching are the proper way of inculcating or evoking loving behaviour. She says:

> If effective teaching on the importance of compassion and brotherly concern were sufficient to bring it into existence, the continuous, imagi-native advertising campaign on behalf of famine and war relief organizations would have resulted in the virtual overturning of the world

economic system, in favor of the 'developing' countries. In fact no such outbreak of love has occurred or is likely to occur, otherwise such advertising would probably be forbidden by law, since the economic stability of the Western world depends on the non-development of the 'developing' countries. A serious outbreak of love in the world would bring the markets crashing down. This may sound shockingly cynical, but an examination of the figures for world trade confirms it. (p. 135)

If you do not love you will not be alive; if you love effectively you will be killed.

The life and death of Jesus dramatizes this state of affairs. His attempt to set up a community of love in Galilee was a threat to the colonialist and clericalist establishment and so he was killed. It was a death, as we say in Canon II, that he freely accepted; he was prepared to totally identify with, to be, if you like, the sacrament of, the condition of his fellow men. He refused to defend his life's work at the cost of compromising what he saw as his mission. He was prepared to see all that he had apparently achieved come down in ruins, to see his fellows deserting him, scattered and demoralized. He accepted all this because he did not wish to be the founder of anything, the man of power who would compel the coming of the kingdom. He wished only to do what he called 'the will of his Father', which was simply to accept the condition of humanity, to seek the fullness of humanity in love and to accept the failure that characterizes loving humanity. This is what the crucifixion says. *Ecce homo*. This is what happens when you are really human. But the primary gospel message is that Jesus was raised from the dead – that is to say that God exists. For the only God we Christians know is He who raised Jesus from the dead. God is what makes sense of the senseless waste of the crucifixion. The existence of God means that the failure, the total failure, which is the act of love is a new kind of triumph.

In the crucifixion Jesus casts everything upon God. The crucifixion says that the coming of the kingdom is not to be an achievement of Jesus but a gratuitous act of the Father's love. The kingdom is to come as a gift.

A gift means an expression of love. When we thank someone for a gift we are thinking through the gift to the giver ('thank' and 'think' come from the same root). To say thank you for a gift (or as the Greeks would say, to make a eucharist of it) is to recognize it, to think of it, as a communication of love. Gift is an expression of an exchange of love. To believe in the resurrection, to believe in God, is to believe that the resolution of the tragedy of the human condition comes as a gift, as an act of love encompassing mankind. The crucifixion-resurrection is the archetypal exchange of prayer and answer to prayer. On the cross Jesus casts himself upon God, not because he has not come of age, not because he lived before the age of technology and therefore lacked the means for constructing the kingdom, not because he needed a 'god in the gaps' to do what science and technology might have done had he lived 2000 years later, but because he was wholly human, wholly free, wholly loving and *therefore* helpless to achieve what he sought. If he had wanted something less than the kingdom, if he had been a lesser man, a man not obsessed by love, he might have settled for less and achieved it by his own personality, intelligence, and skill. But he wanted that all men should be as possessed by love as he was, he wanted that they should be divine, and this could only come as a gift. Crucifixion and resurrection, the prayer of Christ and the response of the Father are the archetype and source of all our prayer. It is this we share in sacramentally in the Eucharist; it is this we share in all our prayer. But the crucifixion, the total self-abandonment of Jesus to the Father is not just a prayer that Jesus offered, a thing he happened to do. What the Church came to realize is that it was the revelation of *who* Jesus is. When Jesus is 'lifted up' – and for John this means the whole loving exchange of the lifting up on the cross and the lifting up which is the resurrection – when Jesus is lifted up, he appears for what he is. It is revealed that the deepest reality of Jesus is simply to be of the Father.

> This is the news about . . . Jesus Christ our Lord who, in the order of the Spirit, the Spirit of holiness that was in him, was proclaimed Son of God in all his power through his resurrection from the dead. (Rom. 1:3–4)

> We are preaching a crucified Christ . . . who is the power and wisdom of God. (1 Cor. 1:23)

Prayer and Sonship

He is not first of all an individual person who then prays to the Father. His prayer to the Father is what constitutes him as who he is. He is not just one who prays, not even one who prays best. He is sheer prayer. In other words, the crucifixion/resurrection of Jesus is simply the showing forth, the visibility in human terms, in human history, of the relationship of the Father which constitutes the person who is Jesus. The prayer of Jesus which is his crucifixion, his absolute renunciation of himself in love to the Father, is the eternal relationship of Father and Son made available as part of our history, part of the web of mankind of which we are fragments, a part of the web that gives it a new centre, a new pattern.

All our prayer, whether the Mass itself or those reflections from the Mass that we call our prayers, is a sharing in the sacrifice of Christ and therefore a sharing in the life of the Trinity, a sharing that is the Spirit. All our prayer is, in a very precise sense, in Spirit and in truth. For us to pray is for us to be taken over, possessed by the Holy Spirit which is the life of love between Father and Son. When our prayer is the prayer of the people of God *as such*, when it is the prayer of *the Church as a whole*, it is a sacramental expression of this life of the Spirit. That is what we mean by the sacraments and this is what we primarily mean by our prayer; but the people of God pray individually too, or in small groups which do not claim to represent the whole Church. And here too their prayer is a living by the Spirit.

So our stance in prayer is not simply, or even primarily, that of the creature before the Creator but that of the Son before the Father. At the most fundamental level, the level which defines prayer as prayer, we receive from the Father not as creatures receiving what they need to make up their deficiencies, but as the Son eternally receives his being from the Father. Our praying is an expression in history of our eternal Trinitarian life. Those who feel that to express our eternal divine life in the form of asking for what we need is a little undignified and unworthy of man come of age, need to be reminded that the Son when he expressed his divine life in history emptied himself, taking the form of a slave . . . and being found in human form humbled himself.

The Spirit prays in us

I remember a 'progressive' theologian providing an unintentionally hilarious account of being tempted to pray as his airplane took off down the runway, and how he sternly rebuked himself for this temptation and was able to preserve his dignity as an adult human being. This kind of crass and vulgar criticism of prayer can only arise because the author's notion of prayer is essentially pre-Christian. Behind it lurks the image of the great power 'up there' whom we can shout at and who, if we are lucky, will hear us and provide us with magical help. You remember all those prayers – particularly extempore prayers – that supply God with the necessary information:

'Almighty Father, as you doubtless saw in *The Times* this morning . . .' or 'Almighty Father, paradoxical as it must seem to you . . .' No, for traditional theology, prayer is not our attempt to gain the Father's attention, prayer is not in fact primarily a human activity, it is something we do in virtue of being divine, it is, to use the traditional language, the work of grace in us, the expression of our trinitarian life. 'Whatever you ask in my name . . .' All prayer that really is prayer is in Christ's name; it is offered in virtue of our identification with Christ, our sharing in the sonship of God. The notion of the needy creature simply appealing to his creator is not merely an inadequate account of prayer; it is not prayer at all. It involves an initiative on the part of the creature, building a city and a tower that will reach up into the heavens. All true prayer is the work of grace, that is to say the initiative is from the Father drawing us into communion with his Son. 'In this is love, not that we loved God but that he loved us . . . We love because he first loved us.' What makes the theologian's story of himself primly deciding not to pray from the highest possible motives so comic is that the man clearly regarded *his* decision as the ultimate truth of the matter. He seems unaware of the depth within the free human decision: the depth of grace. I don't, by the way, at the moment want to go into the whole mystery of freedom and grace – of how a decision can be wholly mine , wholly free, and simultaneously wholly the work of God's grace. If you feel hung up on this perhaps you could just make do with St Augustine's remark that God is closer to me than I am to myself. Grace is not something that comes at me from outside to constrain my freedom, it is a depth within me more central to me than what I call my self.

We must keep this firmly in mind: it is *God* who prays. Not just God who answers prayer but God who prays in us in the first place. In prayer we become the *locus* of the divine dialogue between Father and Son, we are in Spirit and truth. It is when we forget this that we get tangled up about petitionary prayer. There are some people who think that prayer of thanksgiving is OK, but prayer of petition is somehow superstitious. It is hard to see the logic of this. If we are thanking God for what he has done then surely we are seeing it as having been his free gift, an expression of his love, as something that would not have happened but for his personal love for us. If we are allowed to see what has already happened as God's free gift, and thank him, what is wrong with seeing what has not yet happened as his free gift also, and asking for it?

Not manipulation of God

Of course the real objection people make to petitionary prayer is that it looks like manipulation of God. Here is God just about to make it rain for the sake of the farmers and their crops in the fields around Clyst Honiton when he overhears the urgent prayer of the vicar who is running his garden party that afternoon and changes his mind. Then there is always the question whether the louder and lustier prayers of the farmers may make him hesitate again. The critics ask rather smugly how it is possible for God to satisfy everybody, to hear all prayers, since good people frequently want incompatible things?

But all this is to forget that it is God who prays, that my prayer is the action of God's grace in me. My prayer is not me putting pressure on God, doing something to God, it is God doing something for me, raising me into the divine life or intensifying the divine life in me. As Thomas Aquinas puts it, we should not say: 'In accordance with my prayer: God wills that it should be a fine day'; we should say: 'God wills: that it should be a fine day in accordance with my prayer.' God brings about my prayer just as much as he brings about the fine day, and what he wills, what he has willed from eternity, is that this fine day should not be, so to say, just an *ordinary* fine day. It should be for me a *significant* fine day, a sign, a communication from God. It should be a fine day that comes about through my prayer. Now what does that mean? It means that I can truly describe the fine day not just as a fine day but as an answer to my prayer, as a revelation to me of God's love, a sudden privileged glimpse of the generosity of God. The fine day becomes for me a sacrament of the love of God. Not a sacrament in the full sense precisely because it is just *for me* and not a revelation for the whole Church. It is *my* faith that has made me whole.

In the last analysis there is no *essential* difference between an apparently ordinary fine day becoming in my faith, for me personally, a medium of communication with the Father, a revelation in Christ, and the mystery of apparently ordinary bread and wine becoming in the faith of the whole Church the body of Christ himself. Of course there are differences: the answers to my prayers are exuberant scintillations of God's revelation, God just does it for fun now and then, whereas the prayer of the whole Church as such, the sacramental prayer in the strict sense, is always answered. We can be *sure* that the apparently ordinary bread and wine have become the body of Christ; we cannot in the same way be sure of an answer to our personal prayer. Or perhaps we should put it more precisely: the answer to the prayer of the whole Church in the Eucharist is at one level *specified*, the bread and wine become the body of Christ (at another level, though, it is not specified, I mean at the level of what this will mean for those taking part). The answer to my private prayer on the other hand is not specified, it may be answered in ways I do not expect. More about this in a moment, for I must hasten to add, lest there be heresy hunters around, that an ordinary fine day does not change by being an answer to prayer whereas bread and wine *are* transformed into the body of Christ – but I don't at the moment want to go into eucharistic theology. I only want to point to the thing that the two have in common: when God makes it that the fine day shall really be an answer to my prayer, and when God makes it that bread and wine should really be the body and blood of Christ by involving it in the prayer of the whole Church, in both cases he is revealing himself, making us see (in faith of course) the meaning of his love. 'In faith of course' because the bystander will not see the bread and wine as the body of Christ. These revelations like all revelations are a matter of the divine life in us, part of our sharing in the life of the Trinity that we call faith.

Praying for the right things

Another final word about prayer of petition. It is something that I learned from Victor White OP and seems to me well worth passing on. Victor maintained that one important reason why people found it difficult to pray was that they prayed for the wrong things. By this he did *not* mean that they prayed for merely material things instead of for spiritual things; on the contrary he meant practically the exact opposite. He meant that people pray for things they don't really want but have been told that they ought to want. You feel you *ought* to want the grace to be nice to your next-door neighbour or you *ought* to want your mother-in-law to recover from her painful gumboil or you *ought* to want passionately to see a cure for AIDS, but as a matter of cold fact what you *really* want most of all is a short holiday in North Wales. But it would be 'selfish' to pray for that, so you resolutely turn your mind to more high-minded things. Victor maintained that what people call distractions in prayer are just their real wants and concerns breaking in on the bogus wants and concerns that we think are the only suitable ones for prayer. If you get 'distractions', he said, take a good look at them and see what wants and needs they spring from and pray about those – whatever they are. When you are really praying for what you really want you won't be distracted – the prayers of people on sinking ships are rarely troubled by distractions, they know exactly what they want. The prayer of petition is a matter of bringing ourselves, in the form of our wants and needs, into the presence of the Father. If we come before the Father not in our true selves but in a disguised and respectable form, pretending to be high-minded and altruistic saints, then we will not make any contact at all.

Prayer of petition is a form of self-exploration and at the same time self-realization. If we are honest enough to admit to our shabby infantile desires, then the grace of God will grow in us; it will slowly be revealed to us, precisely in the course of our prayer, that there are more important things that we truly do want. But this will not be some abstract recognition that we ought to want these things; we will really discover a desire for them in ourselves. But we must start where we are. Children will never mature if they are treated as adults from the age of two, with no concessions to their infantile emotional needs. Children must begin from where they actually are. Similarly we will never grow in the life of prayer if we begin by imagining that we are John of the Cross. We have to begin in our own infantile imperfect grasping state. All that the Father requires of us is that we recognize ourselves for what we are. He will attend to the growing. He will grant the increase.

I think the process is expressed pretty well in a poem by the Hindu Rabindranath Tagore – which Rosemary Haughton quotes:

> Time after time I came to your gate
> with raised hands, asking for more and yet more.
> You gave and gave, now in slow
> measure, now in sudden excess.
> I took some, and some things I let
> drop; some lay heavy on my hands;
> Some I made into playthings and broke
> them when tired; till all the wrecks and
> the hoards of your gifts grew immense,
> hiding you, and the ceaseless expectation
> wore my heart out.
> Take, oh take – has now become my cry.
> Shatter all from this beggar's bowl:
> put out this lamp of the importunate
> watcher, hold my hands, raise me from
> the still gathering heap of your gifts
> into the bare infinity of your uncrowded presence.

Prayer, then, whatever stage we are at, is an entry into the mystery of the crucifixion of Christ, a sharing into the eternal exchange between Father and Son. That is why prayer is really a waste of time. The incarnate form of our prayer may be concerned with getting something done, forwarding our plans, and the generosity of God is such that he will let himself be incarnate even in these ways. But the very heart of prayer is not getting anything done. It is a waste of time, an even greater waste of time than play. Play is after all something that can be justified in terms of getting something done, some human achievement. I do not mean that play can be reduced to a relaxation that fits someone to return to work – though our own production-obsessed society is in danger of thinking this – but play even valued for its own sake is not a total waste of time, it has to do with a certain kind of human achievement.

For a real absolute waste of time you have to go to prayer. I reckon that more than 80 per cent of our reluctance to pray consists precisely in our dim recognition of this and our neurotic fear of wasting time, of spending part of our life in something that in the end gets you nowhere, something that is not merely non-productive, non-money making, but is even non-creative. It doesn't even have the justification of art and poetry. It is an absolute waste of time, it is a sharing into the waste of time which is the interior life of the Godhead. God is not in himself productive or creative. Sure he takes time to throw off creation, to make something, to achieve something. But the real interior life of the Godhead is not in creation, it is in the life of love which is the Trinity, the procession of Son from Father and of the Spirit from this exchange. God is not first of all our creator or any kind of maker. He is love, and his life is not like the life of the worker or artist but of lovers wasting time with each other uselessly. It is into this worthless activity that we enter in prayer. This, in the end, is what makes sense of it.

Part Two

Incarnation and Sacraments

Seven

Christ and Politics

To begin with I shall say briefly why I think that, if we are to take 'politics' in the ordinary modern sense, political interpretations of the gospels are mistaken. I do not think that Jesus sought political power in order to change society or that either he or his followers were concerned with the political independence of the section of the Roman empire where they lived. In the second part I want to talk of the relevance the gospel has, nevertheless, to the things that do concern politicians in the modern sense. I take it that every Christology implies an ecclesiology; so that section will be a discussion of what, in view of what we have to say about Jesus, is the relationship of the body of Christ to the body politic.

Let us begin with Simon. I do not think that the Apostle whom Luke, both in his Gospel and in Acts, called 'Simon the zealot' could have been a zealot in the restricted and technical sense that the word acquired only some years after the crucifixion of Jesus. Simon was, perhaps, or had been, zealous for the exact observance of the Law and disapproving of other Jews who might have been more free and easy. Maybe he belonged, or had belonged, to a Jewish sect rather like some extreme right-wing, super-orthodox groups in modern Israel. (Or perhaps he just had a nick-name somehow related to this.) Much later 'zealot' also came to mean an organized group engaged not in the defence of the Law against back-sliding Jews but in subverting by violence the Roman colonial rule.

When I say that I think these things you must not suppose that I claim any personal expertise or authority in these matters. I am merely indicating that I have been convinced by E. P. Sanders in *Jesus and Judaism* (1985), and, especially, by the arguments of Raymond Brown in his book, *The Death of the Messiah* (1994).

Brown points out that the Roman direct rule of its province in Palestine by Prefects or procurators falls into two periods separated by the short reign of Herod Agrippa I, between 41 and 46 CE. He argues that Roman rule and Jewish attitudes to it were very different in the two periods; and, of course, the ministry of Jesus belonged exclusively to the first. Much misguided reading of the Gospels, from Kautsky to Brandon and Winter, for whom Jesus was a political activist against colonial rule, arises, he suggests, from treating this first period (when there were Prefects, for example Pontius Pilate, only of Judaea) as exactly like the second, when direct rule extended north into Galilee.

> Too often the final years before the Revolt with their seething discontent and Zealot terrorism have been thought characteristic of the earlier period in which Jesus lived. This has facilitated the creation of the myth that Jesus was a political revolutionary. (Brown, p. 677)

I have, for some years, argued that Liberation Theology is not helped but hindered by a mistaken 'process theology' of God – produced largely by bourgeois academics in Europe and the USA. It is now, I suppose, time to argue that it is not helped either but hindered by misreading the accounts of Jesus in the New Testament.

Brown also notes the particularly savage in-fighting during the century before Christ among various Jewish factions and contenders for power – a bloody history of massacres and crucifixions. The last of the successors of Herod the Great, Archelaus

> . . . was such a bad ruler that, at the request of his Jewish subjects, the Emperor removed him and appointed . . . the first prefect of Judaea . . . after such a baneful history [of Jewish rule] the Roman prefecture represented a more sane and orderly administration, even if foreign rulers are rarely liked. (Brown, p. 678)

We are, I think, entitled to add a pinch of salt to that 'request'; I can think of no successful takeover of a country by a foreign power which did not subsequently turn out to have been 'requested'. Nevertheless, Brown's main point stands.

It is, indeed, hard to imagine anyone actually liking Pontius Pilate, but he was not notably bloodthirsty, either by the standards of the earlier warring Hasmoneans and Herodians or of the later corrupt and repressive Roman colonial rulers. Indeed the whole reign of the (personally detestable) Emperor Tiberius (14–37 CE) which covered the whole public ministry of Jesus was generally recognized as remarkably peaceful (*sub Tiberia quies*, as Tacitus put it) or, as we say in the *praeconium* with which (at least in the Dominican rite) we introduce the liturgy of Christmas: 'In the sixth age of the world, when the whole world was at peace: Jesus Christ, eternal Son of the eternal Father, was born in Bethlehem in Judaea of the Virgin Mary'.

Finally, a Spanish scholar, pleasantly and ironically called Guevara, is quoted by Raymond Brown, in what he describes as 'his most detailed study of the political context in Judaea' as saying 'The response of the sources is very clear: the epoch of the public life of Jesus was a peaceful epoch' (Brown, p. 679).

However, during this peaceful epoch Jesus was undoubtedly crucified. (After typing this article I read in the press that it had been doubted by Mr Enoch Powell: I would like to record my appreciation of this most welcome corroboration of my position.) Moreover, every Gospel indicates that the charge laid against him before Pilate was that he claimed to be 'King of the Jews'. (And this despite the fact that before his trial nobody in the Gospels ever calls him King of the Jews except a legendary Magus at the beginning of Matthew.) There is surely at least a whiff of politics about all this.

A plausible explanation, however, is that the work of Jesus, although not political, and his teaching, although also not political, had a *de facto* political effect. He was a trouble-maker in an unstable society. As E. P. Sanders says, speaking of Jesus' announcement of the end of the temple and, even more, his symbolic attack on the place itself, this

> . . . would have been offensive to most Jews. The gesture, even if it did not raise much tumult, could readily have led the Romans to think that Jesus was a threat to public order. In particular the physical demonstration against the temple by one who had a notable following looms as so obvious an occasion for the execution that we need look no further. (Sanders, p. 302)

Again:

> We can understand [the execution of Jesus] simply by knowing that he spoke of a kingdom and stirred the hopes of the people. His miracles also produced excitement, and excitement carries its own dangers . . . a man who spoke of a kingdom, spoke against the temple and had a following

was one marked for execution; but no one need have regarded him as a military leader . . . the Romans regarded him as dangerous at one level but not at another; dangerous as one who excited the hopes and dreams of the Jews, but not as an actual leader of an insurgent group. (Sanders, p. 295)

There was no insurgent group: none of Jesus' followers was arrested or harassed by the Roman authorities after the crucifixion.

It has to be said, though, that Jesus himself is presented in the Gospels as somewhat ambiguous on the question of his role. The early churches knew of two interrogations of Jesus after his arrest, one by his fellow Jews and one by the Roman authorities, and they give us fascinating (but in historical detail not very credible) dramatic accounts of how they imagined these interrogations took place. As they present it, both interrogations really centred on the question: in what sense is Jesus the *Christos*, the name which after the resurrection, and only after the resurrection, became the commonest title of Jesus. The questioning seems, at first sight, quite different on the two occasions.

In the first, it is what we would call religious, but in the second it is political. The Jewish interrogators are presented as concerned about whether Messianic (Christological) claims about Jesus involve a claim to be in some specially deep (and putatively blasphemous) sense 'son of the Blessed', that is divine, a demi-god. In the Roman interrogation Pilate is concerned about whether the claim is, in the ordinary sense, political: is it a claim to independent kingship. 'Are you the king of the Jews?' In almost every case Jesus replies to this *sy legeis* which has hitherto been rendered in English as 'Thou hast said it' or, as in Brown: 'You say'. We are now, happily, able to be more accurate: since *The House of Cards*, we know that what Jesus said was 'You might very well say that: I couldn't possibly comment.'

There is, of course, no doubt at all that Jesus announced the coming of 'the kingdom', the kingdom of heaven, the kingdom of God or 'your kingdom', as, for example, when Mrs Zebedee came up to him with her sons and said to him 'Command that these two sons of mine may sit one at your right hand and one at your left, in your kingdom' (Mt. 20:20). Jesus replies that that sort of thing is really not his business. His business is to 'drink the cup', to suffer and die. It is the business of his Father to decide what will happen next: the resurrection and glorification of Jesus, the sending of the Spirit and the acknowledgement of Jesus as the Christ (which is what the Church is about).

In the Gospel of John, as a matter of literary device, all interlocutors of Jesus have at least one thing in common: they have to misunderstand him – so that he can develop what he has said at a deeper level. Usually this takes the form of a crassly literal misunderstanding of what Jesus has said: Nicodemus: 'Can a man enter again into his mother's womb.' The woman at the well: 'Give me some of that water, that I may not thirst, nor come here to draw' (though I think she is joking). So also with the people after the feeding of the five thousand. But in the synoptics, too, the people regularly miss the point of what Jesus is doing or saying.

At the big demo on Palm Sunday, Mark reports the crowd as shouting, 'Blessed is the kingdom of our father David that is coming. Hosanna in the highest.' Luke says they shouted, 'Blessed is the king who comes in the name of the Lord'; John has 'Blessed is he who comes in the name of the Lord, even the king of Israel' but adds, 'His disciples did not understand this at first, but when Jesus was glorified, then they remembered'.

So the misunderstanding involved in Jesus' condemnation on a political charge is a sort of culmination of a series of inevitable misunderstandings throughout his ministry. I think this is part of the positive teaching of the evangelists: Jesus is not so much 'the man for others', as 'the man to be misunderstood by others'. His identity, what his place is in the story, his part in the play, cannot be captured in any human categories (including the human category of 'the gods'). Jesus is a mystery. In fact, as John came to see and, at Chalcedon, the Church eventually came to define, Jesus is the Word in which the ultimate mystery, God, speaks himself.

For John, I think, Jesus has no definable place in the story because he is also, in some way, author of the story. That is why Flann O'Brien's *At Swim Two Birds*, in which an author comes under criticism and attack by his fictional characters, is essential reading for any Christologist.

There is a clear implication in, I think, all the passion narratives that the misunderstanding by Pilate is not accidental but manipulated by the chief priests. Their real case against Jesus, it is suggested, has to do with his claims to forgive sinners without the proper religious rituals of repentance, to be closer to God than is the temple, and so on; but, since they wanted him executed, and while religious squabbles in the local alien cult would cut no ice with Pilate, they put the thing in political terms. In a tantalizingly short paragraph, E. P. Sanders notes that Schweitzer, in his *Quest of the Historical Jesus*, had already suggested that

What Judas betrayed (a point on which the Gospels are unhelpful) was that Jesus and his small band thought of him as 'king' . . . Judas conveyed Jesus's pretension to the chief priests . . . it was the final weapon they needed: a specific charge to present to Pilate, more certain to have fatal effect than the general charge of 'troublemaker'. (Sanders, p. 309)

Whether or not this is the case, there remains, I think, a sense in which no attempt to categorize Jesus in either political or religious terms is going to succeed. The Gospels seem to suggest, at least, that there is a certain inevitability here, quite apart from any malicious intention on the part of the opponents of Jesus. It seems to me quite certain that any idea that there was simply a lamentable misunderstanding, which could have been avoided by a little clarification, has to be just wrong.

Consider, for example, the story of the tribute to Caesar. The tribute was, naturally, unpopular but especially with the Pharisees who saw it as an insult to the Lord, the only king of the universe, for his special people to acknowledge the lordship of this primitive idol-worshipper in Rome. So if Jesus had said: 'Yes, the tribute should be paid', he would alienate true and devout Jews. On the other hand the Herodians, who were also present, were not so traditionalist and felt that God's law would allow them to come to an accommodation with Caesar for practical purposes; so had Jesus said that the tribute was not to be paid he would have been speedily reported to the authorities as a subversive.

Clever; but not so clever as Jesus. In the first place he makes the Pharisees produce a coin with Caesar's image stamped on it: thus acknowledging that they are prepared to handle and use an abomination, a graven image, an idol specifically forbidden by the Law. But then he says: 'Render to Caesar the things that are Caesar's and to God the things that are God's.'

Now, if he had meant by this that there are two areas, one the world of coins and trade and secular life which is the business of Caesar, and another, a spiritual realm separate from this which is the preserve of religion and God, he would simply have been opting for the Herodian side, for they were the nearest thing a Jew could get to such a bizarre idea. (This is, need I say, the interpretation taken by all modern liberal individualists: churchmen should not meddle in public politics, nor politicians in private matters of religion.)

It might be that Jesus was taking this position: one area of life where God held sway and another for Caesar, but it seems unlikely that his theology was as bad as that. More importantly, it would not account for the punch-line of the story where it says (in all three synoptics) that when they heard his reply the crowd were astonished at it. If he had opted just for one side of the argument they might have approved or disapproved but hardly have been astonished.

I suggest that they were astonished and perhaps delighted by the ingenious way Jesus evaded the trap set for him. He has devised an ambiguous answer which could satisfy either party, for what he said could have another opposite meaning which would be satisfactory to Pharisees. 'Render to Caesar what is Caesar's and to God what is God's' could also mean: Caesar, under God of course, is welcome to the rest of the world and may lay it under tribute, but this land is *Eretz* Israel and it belongs only to God and was bestowed by God on his own people, the Jews. This concrete interpretation is, in fact, much more obvious than the abstract separation of sacred and secular aspects of human life. It is, of course, one congenial to the Pharisees rather than the Herodians.

There is, then, no formula within which Jesus and his mission can be encapsulated. For Luke, remember, his public life begins with the boy who runs away from home, explaining, when they find him in the temple, that his parents did not understand him.

Jesus, then, was not, we may say, interested in politics or in acquiring political power (Jn 6:15 represents him as actively avoiding it), but the striking thing is how very much politicians and others concerned with power were interested in Jesus. 'The chief priests and pharisees gathered the council and said: "What are we to do? For this man performs many signs. If we let him go on thus, everyone will believe in him, and the Romans will come and destroy both our holy place and our nation"' (Jn 11:47).

The kingdom of God, as Jesus tells Pilate in John's Gospel, is not 'of this world' but it is nevertheless of great interest and importance to this world, and more especially if 'this world' is taken in the sense in which it is most commonly used by John: this corrupt world. This world will hate Jesus and, so he warns his followers, it will hate them as well. The preaching of the kingdom of heaven is threatening to the kingdom of this world – what John the Baptist calls 'the sin of this world'.

It is time now to take a quick look at the implications for ecclesiology of the picture of Christ that I have been sketching. To try to answer the question: 'In what sense was Jesus a political figure?' is also to point to an answer to the question: In what sense is the Church a political institution or related to such institutions? Since I am going to restrict myself to the Roman

Catholic Church, I will begin with a word about what is called 'Catholic social teaching'. I do not think that there is a Catholic social teaching in the sense that there is an accepted Catholic teaching about, say, the Trinity or the Eucharist. Instead there have been an important series of responses on the part of representative Catholics to contemporary social and political situations and doctrines.

Let us start with *Rerum Novarum* (1891). It has, I think rightly, been said that Pope Leo XIII did not address the social injustices of his day: that had already been done by Karl Marx and others. *Rerum Novarum* was addressed centrally to what it described as the 'socialist' response to and critique of liberal capitalism. That liberal capitalism was a disaster for a large proportion of the human race was obvious, and common ground to socialists and the Pope. That it was not a natural disaster but one made by human beings and perhaps curable by human beings was also common ground.

What that highly intelligent and humane man, Leo XIII, saw was that the only serious available critique of the abominations of nineteenth-century liberal capitalism was nineteenth-century socialism and that this would not do. For a majority of European socialists, 'socialism' was an oversimplified doctrine hopelessly in thrall to ideas left over from the Enlightenment, in particular, the Enlightenment' s view of religion: the odd phenomenon that we should call bourgeois atheism.

Leo's problem was to preach the gospel in the face of capitalism without allowing the gospel itself to be oversimplified in a similar way. It was, of course, because Catholics had been slow to preach the gospel in the face of capitalism that when they began they found this rival in the field who had to be coped with. This indeed, was the reason why they (or a small minority of them) began at all. Anyway, whether or not you read *Rerum Novarum* as I do, you may perhaps agree that it was a response to concrete circumstances rather than the handing down of an already developed traditional doctrine. It was simply a matter of preaching the gospel as best you can in a certain time and place.

I do not here want to argue this same point for the great succeeding 'social encyclicals'; but it seems plausible to see *Quadragesimo Anno* as a rather similar reaction to the Thirties world of fascism, and *Centesimus Annus* as a response to the collapse of state capitalism in Eastern Europe – or rather, as with *Rerum Novarum*, a critique of what is perceived as an oversimplified response (in this case of the Western 'market economy') to these events.

I would like now to look briefly at four models of the relationship between Church and society: as alternative, as model, as social cement, and as challenge.

First, then, the model of the Church as *alternative to political society*, even a way of escaping from political society. This model has been popular in our time mainly as an object of abuse, under the name of 'otherworldly Christianity'. The Church is seen as pointing the way to a kingdom of God which is quite distinct from this world. The view is that we should not be too concerned about this world and its problems. Provided they live by the rules, the members of the Church will shortly be leaving this vale of tears and inhabiting an altogether better and quite distinct place. It is no concern of the Church to change the world. We need, of course, to change our individual selves, and this, naturally, involves changing our behaviour towards our neighbours, making sure that we treat them with charity and justice. But that is a very different matter from trying to bring about a just world order. It is an illusion (and perhaps sinful vanity) to suppose we could do any such thing.

The world, on this view, is still in the power of the Prince of this World. True, he has been cast out of the heavens, where he is no longer the Accuser of humankind and has been replaced there by the Advocate, the Paraclete. Satan has indeed fallen from heaven, but fallen to earth: and all that the faithful Christian can expect from this world is persecution at the hands of his agents. Christ's kingdom is not of this world and he reigns only in the hearts of his faithful, secretly. There will be a time when his kingdom will become manifest, but it is not yet.

The illumination I think we might detect in all this is a proper scepticism about the finality of any human achievement. It seems to me that a central contribution that Christianity makes to our understanding of humankind is its understanding of, and ability to cope with, failure. From one point of view, this is exactly what the cross is.

We see this theoretical model concretely represented in the early monastic movement. Here we had groups of people deciding that the life of the gospel could not easily, if at all, be lived in the cities. They went out into the countryside, not because they wanted to be close to 'nature', nor because of its beauty (to which, I imagine, they were wholly indifferent, if not hostile), but because it was not the city, it was not society. Whether in the unstructured groups of desert fathers, or, in a different way, among the Irish monks, or in the organized communes of continental monasticism, we find the idea that the Christian life can best be lived in a Church which is an alternative society and an alternative *to* society.

It is, of course, true that the great monastic communities of the West fairly soon themselves became centres of society; became, in fact, great undying corporations which, by their accumulation of wealth, formed the backbone of medieval rural capitalism. But by that time the model had changed somewhat. So the Church as alternative to the world or to society had respectable and interesting supporters.

I turn, now, to another model, derived, I think, from the first: this is the model of the Church itself as *model for society*. The idea is that, especially in a society consisting largely of Christians, organizations such as parishes or religious communities could be, for example, pioneering testing-grounds for projects of social welfare. This is not an absurd idea for, after all, the state-run schools and hospitals of modern Europe are directly descended from such Church activities in the past, as, indeed, are the universities and the structures associated with marriage. Whatever we say of this though, and however centrally we place the 'option for the poor', it is hard to see such good works as the defining function of the Church or its principal relevance to society and politics.

I would like to move on to the third model: the metaphor of *social cement*. The Church might be thought to provide the social cohesion upon which, in the end, society rests. This, too, has a highly respectable and ancient background. Aristotle seeks to identify the difference between the links that may be formed between separate states and the bonds which unite the citizens of the same state. There can be trade agreements and pacts, he says, between separate states and their individual members, but no amount of such contracts will constitute them as one state or superstate.

The reason Aristotle gives is that the citizens of a state are bound together, not fundamentally by commutative justice, fairness and law, but by what he calls *philia*, political friendship, a recognition that they belong to each other and are responsible for each other. Friendship, he maintains, is much more than mutual benevolence, it involves a certain sharing, a *koinonia*, what Aquinas calls a *communicatio*, a sharing of life between friends.

True friendship, moreover, has to be based on more than a sharing of pleasures or of commercial interests, it has to be a sharing of the most fundamental human requirement, the virtues. Virtues, for Aristotle, are an absolutely necessary (though not a sufficient) condition for human happiness; for virtues are just the cluster of acquired dispositions necessary for living a flourishing human life. So, unless the citizens care about and seek to foster virtue, and thus happiness, in each other and in the community in general, there is no true *polis*: there is just a crowd of businessmen making honourable agreements in order to further their own particular interests. For this reason, Aristotle put at the basis of the state the kind of common life that is expressed in festivals and games and cultural life in general, for it is these things that foster friendship, and, as we should say, a common identity.

Now, if you think that Aristotle has got a point here, then it will not be difficult to, so to say, transpose *philia*, friendship, into a new key. As Fergus Kerr has shown, Thomas Aquinas proposed to treat *caritas* (primarily the love of God for us) on the analogy of *philia*, *amicitia*, and not, as generations of theologians had done, following Augustine, on the analogy of *amor*, the passion of love (Kerr, 1987). *Caritas* means that God shares his life, his Holy Spirit with us, and that consequently we can share it with each other. In Aquinas the model for the plan of salvation is the establishment of a political community: but a political community understood in Aristotelean (rather than, say, Thatcherite) terms. For Aquinas the Church is the sacrament of this community-in-charity: as *Lumen Gentium* put it succinctly, 'the sacrament of union with God and the unity of humankind'.

The Church, then, is the symbolic visibility of God's outpouring of the Spirit in the world. *In the world*, please notice, not just among the members of the Church. The unity sacramentally symbolized and realized in the Eucharist is not the unity of the Church, as such, but of humankind; and it is a unity manifestly not yet achieved, though to love in charity is to have a foretaste or glimpse of it.

It is important to be rather clear about this. What corresponds to the *philia* without which there can be no true political society, is the divine *agape*, *caritas*, that is required if there is ever to be a true humankind: that future unity in charity that will mark humankind's coming of age. It is not the unity of the Church, for this is simply the sacramental sign of human unity. What the sacramental life of the Church is about is the future unity of humankind (and our foretaste of that), not the unity of this or that human society at any point in history. If the sacramental life is the social cement that binds together a particular society, it is merely in the way that festivals and games and a common culture bind it together. One concrete exemplar of the Church as social cement is what we have come to call the 'establishment' of a Church.

We have looked, then, at the Church seen as alternative, as model, and as cement for society. Let me turn now to what I see as a more promising model than any of these: the Church as *challenge to society*. The parallel between this eccelesiology and the Christology I sketched earlier will, I hope, be plain. To put it simply: Christ was not interested in political power, but powerful politicians were very interested in him because they felt threatened. Similarly, the Church (in its sporadic periods of health) is not interested in political power, but these are the very times when those with political power come to take the same kind of hostile interest in the Church.

When Leo XIII spoke of the market economy of capitalism laying on the masses 'a yoke little better than slavery itself', he spoke from within a moral tradition that has much in common with the socialist moral tradition but is not identical with it. The socialist critique of capitalism is based on a fundamentally Aristotelean version of human society, which you can simplify by saying that it is about people before it is about products, though it is about both. The making of people into commodities was noted by both Pope Leo and Karl Marx, who acknowledged his debt to Aristotle more than once.

The difference is partly one of perspective. The socialist is analogous to a doctor who prescribes the right treatment for some baneful disease – working within, let us call it, the 'hippocratic tradition' where he learnt his craft and science. The socialist, like the doctor, is concerned with a particular virulent disease – in his case the chronic condition of capitalism. He is no more concerned with the coming of the kingdom of God, or, indeed, with the coming of any kind of utopia on earth, than is the doctor with curing his patient of death. They are both tackling a specific job, presented to them by a particular juncture in history.

The preaching of the gospel (although of course it takes place at a particular juncture in history) has its perspective not on an immediate and particular objective but on the *eschaton*, on the ultimate destiny of human beings and humankind. That is why, unlike socialism as such, the gospel is not a programme for political action: not because it is too vague and general or too private, but because it is also a critique of action itself, a reminder that we must think on the end.

Central to the gospel is the revelation that our salvation, in the end, comes not by our achievements but by the failure which is the cross, a failure accepted out of Christ's loving obedience to his mission from the Father and for love of his fellow men and women. So if I think (as I do) that all my fellow Catholics should support a socialist immediate programme, it is not because I am a Catholic but because I am a socialist.

The Christian socialist, as I see her, is more complex, more ironic, than her non-Christian colleagues, because her eye is also on the ultimate future, on the future that is attained by weakness, through and beyond the struggle to win in this immediate fight. But even short of the *eschaton*, the Christian is also more vividly aware not only of the need to avoid injustice in the fight for justice (as any rational non-Christian socialist would, of course, be) but also of the need always to crown victory not with triumphalism but with forgiveness and mercy, for only in this way can the victory won in this fight remain related to the kingdom of God.

Without that opening on to a future (and, as yet, mysterious) destiny, what begins as a local victory for justice becomes, in its turn, yet another form of domination, another occasion for challenge and struggle – as we have seen time and time again in the history of the Church and the history of all liberation movements. Remember that even the capitalist revolution could once be regarded rightly as a liberation struggle.

To return to the Church, the sacrament of the divine life in humankind. The sacraments belong, Aquinas reminds us, to the time between, the epoch between the cross, on which our salvation was won, and the *eschaton*, when the fruits of that great sacrifice of love will be plainly, and not just sacramentally, revealed: when there will be no longer faith but vision, no longer a Church but just human beings in and through whose human lives God will be manifested, no longer in alienated, distant form but in our own lives. God will be all in all. For Aquinas, the sacramental and all that belongs to religion and the Church as we know it is part of the time before that, the time of sin.

Like Karl Marx, Aquinas knew that religious cult belongs to human alienation, and that the passing of this alienation would mean the withering away of the Church. But unlike Marx, he knew that the passing of this alienation needed more than the establishment of socialism, or even of communism; it meant a revolution in our very bodies, a death and resurrection.

Eight

He was Crucified, Suffered Death, and was Buried

I don't know whether you've noticed how completely different this article is from all the other articles in the creed. All other articles talk religious language or speak of marvels that only a believer could take completely seriously: 'born of the virgin Mary, on the third day he rose from the dead, the Holy Spirit the Lord and giver of life . . .' and so on. But this just flatly says that Jesus was crucified, died and was buried, rather horrible facts but perfectly ordinary facts that would have been known to any spectator in Jerusalem that day and in fact are quite well known to us. Nobody but a crank has the slightest doubt that Jesus was crucified and died and was buried; it is piece of historical information on a par with the fact that Prince Charlie lost the battle of Culloden. There is no need to be a Christian to know about this, you just have to be ordinarily well-informed.

So already there is a tiny problem here – what is it doing in the creed? The creed is supposed to be full of things that make demands on our faith, on the commitment of the whole man, and the Lord knows what. What is this simple piece of ordinary history doing there? It's as though you had a creed saying, 'And I believe that the Holy Spirit is poured forth in our hearts because of the resurrection of Christ, and that Huddersfield is in Yorkshire'. It's not as though the creed put a religious interpretation on the matter, as though it had said Jesus died as a sacrifice, or he died to make atonement for our sins, or He shed his blood of the new covenant. It just quite starkly states the empirical facts. Indeed, some creeds go out of their way to emphasize the sheer vulgar historicality of the thing by dating it: 'He was put to death under Pontius Pilate.' One word used, 'crucified', does suggest an interpretation of the affair as we shall see. Yet it is precisely not a religious interpretation but a political one. If only Jesus had been stoned to death that would at least have put the thing in a religious context – this was the kind of thing you did to prophets. But nobody was ever crucified for anything to do with religion. Moreover the reference to Pontius Pilate doesn't only date the business but also makes it clear that it was the Roman occupying forces that killed Jesus – and they obviously were not interested in religious matters as such. All they cared about was preserving law and order and protecting the exploiters of the Jewish people.

It all goes to show that if we have some theological theory that only certain kinds of proposition can follow the words 'I believe that . . .' we should be very careful. We can believe that the Holy Spirit proceeds from the Father and the Son, which really isn't an empirically testable statement, and also that Jesus was killed, which is. But this article isn't just an oddity in the creed. This oddity is the very centre of the creed. It is the insertion of this bald empirical historical fact that makes the creed a Christian creed, that gives it the proper Christian flavour. It is because of this vulgar fact stuck in the centre of our faith that however ecumenical we may feel towards the Buddhists, say, and however fascinating the latest guru may be, Christianity is something quite different. It isn't rooted in religious experiences or transcendental meditation or the existential commitment of the self. It is rooted in a murder committed by security forces in occupied Jerusalem around the year AD 30.

Most of the creed is expressed in language that could fairly be called mythological (I suppose it is no longer necessary to insist that mythological language is just as good as any other and at least as likely to tell the truth as any other), which makes it relatively easy to relate it to other mythological forms. There are creation and resurrection myths all over the place and Christianity can be related to them. And a good thing too. What *anchors* the creed is the totally non-theological cross. And I think it is highly significant that in popular tradition (which is where you would expect to find the Holy Spirit at work) the cross is the central image representing our belief. From time to time there are mythological or at least interpretative crosses – crucifixes that show Christ the King in glory, or that show Christ in an attitude of prayer, or with his arms outstretched to welcome all people. But all these, excellent though they are in their own way, are a minority thing. The image that stands at the centre of popular Christianity just shows a dying man nailed to a piece of wood. And this is just a picture of an historical event. I hasten to add that this is not *just* a popular tradition. It is a tradition that very early got itself into Scripture. One of the very earliest Christian writings (earlier than any of the Gospels), St Paul's first letter to the Corinthians, says 'we preach Christ crucified' and 'I decided to know nothing among you except Jesus Christ and him crucified.'

There is then a certain stark and literal simplicity about this article of the creed and I would like to look at it with the same simplicity. There are of course endless interpretations of Jesus of Nazareth, and most of them help to shed some light on him. You can, for example, take the titles used of him in the New Testament; you can tease out what would be meant by calling him Messiah or the Servant or Son of Man or Son of God, or you can unravel what is meant by saying he is light of the world or bread of life. You can examine what is meant by saying that he came to save the world or that he came as our redeemer. And all these are useful things to do. But if you have not started with very simple things these others are likely to lead you into strange pathways. Take the last for example. It is agreed that Jesus is in some way our redeemer – the word is used in connection with him around a dozen times in the New Testament where it is furthermore agreed that it was by his cross that he redeemed the world. But then the questions begin. To redeem means to buy back, as when you give money to the pawnbroker and get back the thing you hocked, or when you pay money to a kidnapper to redeem someone who is captive. And I suppose you would redeem someone from jail or from a debtor's prison by paying the money he owed. People have asked questions like *what* did Jesus pay *to whom* in order to get back *whom*. Most people have thought Jesus was paying a debt due to God that was owed by man, but some have thought he was paying a ransom due to Satan who had captured man. And so people got around to saying that what Jesus was doing on the cross was paying back something owed by man; and pretty soon they were saying that this was why he allowed himself to be crucified.

You get a similar process with the notion that Jesus is our High Priest, as it says in the Letter to the Hebrews. If he was a priest then he offered sacrifice. What did he sacrifice? Himself on the cross, of course. To whom did he offer himself? To the Father, of course. Excellent; and pretty soon people are saying that Jesus went to Calvary in order to offer this sacrifice of our redemption. Then again there were people saying that Jesus like the Servant in Isaiah took on himself the burden and punishment of our sins: 'by his punishment we are healed'. Although he had no sin himself he took on himself the penalty of our sins. And pretty soon they are saying that he submitted to the cross in order to take the penalty of sin off our shoulders and on to his own. Sometimes people have said that Jesus paid the debt or offered the sacrifice or took the punishment of sin *instead* of us – the so-called 'vicarious' theory. And sometimes people say that he did this *in the name of* the whole human race – the so-called 'representative' theory.

Now all these views (and a great many more) can help to shed light on Jesus and are therefore not a waste of time. But they all have one interesting feature in common. They all end up as answers to the questions 'Why did Jesus decide to be crucified? What was the reason for the Cross? Why something so strange as the crucifixion for the Son of God?' Now my belief is that the ordinary Christians who have kept the crucifix or the sign of the cross as their creed – a visual one that is just as good as a verbal one – never had this problem at all. The ordinary people, deep down in their understanding have never had the slightest puzzle about the cross. They have taken it for granted. Why naturally the man was crucified. Aren't we all? Whether they would put it into words or not, they felt deep down that crucifixion really does express what life is about. It is not a thing that is easily acknowledged; for one thing it is something we are afraid to face – that the deep things in life are suffering and death. Not the only things in life of course; and life that is really humanly lived consists in making value out of suffering and death amongst other things. But the deeply significant things are always tied up with suffering. You can tell this by simply listening to the music and poetry of the people. For the most part the really great songs are about love and sorrow and death. I do not believe that this is a morbid aberration. I think that if you can articulate the deep meaning of life in terms of death by means of songs or sacraments, you are free for the wildest celebrations of sheer joy and love of living – these celebrations are freed from the task of carrying the final significance of life and for that reason can be as exuberant as you like. There is a magnificent Irish tune called *Rosin Dubh*, the dark rose (meaning Ireland), which expresses indescribably all the sorrows and suffering of Irish history, and I have hardly ever heard it played without it being immediately followed by the liveliest and fastest air available. This is partly, I suppose, a psychological effect. You simply cannot bear to be left with the ending of *Rosin Dubh*, or the player doesn't want to sound portentous, but partly the exploration of tragedy releases us for simple happiness.

Anyway I think ordinary people have taken the crucifixion for granted in one way; what has made the cross the symbol of hope and consolation is that it is a symbol of God. It says the divine reaches down even to those depths of the human reality, the depths we scarcely dare to explore.

So what I am saying is that the question 'Why did Jesus opt for crucifixion?' is a misplaced one. Of course he was crucified: he was human wasn't he? This is the central thing I want to say: that Jesus died of being human. More than that: all humans die, but he was so human he had to be killed.

He was and is a man like to us in all things but sin. 'Like us in all things but sin' doesn't on the face of it sound very like us. We all I think have a suspicion that if you took away our sins and vices, especially our minor vices, we would first of all be very different people, but also we would be less human and less likeable people. There is something repellently inhuman about the man or woman with no weaknesses who is always rather chillingly perfect. I hardly need to say, I am sure, that this feeling is based on a hopelessly negative idea of virtue. Virtue, whatever else it means, at least means being more human; it would not be virtuous if it did not. Sin, whatever else it means, means being less human, more stiff, cold, proud, selfish, mean, cruel, and all the rest of it. It is not in fact our sins that make us attractive. Weakness, of course, is frequently attractive, but just because it is human weakness, virtuous weakness. There is a perfectly definite virtue involved in letting yourself be helped by others and a perfectly definite vice in declining to be helped. What makes us more human is, of course, being more loving. And sin is a defect in this love. To say that Jesus was without sin just means that he was wholly loving, that he did not put up barriers against people, that he was not afraid of being at the disposal of others, that he was warm and free and spontaneous. That is what really lies behind that portentous sentence 'He spoke as one with authority.' It makes him sound so magisterial and solemn. In fact it just means that what he said came straight from him, warmly and immediately. He was never looking over his shoulder at the textbooks and traditions.

There is, of course, a lot more to be said about the relationship between love and humanity and sin and inhumanity. In fact, when we talk of sin and of love we are operating at a depth in us at which our humanity transcends itself. We are concerned with our divine life. All I want to insist on at the moment is that the fact that Jesus was without sin doesn't mean that he was cold and inhuman, but rather just the opposite. It means that he was liberated, free and spontaneous, really able to love and, as I say, not afraid of others, not afraid of being with others at their mercy.

Any man like this is, of course, at risk. He is going to be first exploited and then destroyed. This is the fact of life recognized by all those ordinary people I was talking about who take crucifixion for granted. This is no world for love. There is a twist or a contradiction in our human life that means we build a world unfit for humans. The only way to get by in it is to restrict your humanity rather carefully, otherwise you will get hurt. The world is not totally unfit for human habitation, but it can take just so much of it. You have to ration your love, keep a wary eye out for enemies if you want to survive. Now Jesus did not ration his love, so naturally he didn't last.

To believe in the cross, as distinct from knowing it happened or expecting it in the circumstances, is to believe that this challenge to the world at the cost of destruction is not only right but the key to what human life is about, that in this act we have the revelation of the divine.

We live in a world that cannot afford too much humanity, too much love. Love is permissible on the surface down to a certain relatively shallow level. But beneath that, what keeps chaos at bay, what keeps our world fairly stable, is not love but domination and fear (Hobbes gives a perfectly accurate account of all this). Any clear, cool, unsentimental look at our world shows us that in the end the last resort of society is to violence, to the appeal to fear; whether it be the threat of punishment or the threat of social collapse. It is not that people go around all the time anxiously living in fear of the police. There is no need for this. But the police and other men of violence are there waiting in the wings in case they are needed. As a matter of fact people do go around in anxious fear, but it is not directed at the police. Sometimes it is just a formless anxiety, a general fear of the world and of other people. This is not just a picture of our own society. It is true in varying degrees of every human society we have yet built – notably it was true of colonial Palestine under the Roman empire. In a subject country massively occupied by Roman troops it was quite obvious that society was based on fear. Roman order was preserved by harassment, torture, and killing.

It was equally true that the religion of the people was based in a more subtle way on fear. Not officially on fear of hell. Hell is not mentioned in the Old Testament as a place of eternal punishment. Nor for that matter is it mentioned in the writings of St Paul. It was Jesus who popularized this idea. Nonetheless the religion of the Jews at the time of Jesus seems to have been based on the domination of God. It was certainly better to be dominated by God than by any human emperor or king. The law of Yahweh was a great deal more humane than the laws of most of the countries round about. But it remains that the covenant relationship between man and God was seen in terms of domination and subjection.

Both the social order and the religious order depended on the imposition of law. The only alternative that could be envisaged was chaos. And Jesus posed a threat to both the political and the religious establishment because he proposed what he claimed was a third possibility: neither domination nor chaos but love. Now this, to the unsentimental eye, is evidently rubbish – unless you have a very special kind of love available. To attempt to sustain an even slightly human society on the kind of thing that we ordinarily know as love is ridiculous and also almost certainly dishonest. People who want to get rid of laws and substitute love are quite often people who find illegal domination easier than using law. What was special about Jesus was not that he produced the theory that people might live by love – that was a tired old theory that had been discredited many times in most people's experience. What was special about Jesus was not that he produced the theory that people might live by love, but that he produced the love. The kind of relationship that he had with his friends, and the kind of relationship he enabled them to have with each other, was something quite new. Here was something that could be the basis of a third possibility, neither law nor chaos.

Or was it? Was there here something really new, or was Jesus just another unconscious charlatan setting up a personality cult of himself instead of the law? I must stress again that abominable as the Roman law was, particularly in the colonies, it was better than some others, and certainly better than the horrors of paganism. It is understood that if someone proposes to dissolve these structures, ramshackle as they are, you want to be pretty sure he has something better to offer than a personality cult.

There can be no doubt that Jesus sounded as if this is what he was offering. His alternative was not a philosophy or a theology or a social theory or a political programme. It was simply himself. Believe in *me*, he says.

The whole question of Jesus turned on whether he really was or was not offering a quite new kind of relationship with people – or as people were subsequently to put it, pouring forth the Holy Spirit. And of course the only way to tell this was to respond to Jesus, to accept him or reject him, to have faith in him or not.

The thing is that your response to Jesus was not just your judgement of him. It was also a judgement of you. Since what Jesus in fact offered was a truly free, liberating relationship, the question really was whether you were prepared to accept this, whether you were frightened by such freedom or whether you were prepared to take the risk. If you did not take the risk then you did not recognize what Jesus was offering; you immediately explained it away.

I say all this so that you will be more able to understand the reactions of the police and the priests, the guardians of the law. It was, as Jesus himself kept saying, so much easier for the poor and the despised and the social outcasts than for those with heavy social responsibilities. The poor could accept him for what he was. The establishment had always to be calculating just where he stood and what his role was in their scheme of things. It was easier for Galilean peasants than for sophisticated city dwellers in Jerusalem. It was easier for the weak than for the strong.

Anyway the religious leaders in general failed to see what Jesus was offering them. They could not open their hearts to him, so hearing they did not hear and seeing they did not see. In consequence they viewed him simply as a blasphemer setting himself up against the Law of Yahweh, against all the religious traditions of the people of God. It was necessary to be rid of him. This would not be too difficult because the colonial powers were naturally suspicious of any popular leader and Jesus had begun to have a mass following particularly amongst the peasants and working class. Generally speaking, as might be expected, the collaborationists who worked in the colonial power were the upper class Sadduceans together with the Herodian party grouped around the Herod family, who had been set up as puppet kings in the territory outside Judea. Judea itself, including Jerusalem, was under the direct rule of Pontius Pilate. Things were made rather worse by the fact that some members of the zealots, the underground revolutionary movement, were associated with Jesus, and although Jesus clearly disagreed both with their aims and their tactics (they were traditionalists looking for a theocratic Jewish state, and their ideology was pretty similar to that of the Pharisees), the Romans would not pay attention to such subtle distinctions. As a popular leader he would be lumped together with the zealots.

The fact that Jesus must in any case have aroused the suspicions of the Romans by the sheer fact of having a mass following not only made it relatively easy to dispose of him. It also gave an added motive for doing so. Caiphas, himself appointed by the Roman authorities, put it quite simply – If we let him go on he will provoke a Roman backlash. We will have an Operation Motorman and our people will be beaten up and killed and have their homes wrecked by the soldiers. Caiphas, in fact, feared that Jesus would provoke what the zealots finally did provoke in AD 70 on a much bigger scale when Jerusalem was ravaged in a hideously bloody act of repression. Of course the author of John's Gospel, who quotes Caiphas, was writing after these events and in the light of them. But there is no need to suppose that he misinterpreted the reaction of the religious establishment.

This I think broadly explains how Jesus came to be crucified, to die, and be buried. Things had come to a head after the Palm Sunday demonstration when it was obvious that Jesus had very widespread and enthusiastic support. It was first necessary to discredit him in Jewish eyes, to get a conviction of blasphemy against him. One Jewish writer on this theme maintains that what was really happening here was that, in order to protect him from the Romans, the Jewish leaders were trying to persuade Jesus not to make dangerous messianic claims. But this theory has not been generally accepted. I think it more plausible to hold that they wanted first to excommunicate him and deprive him of popular Jewish support, and then to see that the Romans did the actual execution job by suggesting that he was a kind of zealot. To present him as an enemy of both the Jewish people and of the Romans was the neatest way of getting rid of him, and they succeeded. There was never much difficulty about getting the Romans to crucify someone. It was the normal punishment for political opposition. In the state in which Palestine was at this time there were probably several crucifixions a week (Josephus records seeing 2000 people crucified at once on one occasion). We naturally see the crucifixion of Jesus as an outstanding and awe-inspiring event, but for the Romans it was just one among many. The Gospels record that two men were executed on the same day as Jesus, and there may well have been a number of others.

That is the death of Jesus as seen from the public point of view, as it might have been reported in the contemporary left-wing press. What about it from Jesus' own point of view? It is clear that very early on Jesus recognized that the love he offered presented such a threat to the establishment that he was sooner or later going to be destroyed. Of course, the evangelists writing with hindsight attribute to him various quite specific prophecies about his death on the cross, and there is no good reason to think these are pure invention; on the contrary, Jesus would have had to be very imperceptive and very foolish to think that he could get away with it. It is only very foolish and inexperienced people who imagine that love is welcomed. Real love is a dangerous, disturbing, and subversive force. If you offer it to the world then, as John has Jesus say, 'The world will hate you.' Jesus knew that his attempt would fail, knew that he would be defeated; but he remained faithful to his mission from the Father.

To conclude, it is clear that if the kind of love that Jesus offers inevitably results in his being crucified, the same kind of thing is going to be true of those who receive his love and are liberated in their turn and able to pass it on to others. Crucifixion in some way is the destiny of every Christian. It does not have to be public execution. That only occurs when the love of Christ takes forms that are recognized as immediately dangerous by the ruling class. But for every Christian his or her death is to be a death that expresses the love of Christ, the Holy Spirit. There are just two kinds of death, the death that, like Christ's death, is the operation of the Spirit, or the death that simply means the organism has ceased to function. To die as Christ did, filled with the Holy Spirit is to conquer death; death then becomes simply the presupposition for the transformation of humanity in the resurrection. But that is another matter.

Nine

Nobody comes to the Father but by Me

In the fourteenth chapter of St John's Gospel we find Jesus saying 'Nobody comes to the Father but by me.' Can we really take that literally? Can we even take it seriously? 'Nobody' (he is talking about the whole human race) 'comes to the Father' (he means God) 'but by me' (he means himself). There are, I think, around four or five thousand million people alive today and countless millions have lived in the past; and most of them (apart from a few eccentrics) have thought about God one way or another, communally or individually. I mean they have thought about the mystery that things are, the mysterious purpose of human life or however they have put it; and they have sought to come to God. There have been great religions devoted to meditating on these things, whole civilizations sustained by some kind of worship of God, there has been endless striving to come to the Father. And now, amongst all these teeming millions, it is being asserted that, after all, nobody comes to God except through this individual carpenter in Palestine.

The egoism is breathtaking. Surely there must be some mistake.

Let us then think about this for a minute or two.

First of all, St John is not saying that nobody sees or understands God except by getting to know Jesus of Nazareth. People can seek to understand God, they can wrestle with this problem or explore this mystery quite apart from faith in Jesus Christ. John does not think they will get very far, for he says 'No one has ever seen God'; but having faith in Jesus Christ will not get them any further. People can seek *a way of life* in which to be united with God, they can try to come to the Father quite apart from faith in Christ. They will not get very far; but they will not get any further by having faith in Christ.

Christians are not people who think that because they have faith they have an advantage, that they are better informed about God than other people or have reached a position closer to God than other people, that they have discovered the secret of coming to the Father. Christians do not claim to have any secret and private knowledge about God or to have discovered any new secret way to the Father.

We come to the Father in Jesus Christ not because he has revealed to us the way by which we may go. (In John 14, Thomas wants to know about this and Jesus tells him that is not the point; that is not what he offers.) We come to the Father in Christ simply because Jesus is the way in which the Father comes to us: not first our way but the way the Father comes, the Father's truth, the life of the Father. And when the Father comes to us in the human life of Jesus it is not to show us how to know, how to be successful at coming to him or successful at anything else. He comes to us, after all, in a complete failure, in one who suffers and is defeated. He comes to us as a condemned and despised and executed criminal.

The *Word* of God is made flesh not to tell us something, not to make us better informed; he does not show us how to teach the world new secrets; what he shows us is our ignorance, our failure to understand. Christians *claim* that they know nothing of God. Christians think that anyone who claims to know God has set up some kind of idol in place of God. Christians say they are in the dark; it is the special darkness they call faith. Christians are not *proud* of being in the dark; they just know that they *are*. Christians are not proud of failing and being defeated by the powers of this world; they just know they constantly will be, if they love as Christ loves. They would much rather not be in the dark and not be defeated, but they don't think it matters all that much because their faith is not in themselves, in *their* success and *their* understanding. Their faith is in the power of God, which appears as weakness, and in the wisdom and understanding of God, which appears as folly. And they know it is by accepting this darkness and accepting this defeat that they will be given victory in light.

The thing that does make Christianity unique, really different from any of the other wisdoms and religions that I know, is not that it has a special secret but that it has no secret at all; it has nothing special to it. It has no way of its own, no truth or wisdom of its own, no life of its own. It has nothing of its own to offer: it just asks us to accept, to submit to, whatever God has to offer. It asks us to accept *the way and the wisdom and the life* which is God's. And if you ask 'What is that?', Christianity will not take you to a book, a recital, a code of laws; it will only take you to a defeated human being hanging from a cross. For the secular world looks for wisdom but we preach Christ crucified . . . the power of *God* and the wisdom of *God*.

I am sure you all know the nasty story of the ecumenical gathering when one Divided Christian says to another: 'After all, aren't we all going to the same God, you in your way, and I in his?' But that really is what the Gospel says. It makes no claim to know the way, except to refuse to believe in any such claims. There is no Christian way of perfection that is better or worse than anybody else's: the actual gospel is that we do not need it since God is taking humankind, the human race to himself. There are, indeed, ways we can learn to be more human, to grow in human virtues; and from the Ten Commandments onwards Jews and Christians have played a large part in this search for human decency. There are no ways we can learn to become divine, to come to the Father; making us divine is God's business.

It was always an illusion to suppose that by wisdom or ascetic practices, by meditation or by building the Tower of Babel, we could come to the Father. The good news is that the Father comes to us. In one way, a negative way, Christians do perhaps understand God better; because they won't have any substitutes, any idols, any gods. They have the sort of clearer, unclut-tered understanding that atheists have – except that most atheists cultivate some little idol of their own on the quiet. But apart from that, Christians don't expect or want *their* understanding of God to improve; they want to be taken over by God's understanding of God – and they don't mind much if, at the moment, this seems like nothing but greater ignorance for them.

This is what John is talking about at the beginning of his Gospel when he calls Jesus the Word of *God* made flesh. Jesus is God's Word, God's idea of God, how God understands himself. He is how-God-understands-himself become a part of our human history, become human, become the *first* really thoroughly human part of our history – and therefore, of course, the one hated, despised, and destroyed by the rest of us, who wouldn't mind being divine but are very frightened of being human.

In Jesus, says the Christian, we do not understand God but we can watch God understanding himself. God's understanding of God is that he throws himself away in love, that he keeps nothing back for himself. God's under-standing of God is that he is a love that unconditionally accepts, that always lets others be, even if what they want to be is his murderers. God's under-standing of God is that he is not a special person with a special kind of message, with a special way of living to which he wants people to conform. God's understanding of God could not appear to us as someone who wants to found a new and better religion, or recommend a special new discipline or way of life – a religious code laid upon us for all time because it is from God. God's understanding of God is that he just says: 'Yes, *be*; be human, but be really human; be human if it kills you – and it will.' The Law of God is a non-law; it has no special regulations. The Word just says: 'I accept you as human beings; what a pity you have such difficulty in doing this yourselves. What a pity you can only like yourselves if you pretend to be super-humans or gods.' God could never understand himself as one of the gods; only as one of the human race.

Let us be absurd for a minute and try to imagine what it means for God to understand himself. I don't mean try to think or understand it (of course we cannot do that). But let us try to *imagine* understanding that limitless abyss of life and liveliness, that permanent explosion of vivacity and awareness and sparkling intelligence and, of course, humour. And remember that in understanding himself God will thereby be understanding all that he has done and is doing, all that he holds in being, every blade of grass and every passing thought in your mind. The concept he has of himself in all this is his Word. This is what is made flesh and dwells among us in the human suffering and dying Christ.

And in contemplating his life in this Word, in this concept, in contemplating all he is and all he does, God has surely a huge unfathomable joy and immense excitement and enjoyment in all the life that is his and all the life he has brought into being. God takes immensely more joy in one little beetle walking across a leaf than you can take in everything good and delightful and beautiful in your whole life put together. If he gets that pleasure from one beetle he has made, think then what joy he takes in being God. This limitless joy is what we call the Holy Spirit.

To be able, through faith, to share in Christ, in God's understanding of himself, to be in Christ, is to be filled ourselves also with this joy, this Holy Spirit. It is a joy so vast that we can only faintly sometimes experience it as our elation and joy – just as our sharing in God's self-understanding hardly at all seems to us an understanding, a being enlightened. We have a life in us, an understanding and a joy in us, that is too great for us to comprehend. Quite often it has to show itself as what seems its opposite, as darkness and suffering. The Word of God is Christ crucified. But it is God's way and the truth of God and the life and joy of God. And this is in us because we have faith. We have been prepared to go into the dark with Christ, to die with Christ. And we know that this means that we live in Christ. And that life, the divine understanding and joy that is in us, will one day soon show itself in us for what it truly is. And we shall live with the Father, through the understanding which is the Word made flesh, in the joy which is the Holy Spirit for eternity.

Ten

Aquinas on the Incarnation

In *Summa Theologiae* 3a,16 Aquinas looks at the things that can truly be said of Christ in virtue of the union in one *esse*, one *persona*, of the nature of God and of man.* For Aquinas, the nature of a thing governs what can be said of it. To know the nature of a thing is to know how to talk about it, thus the union of two natures in Christ means, for Aquinas, that we have two ways of speaking about him – only one of which we understand. In virtue of his human nature we speak of him in exactly the same way that we would speak of any other human being. In virtue of his divine nature we can also say more enigmatic and mysterious things such as that he forgives sins or is our redeemer.

In order to understand Aquinas's treatment of such statements it is first necessary to remind you of his theory of the proposition in general. Aquinas did not hold what has come to be called the 'two-name' theory of the proposition: this is the theory that in a proposition a subject and a predicate are linked by a copula. The subject stands for one thing or class of things, and the predicate stands for another, and the copula shows how these classes overlap: 'All men are mortal' in this view says that the class of men is wholly included in the class of mortal things. I only mention this absurd theory because at one time it used to be found in logic textbooks called 'scholastic' and even 'Aristotelean'. In fact it has nothing whatever to do with Aristotle and had its origins, I think, among the Jansenists of the school of Port Royal. Aquinas's own view is altogether different. For him a simple proposition consists typically of two parts, not three: a subject and a predicate (roughly speaking, a noun and a verb). The so-called copula is just the verb 'to be' when it is used to construct the predicate. If instead of saying 'John sings'

---

* In what follows, and except as indicated, English translations of *Summa Theologiae* 3a,16 are taken from Volume 50 of the Blackfriars edition.

you prefer to say 'John is singing' then you have a copula. But there is no logical virtue in doing so. If, instead of saying 'All men are mortal', you say 'All men die', you have just as perspicuous a logical form (not to mention a better English sentence).

Now for Aquinas the words in the two parts of a proposition function in quite different ways. (For the 'two-name' theory, they function in the same way – to denote classes.) Terms in the subject place, he says, are to be taken 'materially', and those in the predicate place are to be taken *'formaliter'*. Without going too far into this, what he means is that the subject words are there to stand for, to identify what you are talking about, to refer, while the words of the predicate are there to say something about it, they are taken as to their meaning (*formaliter*). For Aquinas, identifying something is not the same as saying something about it. If you say 'The President is in the White House' you are, for him, enunciating the same truth as when you say 'George W. Bush is in the White House', even though to be President of the USA and to be George W. Bush are not the same thing. In those two propositions 'the President' and 'George W. Bush' are fulfilling the same function of identifying the one you want to talk about. When you identify Bush as the President you are not asserting that he is President. You are just taking for granted that people know who the President is. The thing you are asserting is that he is in the White House. And this can be just as well asserted by saying that George W. Bush is in the White House. Any word or phrase will do in the subject place provided it makes clear what you are talking about. Very often this will be because the words you use in the subject place could be predicated of the subject. For example, 'the President' serves to identify George W. Bush because the proposition 'George W. Bush is the President' is true (in 2001, anyway). But this proposition is not being enunciated when you say 'The President is in the White House.' It is just part of the background.

Now the relevance of all this to talk of the Incarnation is this: since the one person (Jesus) is both divine and human, we can identify him either with divine or with human terms. So long as what we are doing is simply identifying Jesus, it makes no difference whether we call him Son of God or son of Mary. Thus so far as words in the subject part of the sentence are concerned it makes no difference whether we use identifying phrases derived from Jesus' divine nature or his human nature.

Thus we might say 'The friend of Peter and Andrew sat down by the well.' Or we might say 'The Son of God born of the Father before all ages sat down by the well.' And these are exactly the same proposition. They are both simply asserting that Jesus sat down by the well. (They are the same proposition in that one is true if and only if the other is true.) They are the same proposition because 'The friend of Peter and Andrew' and 'The Son of God born of the Father before all ages' are both simply being used to identify Jesus. The first proposition does not include the assertion that Jesus is a friend of Peter and Andrew. The second does not include the assertion that he is Son of God, etc. These assertions are not included in what is said. They are simply taken for granted.

For Aquinas, what is formal to a proposition, what makes it the proposition it is, is the predicate not the subject terms. It doesn't matter much what you use to identify the subject, but if you change the predicate then you have a new proposition. So to say 'Jesus is Son of God' is to say something quite different from saying 'Jesus is son of Mary' because here 'Son of God' and 'son of Mary' are in the predicate place. But to say 'The Son of God died on the cross' is to make the same assertion as is expressed by 'The son of Mary died on the cross.'

We now come to the word '*qua*' or 'in virtue of being'. If you say 'Mr Tony Blair *qua* Prime Minister chairs the meetings of the Cabinet', you mean that it is just because Mr Tony Blair is Prime Minister that he does this. You mean that his being Prime Minister is a condition of his chairing the meetings. So your proposition is a complex one, it asserts (1) that Mr Tony Blair chairs the meetings, and (2) that he is Prime Minister, and (3) that it is because of being Prime Minister that he chairs the meetings (which seems an enormous lot to unpack out of the little word '*qua*', but there it is).

What is important here is that what follows the *qua* is part of the predicate of the proposition. It is part of what is being asserted.

Now consider the proposition 'God sat down by the well.' This for Aquinas is a perfectly proper and true utterance since 'God' is one of the ways in which you could identify Jesus; 'God', here, is in the subject place and is being used to identify what is being talked about.

But if you said 'Jesus *qua* God sat down by the well' it would be very different. This would assert (1) that Jesus sat by the well, and (2) that Jesus is God, and (3) that it is because of being God that he sat by the well.

Now since the third of these is false the original proposition is false. The word '*qua*' is important because we are to be concerned with natures, and a nature is that in virtue of which things are true of a thing, or can be said of a thing. To say that Jesus has two natures is to say that he has, so to say, two *quas*. He does some things *qua* human and others *qua* divine. This does not mean that he had two sources of power and could switch from one to the other, like having an emergency engine on a sailing boat. It means that there are two levels of talking about him, or that he exists at two levels.

Another little phrase of importance in talking about the incarnate word is 'as such'.

'God sat by the well' is fine, but 'God *as such* sat by the well' is the same as 'God (i.e., Jesus) *qua* God sat by the well', which is false.

Similarly, 'This man created the world' is fine. But 'This man *as such* created the world' is false.

But let us look at Aquinas's own examples.

3a,16,1: 'Is this statement true, "God is a man"?' Aquinas replies that 'God is a man' is true because 'the person of the Son of God, for whom the term "God" here stands (*pro qua supponit hoc nomen Deus*) is a subject (*suppositum*) subsisting in human nature' and since 'the term "a man" may [therefore] truly and literally be predicated of the term "God" when the latter stands for the person of the Son of God'. (Aquinas is, of course speaking loosely here, it is not the word 'man' that is predicated of the word 'God'; but what the word 'man' means is predicated of what the word 'God' stands for or identifies.)

The first objection to this is that the proposition 'God is a man' is *in materia remota*. A proposition *in materia remota* would be, for example 'Thursday is green' – when, as Aquinas puts it: 'Two forms cannot come together in the same *suppositum*.' The kind of thing that is Thursday just isn't the kind of thing that could be green. The thing seems to depend on the meaning of 'Thursday' and of 'green'. Now the objector argues that the meaning of being God is so totally different from the meaning of being man that the kind of thing that is God just couldn't be the kind of thing that is man. But when you have a case of two forms, even quite different and unrelated forms, that can come together in one *suppositum*, then you have not got *materia remota*: for example, if the same man is both white and musical you can sensibly say 'the white is musical', even though being white and being musical are quite different. Such a proposition is said to be in *materia contingenti*.

Aquinas points out that *au fond* it is not precisely the difference of forms or of meanings that make for nonsense. It is their not being able to come together in one *suppositum*. And he argues that, although to be divine and to be human are totally different (*maxime distantes*), this is not the important thing; the significant thing is that through the mystery of the Incarnation they do come together in one *suppositum*. But it is not just as with 'the white is musical' for, in the case of the Incarnation we have not simply an accidental conjunction of forms. Neither the being divine nor the being human belongs to the *suppositum 'per accidens'* but *'secundum se'*. Being human is a matter of what Jesus is as Jesus; and being divine is a matter of what Jesus is as Jesus. So, says Aquinas, the proposition 'God is a man' is neither in *materia remota* nor in *materia contingenti*. It is in what Aquinas calls *materia naturali*. He means by this that it belongs to the same class of propositions as, for example, that a man is rational. 'Being a man' is predicated of God not *per accidens* but *per se*, not however by reason of the form signified by 'God' (the meaning of 'God') but by reason of the *suppositum* which becomes the hypostasis (the subsisting subject, the independent, concrete, substantial reality) of the human nature. Thus 'God is a man' is *per se*, but not in quite the same way as 'A man is rational' is *per se*. 'A man is rational' is *per se* and not *per accidens* because a man as man (because of what it means to be human) is rational. But 'God is man' is *per se* and not *per accidens* not because of the meaning of 'God', not because God as God (because of what it means to be divine) is a man, but because God as this person, this hypostasis, is the hypostasis of the man.

Aquinas, you see, is here steering his way between (a) saying that God is a man because of some merging of the natures of God and man (a matter of the meaning of being God and the meaning of being man), and (b) saying that the union of divinity and humanity is accidental, like the union of whiteness and musicalness in one man. The union is non-accidental, but not non-accidental in the way that other unities are (e.g., man and his rationality).

What Aquinas is here saying is that it is not merely a contingent fact that God is man. It is not a contingent fact like the fact that John is singing. It is non-contingent much the same way as the statement that John is human is non-contingent. Of course 'John is human' might not be true, but only if John doesn't exist; John cannot cease to be human in the way that he can cease to sing; he can't take it or leave it alone. In the same way, it might not have been the case that God became man, and for a long time it was not the case that God became man. But when it happens it is not a contingent fact. God did not take on humanity like John might take on singing.

Aquinas, naturally enough, argues that just as you can say 'God is a man' so you can say 'A man is God' (3a,16,2). But then he comes to consider two other propositions: 'God was made a man' (3a,16,6) and 'A man was made God' (3a,16,7). The first of these he allows but the second presents problems.

He points out, of course, that the truth of the first proposition, 'God was made a man', does not entail any change in God. All that it says is that whereas previously it was not true of God that he was man, it became true about 2000 years ago. What happened was that a new relationship was set up between God and human nature, but this relationship, so Aquinas argues, is not based on any change in God but on a change in human nature which becomes the human nature of the Son of God. God does not change by becoming man any more than I change by becoming an uncle.

'A man was made God' would be fine, Aquinas says, if it meant simply 'It became true that a man is God.' But, so he adds, this is not the natural meaning of the sentence. The natural meaning is that the *suppositum* that 'this man' stands for (the *suppositum* that is identified by this term in the subject place) became God. But the *suppositum* that it stands for is the Second Person of the Trinity and it cannot be the case that the Second Person of the Trinity became God. So we can't say, says Aquinas, that a man became God or that he began to be God, or that he was made God (*factus est Deus*), even though we can say that God became man or that God began to be man, or that God was made man. It is just this logical point that Aquinas is referring to when he speaks of Christ not having a human '*personalitas*' or human 'existence' (see below). It has nothing to do with Christ not being a human person.

In 3a,16,8 Aquinas asks whether we can say that Christ is a creature. It will be clear from the principles that we have already established that we can; for 'Christ' in the subject place simply identifies what is being talked of. So it is legitimate to say that Christ is a creature just as we can say he suffered and died and was buried. We mean of course that Christ, *qua* human, is a creature. But as a matter of fact Aquinas is not keen on saying that Christ is a creature because, he says, it would be so misleading to do so, and its most natural meaning could sound Arian. He says it would be as misleading as to say that the Ethiopian is white. Technically you could say this because of his teeth. But it would be misleading.

With better reason Aquinas (3a,16,9) disallows 'That man (pointing to Christ) began to exist', for 'That man' in the subject place stands for the *suppositum* (*terminus in subjecto positus non tenetur formaliter pro natura sed magis materialiter pro supposito*) and the *suppositum* in question is the Second Person of the Trinity, who did not begin to exist. Aquinas is, of course, aware that you can use the same sentence to mean different things, and he allows that someone might use the sentence 'This man began to exist' to mean 'This man, as man, began to exist' (or 'This man, as such, began to exist'), which would be fine. But, as with respect to 'Christ is a creature', he advises against 'This man began to exist' (said pointing to Christ) on the grounds that it is a sentence which would be used with an heretical meaning by the Arians.

Finally Aquinas asks whether you can say 'Christ as man is a subject (*hypostasis*) or person.' And he says clearly that, if you are asking whether Christ is a human person, then the answer is 'Yes' since 'whatever subsists in human nature is a person' (*omne enim quod subsistit in humana natura est persona*). But, Aquinas adds, 'Christ as man is a subject or person' could mean that 'the human nature in Christ ought to have its own personality, having its causal origin in the human nature'. And, so Aquinas continues, 'in this sense, Christ, as man, is not a person; for his human nature does not exist by itself apart from the divine nature, as would be required if it were to have its own personality'. This is the point to which I referred above. Aquinas's meaning is that his human nature does not define the existence (*esse*) of Christ in such sense that there would be an existence of Christ according to his humanity and another according to his divinity. For Aquinas, Christ is one existence, divine and human.

He puts this very nicely in 3a,17,2 (my translation):

In Christ whatever pertains to the nature is twofold, whatever pertains to the hypostasis is single. Now to be (*esse*) pertains to both nature and hypostasis: to the hypostasis as *that which has* being, to the nature as *that by which* something has being. For we speak of a nature as we speak of a form – as 'being' in the sense that by it something is (*by* whiteness something *is* white; *by* humanity something *is* a man).

A form or nature that does not pertain to the being-a-person of some subsistent hypostasis does not simply speaking make that person be; it only makes him be in some respect: to be white is indeed a being that Socrates has, but not insofar as he is Socrates, just insofar as he is a white thing. In this (accidental) sense of being there is no reason why one person should not have many 'beings': Socrates can *be* white and *be* musical, and these 'beings' are different. But the being that belongs to the hypostasis or person *as such* cannot be multiplied like this, for it is impossible that one thing should have more than one existence.

If therefore the Son of God acquired human nature not hypostatically or personally but accidentally, as some have held, we should have to say that in Christ there are two existences, one as he is God, the other as he is man. Just as in Socrates there is one being in that he *is* white and another in that he *is* a man, for being white is not part of being Socrates as this person.

Contrast this with *being* equipped with a head, or *being* corporeal or *being* alive. All these in fact make up the one being, the person Socrates. So from these there is but one being in Socrates. Now suppose that after Socrates is constituted as a person he acquires hands or feet or eyes (like the man born blind); from these he would not acquire a new being but only a new relation to these things in that he would now be said to be in respect of these and not just in respect of what he had before.

Now human nature is joined to the Son of God hypostatically or personally and not accidentally. Consequently with his new human nature he does not acquire a new personal being, but simply a new relation of the personal being that is already there to human nature, so that this person is now said to subsist not only in respect of a divine nature but also of a human nature.

Aquinas is looking for something that might be acquired and yet not be accidental; something that once acquired simply contributes to the *esse* that is already there. There is a difference between, let us say, becoming a postman and becoming sexually mature. Being a postman is accidental to you, and so it is by two separate acts of being that you are a postman and are human. Being sexually mature, although it is something you acquire and grow into, once acquired is part of you. It is not by two acts of being that you are grown up and are human. You do not just happen to be grown up, as you happen to be a postman. Being grown up is a new way in which you are yourself. Now in the Incarnation the Son of God has acquired a new way of being himself, it is as though he had grown up or achieved sexual maturity (in fact he did achieve sexual maturity).

Of course Aquinas is not here trying to fit the mystery of the Incarnation into our own categories of thought. He is not saying that becoming a man is for God just like a man born blind acquiring the sight that belongs to him, or a child becoming a man. For one thing, of course, any such example must begin with something imperfect receiving the perfection that belongs to it, and this is hardly the case with the Incarnation. Aquinas is not saying this is just how the Incarnation was, rather he is rejecting any attempt to force the Incarnation into other categories, to say that the humanity must be accidental to the divinity, or the divinity must accidentally have supervened on the humanity.

The Incarnation remains a mystery. But, perhaps, Aquinas can help us to see that we don't therefore have to talk nonsense about it.

Eleven

Eucharistic Change

Let's begin with some misconceptions about what the Catholic tradition says happens when bread and wine are consecrated. The Council of Trent did not decree that Catholics should believe in transubstantiation: it just calls it a most appropriate (*aptissime*) way of talking about the Eucharist, presumably leaving it open whether there might not be other, perhaps even more appropriate, ways of talking. You could say that the Council sanctioned and recommended this theology, whereas, for example, the Anglican Thirty Nine Articles are rather less liberal: they forbid it as 'repugnant to the plain words of Scripture'. It is likely, however, that the authors of that document did not quite understand the meaning of that doctrine and fairly certain that a whole lot of Catholics don't either.

Perhaps we could start with a caricature of the doctrine which I think would be taken for the real thing by a great many Christians, whether they accept or reject it. The caricature goes like this: at the consecration, the bread and wine change into a different kind of substance, flesh and blood, in fact the flesh and blood of Christ; but this is disguised from us by the fact that to all appearances the bread and wine are unchanged. This is so that we can eat the flesh and drink the blood of Christ without being disgusted by the cannibalism involved. The miracle here is a kindly deception which protects us from seeing what we are really doing. If we could only peep behind the residual appearances we would discover human flesh and human blood. (There is a famous medieval legend about a priest being confirmed in his faith in the reality of the eucharistic change when he saw the host bleed.)

Now this is not the doctrine of transubstantiation, at least as understood by St Thomas Aquinas. First of all, for him, the change is of a completely different kind from the change of bread and wine into another kind of stuff (which he would call a 'substantial' change); and secondly the appearances of bread and wine do not become the misleading appearances, the disguise, for the new stuff, so as to make it palatable. They become the signs which reveal to us the new reality. In all sacraments God shows us what he does and does what he shows us. In six of the sacraments he makes present and shows us by signs the power of Christ to save us; in the central sacrament of the eucharist he makes present Christ himself and shows him to us by signs which indicate what he is, the unity of his faithful in charity. 'For he is our peace who has made us one.'

St Thomas talks of transubstantiation in language borrowed from Aristotle: he speaks of substance and accidents. If you tell somebody what sort of thing something is (a horse, an electron, etc.) you are telling him of its substance. If you are giving him further information (where it is, how high it is, how intelligent it is, etc.) you are telling him its accidental characteristics. It is important to an Aristotelian that a thing may lose some accidental characteristic (it may move, shrink, grow stupider, etc.) without ceasing to be the same identical thing; whereas if it should lose its substance, its essential character, it perishes, ceases to be this thing and turns into something else (as when the horse dies, it is no longer a horse but has changed into a corpse). This seems a fairly common-sense account at least of the organic world in which it is usually fairly easy to agree on what sorts of things there are (horses, onions, human beings) and not too difficult to observe them beginning to exist (being born or whatever) and ceasing to exist (dying). It differs considerably from our modern physicist's way of talking but it seems bizarre to claim that it is unintelligible to us. Amongst the accidental characteristics of things around us are their appearances: size, colour, taste, etc., by which usually we recognize them for what they are. Unlike St Thomas, the Council of Trent speaks not of accidents but of appearances (*species*), saying that to all appearances the consecrated elements are still bread and wine and no investigation of ours could tell us anything different, but we know by faith that what they are is no longer bread and wine but the sacramental presence of the body and blood of Christ.

It is important to recognize that in using Aristotelean language St Thomas is not giving an 'Aristotelean' explanation of the Eucharist. He uses it because it was the common philosophical currency of the time; but he uses it to give an account of something that simply could not happen according to Aristotle. Transubstantiation, like creation or incarnation, does not make sense within the limits of the Aristotelean world-view. St Thomas uses

Aristotle's language, but it breaks down in speaking of the Eucharist. It doesn't break down because there is some more accurate language in which the whole thing can be explained. It breaks down because it is language. We are dealing here with something that transcends our concepts and can only be spoken of by stretching language to breaking point. We are dealing here with mystery.

Those who wish to replace talk of transubstantiation by talk of transignification are quite reasonably claiming that in our culture we are more familiar with talk of meanings than of substances. And meaning seems the obvious category in which to speak of sacramental signs and liturgy; for one thing we are less likely to imagine that the Mass turns on a specially mysterious chemical process.

There is much in this so long as it does not sound like 'Really its only a change of meaning' (for the meaning in question has a special profundity about it) and so long as it is not taken to be saying that the bread and wine, while remaining what they were, are 'deemed' (by the Church, or even by the individual believer) to be the focus of the presence of Christ to us in his bodily humanity (for this sounds to much like 'deeming' a piece of stage furniture to be the Castle of Dunsinane). On the other hand to say that it is God who does the deeming would take us straight back to something like transubstantiation, for if God deems something to happen it must happen, and come about in the created world (for nothing can happen in the eternal immutable Godhead). Moreover not even God could deem something both to be and not be bread and wine – except in different senses; and that takes us back to where we were before we talked of 'deeming'.

A guiding principle in our thinking about this matter must surely be that anything which seems to take the scandal or mystery out of the Eucharist must be wrong, whether it be couched in terms of substance or of meaning.

If we are to understand what the notion of transubstantiation is saying, or trying to say, we need to reflect on the difference between the way appearances tell us something and the way in which signs tell us something. It is only in a metaphorical sense that, in English, we can say, for example, 'The smell of bitter almonds tells you that it is cyanide'; but, of course, smelling of bitter almonds is no part of telling you anything. It is simply a physical reality and it is you who tell yourself it is due to cyanide because you have read enough detective stories to know this.

It is not literally true that 'appearances are deceptive'; they are just there; it is people who may use them to deceive you, or you may deceive yourself by jumping to conclusions. On the other hand, signs, conventional signs, like words or flags, for example, are part of language and as such they are part of telling. (We even have a special name for deceiving by the use of conventional signs: we call it lying.)

There is, then, a lot of difference between the appearance which simply shows you a thing and signs which are part of telling you something about it. I labour this point because it is an important part of St Thomas's teaching on the Eucharist that the accidents of bread and wine cease to be the appearances of bread and wine, but this is not because they become the misleading appearances of something else. They cease to function as appearances at all, they have become signs, sacramental signs through which what is signified is made real.

Before the consecration the appearances were there because the bread was there; they were just the appearances of the bread. After the consecration it is the other way round; the body of Christ is sacramentally there because what were the appearances of bread (and are now sacramental signs), are there. So with unconsecrated bread the accidents can remain (and vary) so long as the bread still exists: how very bizarre if they were to stay on (like the Cheshire cat's grin) when what they are accidents of isn't there. But after the consecration the body of Christ is sacramentally present just so long as the signs are there. The important consequence of this is that these signs are not the appearances of Christ's body: they are no longer the appearances of anything. The colour and shape of the host is not the colour and shape of Christ's body; the location of the host, its being on the altar, does not mean that Christ's body is located on the altar; the fact that the host is moved about, say in procession, does not mean that Christ's body is being moved about. When we do things to the host, such as eating it, we are not doing anything to Christ's body. What we are doing is completing the significance of the signs. For bread and wine are meant to be eaten and drunk, to be our food; and food, eating and drinking together is, even in our secular lives, a sign expressing friendship and unity. This is why Jesus chose it to be the sign which would tell us of the real sacramental presence of his body given for us and his blood poured out for us – the body of Christ which is more deeply our food, our 'bread and wine', than is the ordinary bread and wine with which we began.

I have said that St Thomas uses Aristotelean language to propound what Aristotle would have found unintelligible because, of course, the whole biblical teaching of creation, the incarnation and Christ's humanity as the sacrament of God's love for us, and the sacraments of the Church, are utterly outside Aristotle's ken. For Aristotle, when bread becomes human flesh (as when you eat it) it is because a 'substantial change' (cf., 'chemical change') has taken place. This means that matter which at one time had the substantial form of bread now has the form of flesh. It is by such changes that old things perish and new things come into existence – by being made out of some predecessor. Aristotle did not think that everything *does* come into existence: he thought there were imperishable beings that could never have started to exist and that coming into existence belongs only to those inferior parts of the universe which have to be made out of a predecessor and which perish by being turned into a successor. So, for him, the entire universe itself could not have come into existence – there would be nothing for it to be made out of. So Aristotle gives us an interesting analysis of coming into existence by substantial change, but had no notion of creation. St Thomas, however, believing in creation, believed in a new and different kind of bringing into existence. He thought there was a kind of cause which did not merely give a new form to the matter of already existing perishable things, but simply brought things into being when there was nothing there before. The creative act of God does not just deal in the forms of things – making one kind of thing into an individual of another kind with a different form. It gives sheer existence to the whole thing. Causes within nature give things the form by which they have existence; God gives things existence itself. God is the reason why there is a world of natural causality; and every natural cause can only give existence because it is an instrument of the Creator, the source of all existence.

Now, says St Thomas, it is this depth of divine causality that (without using any natural causes) is going on in the eucharistic consecration. The bread does not turn into the body by acquiring a new form in its matter; the whole existence of the bread becomes the existence of the living body of Christ. The body is not made out of the bread, as ashes are made out of paper by burning it (a chemical change). Something has happened as profoundly different from chemical change as creation is. It is not that the bread has become a new kind of thing in this world: it now belongs to a new world. As far as this world is concerned, nothing seems to have happened, but in fact what we have is not part of this world. It is the kingdom impinging on our history and showing itself not by appearing in the world but by signs speaking to it.

So what we have in the Eucharist is first a perfectly ordinary ritual-religious meal symbolizing our friendship and unity. Then it begins to belong to what is beyond our universe, beyond space and history. What was hitherto just a religious word spoken by people has become the Word spoken by God, the Word made flesh that dwells amongst us. We begin with a ceremony in a church and find ourselves in the kingdom; no longer simply talking or thinking about Christ, but in his bodily presence.

The change is so tremendous that it is quite imperceptible. In fact, St Thomas says it is not a change (*mutatio*) at all, for such a change means a re-adjustment of our world – as when one thing is altered or changes into something else. This clearly makes a perceptible difference. But transubstantiation is not a change, just as creation is not a change. What the bread has become is the body of Christ, which is to say the kingdom itself – for Christ does not inhabit the kingdom, he, his body, his human way of communicating with other humans, is the kingdom of God. It is by the union of his body and ours that we belong to the kingdom. Now the kingdom, the glorified body of Christ, is not something that could be seen within our world as part of our world; if it is to be manifest among us it can only be by signs, by sacramental signs. And this is just what the Eucharist is.

What happens in the Eucharist is not, of course, happening to Christ. He does not literally 'come down' on altar after altar. What happens occurs to the symbolic meal which we share in expression of our faith and love. But nor is this happening an event within the parameters of our creaturely world, to be monitored by scientific or historical investigation. It is the event, the advent, of grace. Indeed the Eucharist with its satellite sacraments is the paradigm source of all grace. By it the Church participates in the divine life through sharing in the grace of the one mediator between God and humankind, the man Christ Jesus.

'The bread which we break, is it not a participation in the body of Christ? Because there is one bread we who are many are one body . . .' Bread is not the name of a chemical substance, although certain such substances have to be there for it to be bread. Bread is stuff we eat: a particular stuff we eat, but still, primarily, to call it bread is to speak of it as what we have for meals. To be bread is to be nourishment, to play a part in human life. Bread and wine in any circumstances are potentially symbols of human community, of being one. Now in the Eucharist this meaning is deepened and what was common bread becomes the sign, the sacramental sign, the sign in God's language, proclaiming that our human community is a community in God's life. What was our bread has become the bread of heaven and it would now be sacrilegious to see it and treat it as ordinary bread. To say, as Trent does, that in the consecrated host 'the substance of bread does not remain', is not like saying that zinc or wool is not bread. If we think that the consecrated host is ordinary bread we are not making the same kind of mistake as we would if we thought a model of a slice of bread in fibreglass was ordinary bread. Our mistake lies in not recognizing that it is so much bread in the symbolic sense, as far as the human meaning of bread is concerned, that to call it ordinary bread is to misdescribe it. In St Thomas's language it would be to treat the appearances as accidents of bread when really they are the divine sacramental signs of Christ's body. They belong to a new language.

To say that the appearances of the host are not in truth accidents of bread, but only mistaken for such accidents by one lacking faith, may seem less odd if we notice other quite different contexts in which we make the same kind of mistake. Until fairly recently nearly everybody thought that arching over us is a large vault which is blue unless obscured by clouds. This is what the book of Genesis calls 'the vault of heaven'. Common speech retains this picture and we ask 'What colour is the sky?' But just as in the Eucharist we know better by having faith, so in this case we know better by having physics. We know, when we think about it, that what is causing our sensation of blue is not that there is a blue object called the sky. The sensation is not due to the reflection of blue light from a surface but to the refraction of light so that we are only affected by the blue end of the spectrum of white light. We over-hastily assume that the blue is an accident of the vault of heaven, but there is no such thing. The blue of the sky is nothing so nonsensical as an accident without anything to be accident of (cf., the Cheshire cat's grin), it is only what might easily be mistaken for an accident. Similarly the colour and shape of the host are nothing so nonsensical as accidents which are not the accidents of anything; they are just what might easily be mistaken for accidents of something and would certainly be so mistaken if we did not have faith that they are no such thing, but signs of the presence of Christ. It is, of course, miraculous that these signs, these appearances, should remain when they have ceased to be accidents. It is not a natural phenomenon like the apparent blue of the sky. My comparison is not intended as an explanation of the eucharistic miracle. It is intended merely as an attempt to show that it does not involve sheer contradiction. And this is the most that can be done with any miracle.

What happens, then, when we consecrate is that the body and blood of Christ become present as our food and drink to constitute our sharing in the coming banquet of the kingdom. This happens not by any change in Christ himself but by a miracle, comparable to creation, in which the whole existence of our bread and wine becomes the existence of Christ. The bread which was present naturally is converted, not by any substantial change, but by the creative power of God, into the body of Christ which is present not naturally but sacramentally.

Instead, therefore, of the body of Christ manifesting itself to us in his own accidents, in his glory, it is manifested to us in sacramental signs. What had been the appearances of bread and wine become, through this miracle, the signs in which Christ shows himself, his presence to us. They become the language in which God speaks to us and which we hear only in faith; they become the Word of God, they become Christ, that Word made flesh and dwelling among us.

Twelve

The Eucharist
as Language

Plainly, the Eucharist can be studied in the light of a great number of disciplines: anthropology, history, sociology, and so on. It seems reasonable, however, to suppose that, first of all, it is a matter of theology. By theology I do not now mean the study of religions but rather a study within a religious tradition. In other and more classical words, it means 'Faith seeking understanding.' I shall be looking at the Eucharist from the inside, so to speak, rather than as a detached observer.

> In many and various ways God spoke of old to our fathers by the prophets; but in these days he has spoken to us by a son whom he appointed heir of all things, through whom he also created the world. (Heb. 1:1–2)

I take as my starting point this tremendous claim in the Epistle to the Hebrews. I am not concerned, for present purposes, with whether this Epistle falls short of Chalcedonian Christology or even that of John, but simply with the notion that God 'spoke to our fathers' and that he has 'spoken to us' by the Son.

In what I would call the mainstream Catholic tradition (elegantly set forth in Eph. 1:3–10), God's revelation of the 'mystery of his will, according to the purpose he set forth in Christ as a plan for the fullness of time [is] to unite all things in him, things in heaven and things on earth'.

This revelation is presented to us by the prophets (in the words of Scripture) but most definitely in the Word made flesh dwelling among us. And the dwelling among us which took place historically in the life, death, and resurrection of Jesus (giving rise to the preaching of the New Testament) thereby takes place sacramentally in the mysteries that constitute the institutional Church. These are the continuing presence/ absence of the Word of God, centring on the Eucharist.

Of course, all these propositions are highly debatable but my purpose is not to offer an apologetic defence of this view but simply to admit to what I am taking for granted as background to the proposition that I do want to discuss. This is the proposition that the body of Christ is present in the Eucharist as meaning is present in a word.

Three or four decades ago a number of Roman Catholic theologians, uneasy with what they took to be the traditional doctrine of transubstantiation as an account of the real presence of Christ in the Eucharist, proposed to substitute a doctrine of 'transignification', according to which it was not that the *being* of the bread and wine became the being of Christ, but that the *meaning* which the bread and the wine had as a symbol of our unity in the body of Christ changed. This, presented as an *alternative* to transubstantiation, sounded suspiciously close to the proposition that a piece of fabric with some pattern or other should be the national flag and, on ceremonial occasions be saluted as an expression of patriotism. This is perfectly reasonable behaviour, but it makes the flag only an emblem whose meaning is supplied by the opinions and aspirations and bonds of friendship in the human society in question. The proposition that the Eucharist is something much the same seemed to empty it of its mystery, not to say its interest. It is true, as I shall be trying to argue, that human language itself, whether of flags or of words, is a kind of mystery, something that in a way transcends our understanding even while being the means of our understanding. But, of course, for the tradition from which I speak, the mystery of the Eucharist is much deeper than this. For the Church is not founded on the opinions, aspirations and friendships of its members. It creates and sustains these; and 'the Church's one foundation is Jesus Christ the Lord . . .'

The Eucharist is the creative language of God, his eternal Word made flesh. The *aspirations* are the hope engendered by the resurrection, the *opinions* are the faith which is the word of God, and the *friendship* is the *agape* that God has given us that we might share it with all humankind. The 'society' whose 'emblem' it is (I put both these words in scare-quotes to indicate that they are both being used analogically) is the society which is 'the body of Christ' whose emblem is (in yet *another* analogical sense) 'the body of Christ'.

A word, now, on the philosophical background to talk of transubstantiation. For Aristotle, as for Aquinas, a substance exists by being a certain kind of thing, having an essence which distinguishes it from other kinds of things. ('No entity without identity' as Quine used to say; 'It is form that gives *esse*' as Aquinas used to say). To say that Fred exists is not to attribute to him a property called 'existence', there is no such property, it is to say of him that he truly *is a human being*; being a human being *is* what it takes for him to exist. This predication, they would say, is in the category of substance (simply answering the question: 'What is it?'). True statements in other, accidental categories (such as 'He is sitting down' or 'He has a cold'), although they presuppose, they would say, the existence of Fred, do not *directly assert* that he exists. Material substances exist (as does everything other than God) by being some kind of thing, and exist over against the possibility of changing into other kinds of things – for this is what being 'material' implies. They are contingent, not in the later rationalist sense (that we can conceive them not being) but in the medieval sense of being contingent on how they will be affected by the other things in the universe. In the medieval sense not all creatures are contingent. That such substances (and, for that matter, non-material imperishable 'necessary beings' like Angels) should also exist over against the deeper possibility of there not being anything at all, nothing to be made out of, nothing to be made into, would be a thought quite foreign to Aristotle. And of course, that it *is* a real thought is something that needs to be demonstrated. Aristotle had a metaphysics of *substance* and form; Aquinas developed a deeper metaphysics of *esse* and creation.

Étienne Gilson was, I think, quite right to argue that the notion of *esse* (existence over against the possibility that nothing whatever might have existed) came to medieval European thought not from classical Greek philosophy, but from the biblical doctrine of creation. Since it was generally agreed by advocates of both transubstantiation and of transignification that the consecration of the bread and wine made no chemical or physical or other scientifically detectable difference to these elements, the choice seemed to be between a deeper metaphysical transformation of the elements or a change in *our* interpretation of their significance. Of course, for transignificationists this change in our perception was an act of faith, a real supernatural activity in us of the Holy Spirit. But it seemed to be something that had to do with us, in us, rather than with the bread and wine themselves. It sounded like nominalism (this was the view that the meaning of things is simply put there by us and the language we use).

The most coherent exponent of transubstantiation, Thomas Aquinas, was quite clear that it was a matter of metaphysics. He argues that the Eucharist is not a question of the substance of bread becoming the substance of a human body (this kind of substantial change is familiar enough and takes place whenever we eat a slice of bread); it is a miraculous transformation at a deeper level, which Aquinas compares to creation, in which the *esse* (the existence) of this piece of bread and this cup of wine becomes the *esse* of Christ. This transformation of a substance into another *particular* existent, as distinct from a different kind of thing (as in ordinary substantial change) would have been completely unintelligible to Aristotle as, of course, was the notion of creation and, indeed, the whole notion of *esse* in Aquinas's sense.

My next task, then, is to give some account of 'meaning'. This philosophical task may seem rather distant from doing theology as such, but if faith is 'seeking understanding' it had better not be confused about understanding. I shall be arguing that meaning is never subjective 'just in the mind'. But nor is it 'objective' in the sense that most people would reckon that leopards and trees are objectively there (or not).

'When I use a word,' Humpty Dumpty said in a rather scornful tone, 'it means just what I choose it to mean – neither more nor less . . .' 'The question is,' said Humpty Dumpty, 'which is to be master – that is all.' He was, of course, talking nonsense. Words are for communication, which means common use, and cannot function unless there is a conventional agreement about their meaning. As Wittgenstein has convincingly shown, there can be no such thing as a private meaning. Meaning *belongs to the language itself.* Though, of course, in the development of language throughout human history, there is the creation and appreciation of new meanings, which is the intellectual life of a human society and is the intellectual life of particular individuals who share in the task. This is a point well brought out by Peter Geach in *Mental Acts* (1957) in criticizing the form of behaviourism he detected in Gilbert Ryle's *The Concept of Mind* (1949). The same point was made by Thomas Aquinas in the *De unitate intellectus contra Averroistas.* The understanding of meanings is the work of human intelligence, by which we transcend our individuality, but it comes about by a power of the human soul, which is always the substantial form of an individual human body. For Aquinas, concepts, unlike sensations, are not the private property of individuals but do arise from individual material animals transcending their individuality and hence their materiality. As Aristotle knew, thoughts, unlike sensations, have no corporeal organ. Brains do not think; they are the co-ordinating centre of the structure of the nervous system which makes possible the sensual interpretation of the world, which is itself interpreted in the structure of symbols, language, which we do not inherit with our genes but create for ourselves in community.

Britain recently had a prime minister who notoriously said, 'There is no such thing as society; there are only individuals and their families.' I will argue that there is a kind of objectivity to meaning just because there is such a thing as society and, moreover, that there is a symbolic relationship between language and society; one cannot exist without the other. And both are essential to (of the essence of) being human. I shall claim that the sacraments which centre upon the Eucharist are the language which makes a certain 'society' possible, and that it is this society that makes this sacramental language meaningful, and that what makes *this* language distinct from others is that the society in question is the mystery of the people of God. Of course, anything that is actual is 'of God', created and thus kept in being by the creative act of God. But the people of God are not simply God's creatures. They are the outcome of his personal convenantal love, the Holy Spirit, so that we are *children* of God sharing by grace in his own divine life. The sacramental language is the language granted to us in which this mystery is to be expressed and lived out in human and material terms.

The word 'sacrament' is, like so many theological words used *analogically* (as with 'sin' and 'love' and many of the words we use to speak of the unknown God). The first and greatest sacrament is the culmination of scriptural revelation (in the perspective of *Hebrews*) in the Word made flesh, the humanity of *Christ*, the image of the invisible God. Secondly, we speak analogically of the *Church* as 'sacrament', 'a sign and instrument, that is, of communion with God and of unity amongst all humankind' (*Lumen Gentium* I). The document of the Second Vatican Council from which these words come is in a medieval tradition which sees sacraments not simply as 'outward signs of inward grace' but as taking in the whole sweep of salvation history, past, present, and future, and sees humankind as something mainly for the future: 'while people of the present day are drawn ever more closely together by social, technical and cultural bonds, it still remains for them to achieve full unity in Christ.' That seems to me the ecclesiastical understatement of the century.

After the humanity of Christ and, then, the community of the Church, the third analogical use of 'sacrament' we use is when speaking in the plural, of the '*sacraments of the Church*' – Baptism, Eucharist, etc. My own view, which I do not have a chance to expound here, is that discussion of these has to be a discussion of the constitution and structure of the People of God, which is neither political nor invisibly 'spiritual' but precisely *sacramentally* visible. Suffice it for the present to say that the Eucharist in my view, which is not at all original, is the centre of the sacramental life. Other sacraments are sacramental by their relationship to the Eucharist.

But, back to the objectivity of meaning. In order to understand this, we first need, I think, to distinguish clearly between *sense experience* and *understanding*. Aquinas said that to make this distinction was one of the great achievements of Aristotle; but since then the blight of empiricism, among other things, has badly obscured it. To elucidate it, we need to think first about animal life.

It seems to me characteristic of animals that, unlike lifeless things like bits of glass and computers and volcanic rocks, they have purposes and a point of view and they *interpret* and *evaluate* the world in which they live. They find bits of their world frightening or edible or pleasurable or sexually attractive . . . or whatever. Animals do not have to be taught to groom each other; lambs do not have to learn to run away from wolves. Moreover, they manifestly do some things willingly and some things, under coercion, unwillingly.

It was by way of Avicenna (Ibn Sina, the eleventh-century Persian philosopher) that the medieval Europeans learnt of what they called the 'interior sense powers'. These were, first the *sensus communis*, the power of coordinating the deliveries of different exterior senses, to produce what in the early twentieth century we began to call the Gestalt as the meaningful object of sense experience. Secondly, there was the *imaginatio* or *phantasma*, the power of retaining such experience for future reference. Thirdly, was the *sensus aestimativus* (or *cogitativus*) that I have called the evaluative sense-power, by which the animal feels that something is dangerous or edible or whatever. Finally, there is the *sense-memory*, the awareness of time and temporality, the power of recalling experiences of the past. In linguistic animals there is also a quite distinct power which is not a sense but the 'intellectual memory', which is not concerned with time as such but is the power of *recall* by which what we have learnt and not forgotten is brought to mind when we are not at the moment thinking about it – like your address or the capital of Spain or Newton's second law.

So I want to argue that the sensuous bodily life that, broadly speaking, we share with non-linguistic animals, is primarily about finding *meaning* in the world. This is sense-experience – not simply being struck by some mythical 'sense data,' but being struck by the *significance* of surrounding things for the animal itself 'from its own point of view'. Such an experience gives rise to animal behaviour (if a bit of its world strikes an animal as edible it will tend to try to eat it). Not all such response is as simple as this. If, for example, a male animal perceives a fellow male of the species as threatening and aggressive, his response may be the performance of a ritual action of, say, submission which will divert the other's aggression. Ritual behaviour amongst non-linguistic animals is extremely common in moments of crisis, both in danger situations and courtship, and it is one of the features of behaviour that we should be careful *not* to confuse with language. The reason for this is that it is genetically determined by the animal's inherited DNA and quite as automatic as any other triggered response.

But in any case, every non-linguistic animal's response to its world is mediated by, and determined by, the meaning it discovers in it by its senses. What it *desires* to achieve or avoid (which is to say what it will *tend* to achieve or avoid) is conditioned by, indeed is *defined* by, its sensual interpretation of its world. Meaning can only be understood in terms of the larger notion of structure.

Meaning, in a perfectly general sense, is, I would maintain, always the role or place or function that some part of the structure has within that structure. What does it *mean* to be President of the United States? To answer this you have to give some account of the *structure* of the US government and society. What does 'perhaps' *mean*? It is a word, an adverb, qualifying a statement to express possibility with uncertainty. You have thus placed 'perhaps' within the *structure* of language in which it has a part to play.

Now consider seeing. It begins with light of some kind falling on the retina of the eye. In consequence of this, because the eye belongs to the structure of the bodily nervous system, certain things occur in the brain and, in consequence of *this*, certain tendencies may arise in the muscles of the animal's limbs and so on. The point of this is that the eye, because it belongs to the structure of the nervous system, is *relevant* to other parts of the animal's body. What happens in the eye is *meaningful* for the animal. It is this meaningfulness of the eye that we call 'sight'. The eye does not see; it is the whole animal that sees because of what has happened in the eye and elsewhere. The eye is an instrument of seeing (so the Greeks called it an 'organ', which means instrument). Animals see and hear and feel because the behaviour of parts of them is relevant to the whole. We call it an *organic* whole.

The non-linguistic animal's interpretation of its world is expressed in its behaviour, and only its behaviour. There is a superstitious view that the brain is what sees. This is quite false. The brain is the coordinator, the 'nerve centre' of the nervous system (and even this is not true in all animals). The notion that the brain sees is only a degree less absurd than the notion that the brain understands or thinks. The brain is not even the organ of understanding but rather part of the sensitive infra-structure necessary for understanding.

So: the non-linguistic animal's interpretation and evaluation of its world is expressed in its behaviour and *only* in its *behaviour*. The linguistic animal's interpretation of its world is expressed also in its *language*. So we must now turn to language and understanding.

The extraordinary thing about human animals is that they possess more than an inherited, genetically supplied nervous system which is the structure that makes meaningful *sense-experience* possible; we human animals also possess an (enormously more complex) brain structure which will serve as the necessary infra-structure of meaning that *we do not inherit but create for ourselves*: the structures of language. Nobody could have a gene for the Polish language; and if she could, Polish could not be a language.

As when we and our fellow animals *experience* our world we take it up into our inherited, more or less *genetically determined* bodily structures, *so* we *understand* as we take this experience up into our *socially* created structures of language. So our understanding, our use of language, requires sense-experience as *that which* we interpret and 'comment on'. But also, in order to use the meanings we understand, we need what Aquinas calls the '*conversio ad phantasmata*': a reference *back* to the interior sense-power of *imaginatio* in order to recall and actually reflect upon what is latent in our intellectual memory but which needs bringing to mind. This selective recall of what we have in the intellectual memory is, for Aquinas, at the heart of the human capacity for free choice. The necessity for the *conversio ad phantasmata* shows us why what we have called the 'bodily infra-structure' of human linguistic intellectual life is so important, and it is why, for example, brain-damage inhibits thinking. This is not, as I have said, because the brain is the organ of understanding, but because the brain is an important part of the 'infra-structure' upon which human understanding depends.

To make a language is to take certain material things (noises, marks on paper or cuts in stone . . . etc.) and to use them not as tools for their *causal* efficacy, as we might a hammer or a sword, but as *symbols*, as having an externally imposed meaning, imposed by our *convention*. Of course, no amount of study of the *intrinsic* meaning (the *natural form*) of the material thing which happens to be used as a symbol will reveal what its *linguistic* meaning is. You have to go amongst the community who use it and share their life so that you will come to appreciate how it is to be used in accordance with their conventions.

That assertion demands a very important qualification. It is not true that it is only the *conventional* and not the *natural* properties of our symbols that matter in language. The full, complete and perfectly precise use of language is what we nowadays call poetry. In listening to or reading or writing a poem, we pay attention not only to what I shall call the conventional 'dictionary meaning' of a word but also its sensual value, how we interpret it subjectively through our particular natural bodily nervous system, its rhythm and how it sounds and feels along the nerves. And this is not only true of the limited area we call poetry but also of normal human conversation. In fact to use language attending *only* to its dictionary meaning demands a special skill, but a very important one, for on it depends the development of all scientific disciplines: indeed, it is largely this that defines our use of words like 'scientific' and 'logical'. But poetry is language trying to be bodily experience, as music is bodily experience trying to be language. And science is language trying to be universally available regardless of particular languages.

It is when our language is stripped down to its dictionary meanings that we can confidently say that all human languages are inter-translatable, so that when we learn 'our own' language we are not simply fitting into the customs of our tribe, but, potentially, hearing or speaking to the whole human race, past, present, and to come. To understand a meaning at the human linguistic level is just to have a skill in using a symbol, let us call it a word. Now, there is, as I have suggested, an important difference between understanding a linguistic meaning and having a sensation, even though both are a matter of meaning, though at different levels. I can reasonably expect another member of my species to have roughly the same sensations as I have. It must be much the same for him or her as for me to be hungry or angry or frightened. If this were not so we could never learn the words 'hunger', 'anger' or whatever.

Now it is not so with understanding linguistic meanings. Here it is necessary not simply that another should have *similar* meanings in mind; it is necessary that he or she have *identical* meanings in mind. It is necessary that we should agree on at least the 'dictionary meaning' of the words, otherwise we shall be at cross purposes.

Fortunately it is not difficult to resolve such misunderstandings because

it is a feature of language that we can talk about talking. In our sensual interpretation this is not possible, or at least not in the same way. (The interior
evaluative sense [the *sensus aestimativus*] comes close to sensing a sense –
as the alternative medieval name for it, *sensus cogitativus*, implies).

Sensations remain my private property or yours. Thought, however, transcends my privacy. To repeat myself: in the creation of language we reach
beyond our private material individuality to break into the non-individual,
non-material sphere of linguistic meaning. This does not, of course, mean
that we cease to be material animals. But we are the material animals who
have a way of transcending our individuality so that the community we form
with others is something entirely new.

The human *polis* does not rest upon interacting self-interests, as Aristotle
thought our international relations did. But the *polis* itself rests, as Aristotle
thought, on *philia* (Pol. III.9). What distinguishes citizens from foreigners in
the true *polis* is that our moral bonds with the foreigners are those of a particular kind of commercial justice, whereas what unites citizens is *philia*,
friendship, which involves the capacity to transcend our individuality and
our individual interests. And with this we are not far from 'Greater love hath
no man than that he lay down his life for his friend.'

And here we come to the central meaning of the Eucharist. With the irony
or paradox typical of the New Testament, it is a celebratory feast which is
about defeat and death. It is both about the worlds of sin and about the
redemption of this world within, but from beyond this world by grace. It is
misunderstood if either of these facts is forgotten or played down. It is an
agape, a love feast, but it is saying that love is best represented in our kind
of world by an acceptance of death: an acceptance of murder, indeed. But
this is not presented as a philosophical or sociological discovery. It is not
presented as a doctrine at all. The last supper, the festival celebrating liberation from slavery, takes place under the shadow of the immanence of
calvary, and these irreconcilables like presence/absence cannot coexist on
paper but only in person, in the human person of Christ. Not in what he illus-
trates or what *he stands for* but in *himself*. That is why transubstantiation is
right. The Christian Church as I see it does not first of all preach a doctrine:
as Paul said, we preach 'Christ crucified'. Sure, over the centuries we have
quite rightly developed doctrines, but these have been articulated in order to
prevent misunderstandings, especially facile simplifications.

Like Karl Marx, Thomas Aquinas thought that the Christian religious cult
belongs essentially to an age of alienation, or as he put it, of sin. And by the

use of this word 'sin' he indicates that the alienation is deeper than anything Marx understood. Sin, for St Thomas, was an option for some perceived good which, in the circumstances would be *incompatible* with friendship, *agape*, with God, and that means alienation from the very roots of our existence and from our sharing in divinity. For Marx, religious cult was merely a symptom, certainly not a cause, of human alienation. It was neither the cause nor the cure, but simply 'the painkiller of the people' giving an illusion of well-being. With the elimination of the market economy, which has to treat human beings as commodities, religion, Marx thought, would simply fade away much as being greedy for sweets fades away as we grow up. Aquinas would have seen this as too optimistic; his thought is more complex. He sees the sacramental order as essentially God's word in our symbolic linguistic mode but, like Paul, he sees it also as a possible occasion of sin. In a famous passage from 1 Corinthians 11, Paul roundly tells the Corinthians:

> When you come together it is not for the better but for the worse. For in the first place, when you assemble as a church, I hear that there are divisions among you . . . When you meet together it is not the Lord's supper that you eat. For in eating, each one goes ahead with his own meal and one is hungry while another is intoxicated . . . do you despise the church of God and humiliate those who have nothing?

And Paul goes on

> It was on the night he was *betrayed* that the Lord Jesus took bread and having given thanks broke it and said 'This is my body'. (my emphasis).

Like the historical death of Christ, the sacramental commemoration (and even celebration) of it takes place in a world of sin.

A Church which is not a challenge to the values of such a world is one which, as Paul says, 'does not discern the body'. But the body is *there* to be 'discerned' and they are 'profaning the body and blood of the Lord' which is *there* to be profaned. For the Eucharist is the Word of God and not the word of man. We *make*, as well as *are made by* our human language. But we do not make the meaning of the Eucharist. If it is anything of interest, it is the Word of God and thus a word of power: the creative word that says 'Let there be light' – and there was light; the re-creative word that said 'This is my body and my blood' – and so it is. What the bread and wine have become is clearly not an icon, picture, reminder of Christ, but Christ himself, and him crucified, the only one who can reconcile the opposites, who can bring life out of death.

A Church which celebrates the Eucharist while ignoring what we should nowadays call 'the fundamental option for the poor' is 'eating and drinking judgement upon herself' as Aquinas thought; it is using the language of God to tell a lie.

Medieval Eucharistic theology distinguished three levels of meaning in the eucharistic language. There was what was simply a sign (*sacramentum tantum*) visible to anyone, a ritual meal, like a party which could be studied as well by atheist anthropologists as by Christians. This sign, however, is a God-spoken word which reveals itself to our faith at two levels. First there is the significance of *this* world (characterized by both grace and sin), this still-alienated world. The sign is that of the Church witnessing to this world and challenging it with the revelation of the gospel of love. This the medievals called the *res et sacramentum*. This *res* means what is signified by a sign; *sacramentum* means a sign itself. So at this level of meaning we have what is signified by the ritual meal, our human word of friendship. For now it signifies and thus realizes the incarnate Word of God at the moment of his supreme expression of love for us (what John calls his 'hour' and his 'lifting up') when his body is broken in death (as symbolized by the separation of body and blood). Here he reveals his loving and obedient faithfulness to his mission from the Father, the mission to be the first totally *human* being, living, as we are meant to, by love, by transcending his individual self and self-interest and thereby being totally vulnerable, not seeking to evade or resist whatever his brothers or sisters would do to him. It was this loving acceptance of defeat at our hands that won for this first really human being his defeat and our being given a sharing in his resurrection.

This real presence, then, of the incarnate Word of God in his meaning of victory-through-accepted-defeat for himself and for us, is the *res*, the thing directly signified by our eucharistic token meal. But this *res*, the sacramentally real presence of the body of Christ, is also itself a sign, a *sacramentum*, of a deeper *res*, a deeper reality, indeed the deepest reality.

The sacramental order of this world points towards and partially realizes a further third level of meaning, the ultimate mystery that is signified-and-not-a-sign of anything deeper (*res tantum*). This is the *agape*, the *caritas*, the love which is the Godhead. The liturgy of the Eucharist and its attendant sacraments, our life in the Church, is itself a sacramental sign and realization of our life in the kingdom.

Then there will be no more Eucharist, no more sacramental religion, no more faith or hope. All this will wither away. And there will be simply the unimaginable human living out of love which is the Spirit of God in eternity.

Part Three

People and Morals

Thirteen

Sense and Sensibility

'All the perceptions of the human mind resolve themselves into two distinct kinds, which I shall call *Impressions* and *Ideas*. The difference betwixt these consists in the degrees of force and liveliness, with which they strike upon the mind, and make their way into our thought or consciousness. Those perceptions, which enter with most force and violence, we may name *impressions* and under this name I comprehend all our sensations, passions, and emotions, as they make their first appearance in the soul. By *ideas*, I mean the faint images of these in thinking and reasoning; such as, for instance, are all the perceptions excited by the present discourse . . . I believe it will not be very necessary to employ many words in explaining this distinction. Every one of himself will readily perceive the difference betwixt feeling and thinking' (David Hume, *A Treatise of Human Nature*, I,1,1)

I

I want to argue that the arrival or emergence of the linguistic, human animal marks a huge change or development in the animal kingdom; not just an improvement, a particular lucky adaptation, but a revolutionary change such that the very notion of being an animal is radically changed. In developing my case, I shall be suggesting that Hume made some big mistakes.

A few weeks ago I watched one of those splendid BBC nature programmes on television. This one was about chimpanzees. The point of the programme was the great similarity between chimpanzee behaviour and ours – and, indeed, in many respects their behaviour was uncannily like ours. And, as though to hammer home the point, we were told that we share over ninety-eight per cent of our genes with the chimpanzees. The moral we were clearly expected to carry away was that really we are not that different from the chimps.

It was only some time afterwards, when I had got over the spell of the film, that I recognized that I had been watching a film made by human animals about chimpanzees. And I knew for sure that I would never watch a film made by chimpanzees about human animals. The reason for this a-symmetry (what I have called a huge difference) was quite clearly that human animals are linguistic and chimpanzees are not. It is language that makes us able to develop a technology and a science of chimpanzees (and, moreover, to develop a technology of television).

And the reason for this is that language always contains a sign for negation. And it is because of this that in language we can ask *questions* (no other animals can ask questions); and because of this we can, by language, come to know *truth*. For us, *truth* is in the answering of asked questions.

Let me point out that these thoughts give rise to another one. If it is really true (as I believe) that there is a catastrophic or revolutionary difference between non-linguistic and linguistic animals, and if it is also true that we differ by less than two per cent in our genes, then our genes must have very little to do directly with our having language. I leave you this thought to ponder on, whenever you hear Dr Richard Dawkin, or anyone else, tell you that all that you are and do and can do is determined by your genes and DNA.

II

Hume writes: 'Every one of himself will readily perceive the difference betwixt feeling and thinking.' Hume, I think, is being over-optimistic. He himself, it seems to me, does not at all perceive the difference in question.

Thomas Aquinas thought that one of the greatest achievements of Aristotle was to have given a clear account of this difference between feeling and thinking. This is what I also want to do, following Aristotle and Aquinas but taking as my starting point the phenomenon of language.

The first part of my central thesis is going to be that all animals both *interpret* and *change* the world in which they live, and do so by the medium of their senses. To repeat: all animals, including ourselves, interpret, *find significance* in their world through their bodily senses. This is what senses are: not bits of the body but *functions* of bits of the body. Significant functioning parts of the structure we call the nervous system. Thus the eye is not a sense but an organ of the sense of sight. The sense of sight belongs to just those animals which in their nervous structure interpret their world differently when it is lit up and when it is in the dark. Senses belong to *animals*, not to sense organs. *Eyes* do not see: cats see with their eyes.

For all animals, including ourselves, in the interpretation they give of their world, the significance they find in their world is shown in their *behaviour*, in how they change their world by what they do. So an animal with a sense of sight will show that it has seen part of its world as edible by activating a tendency to go and eat it. It will show that it sees part of its world as dangerous by activating either a tendency to attack it or to avoid it. An animal has many senses, though all have their roots in the primary sense organ: its skin, its bodily surface, the *locus* of the interchange between itself and its world. It may have many, sometimes conflicting, tendencies to action of different strengths or urgencies; its behaviour will spring from the sum of these tendencies.

The second part of my thesis is that we human animals (and only human animals) have also another structure by which we find significance in our world. This is language. By having language we not only have a *sensual* interpretation of our world (like all our fellow animals); we also have an interpretation *of that sensual interpretation itself*; which I shall call 'understanding'. To repeat: this capacity for producing an interpretation of our sensual interpretation, by language, by talking about it, is unique and exclusive to us. No other animals talk, either to each other or to themselves.

From now on I should like to call our sensual interpretation of our world our *experience*. And I shall call our linguistic interpretation of our experience our *understanding*.

I have said that experience, the delivery of our senses, finds *significance* in the world of the animal, and because of this the animal (unless it is ill or otherwise defective) behaves appropriately in its world. What, then, is significance? Significance or meaning is the relevance of a part to the structure to which it belongs. The meaning of being president of the republic is the part she or he plays in the structure which is the political life of the republic. This is what you would explain if you wanted to explain the meaning of the presidency. Again, the meaning of, say, the word 'perhaps' is the part it plays in the structure which is the language to which it belongs. Similarly the meaning of 'elephant' is the part it plays in the language. I say this to indicate that I reject the notion that the meaning of the word 'elephant' is ever an elephant, or that you could teach someone the meaning of the word 'elephant' by, say, painting an elephant and pointing to the painting. No concrete individual object can be the meaning of a word – fundamentally because we do not *understand* concrete objects; we can only *experience* them as meaningful sensually. We may use the word 'elephant' to talk about, to refer to, a particular elephant, but this is not the same as saying that the elephant is what the word means. The meaning of a word, like the meaning of being president, is a matter of the rules governing its position in a structure.

The body of any animal such as ourselves is an organic unity, one in which parts are intrinsically related to other parts and make a difference to other parts. The parts of an organic body are organs (instruments) which relate to each other through a bodily structure we call the nervous system, centred on the brain. As the eye is the organ of sight and the nose the organ of smell, so we could say that the nervous system is the organ of experience in general. Or we can say more succinctly that the brain is the organ of experience. (It is not, as many suppose, the organ of *understanding*. There is no organ of *understanding*.) Remember that by 'experience' I am meaning that interpretation of our world which is provided by our *senses*. This interpretation is not a matter of understanding or thinking, but the work of sense experience itself. In saying this I am rejecting what I think of as the empiricist view of the senses such as Hume took for granted: that sensation is simply a matter of 'impressions', the production of raw 'sense data' by the physical impact on us of other objects. Ever since the Cartesian revolution (the revolution initiated in the seventeenth century by René Descartes) philosophers have tended to suppose that all finding of meaning in our world is the work purely of the mind, a spiritual entity that lurks somewhere inside the head, and that non-human animals that lack a mind are simply machines which do not give any interpretation to their world at all. I think that, in Europe, we have happily seen the demise of the Cartesian epoch, at least among philosophers (though not always amongst biologists), and this has been in great part due to the work of Wittgenstein, but also of those Gestalt psychologists who showed that for non-linguistic animals, such as apes, experience comes not as raw bits of disconnected sense data but as meaningful patterns. In this we have returned in a way to pre-Cartesian modes of viewing our non-linguistic fellow animals, well aware that they can be angry, can fall in love, can be submissive or domineering, that they can play and can learn by imitation . . . and so on. All this had been temporarily suppressed (for nearly three centuries) when, because of the dramatic expansion of human technology during and since the seventeenth century, the *machine* became a dominant image for explanation of the world. (You thought you understood, say, animal behaviour when you could suggest how a machine might be made to do the same things. What is now becoming much clearer to us is that machines are just imitation animals; as statues are just imitation people.)

So in sense-experience what takes place in, say, the retina of my eye is relevant to what happens in my feet and hands, and this whole pattern of relevance is what we call 'seeing'. Within the structure of the nervous system what happens in one part of the body is meaningful, significant, for another part. It is because of the structure of the nervous system that experience delivers to the animal the meanings of its world. The world has meanings for the animal that call forth appropriate behaviour patterns. A billiard ball moves simply because it has been hit by another ball. In an animal its behaviour is indeed due to the world outside it; but this is *mediated by experience*, by the meaning its nervous system reveals in the world.

One important thing to notice here (and we will be coming back to it again later) is that your nervous system is yours and not mine. A nervous system is an individual material thing and its shape is determined, at least in large part, by the genes that the animal who has it has inherited. If two animals belong to the same species, they will ordinally have very similar structures of the nervous system – structures in which their world is made sensually meaningful to them. But there may be slight differences. All sparrows will have broadly the same experience of their world, but it will be widely different from that of, say, whales or duck-billed platypuses. In other words, the experience is always subjective, depending on bodily structure. Or, as we may say, while returning to ourselves, it is mine and not yours, however similar they may be. How the world looks is always how it looks *to me*.

We now come to the special structure of meaning that is the exclusive property of linguistic animals, human beings. This is language. Language is the non-inherited but home-made 'nervous system' for interpreting deliveries of the inherited nervous system. If a nervous system is the inherited bodily structure which makes possible the sensual interpretation of the world (experience), language is the structure which makes possible the interpretation of experience itself (understanding). Because we have language, we do not just have experience. We talk about it, making it meaningful within the structure of our language. We are born with our nervous systems already in place. We are not born with a language, merely with a capacity for developing or learning a language. Any language is a human artefact – not indeed the work of an individual artist but one that develops or is impoverished over many generations, and which is handed down from the older to the young. This is tradition.

Some elementary words, now, about evolution and natural selection. In animal reproduction the parent passes on to its offspring the genes which it inherited from its own parents. In sexual reproduction, of course, where there are two parents, the offspring receives half its genes from each, and this makes for richer possibilities of variation in the descendants. The genes function as plans or maps according to which proteins in the offspring make more proteins as the new offspring develop. It is quite important to see that (*pace* Professor Richard Dawkins) the genes do not do anything; they are, as I say, the plans according to which proteins operate. Genes do not bring about the development of the new animal any more than your road map will drive your car to Canterbury.

Central to Charles Darwin's account of evolution (and where he differs from his predecessor Lamark) is that parents pass on only what they have received genetically from their own parents, though this may have been subject to minor random modification due to radioactivity or whatever. Such modifications are usually harmful, quite often neutral, and of no evolutionary effect one way or the other. But just occasionally, especially if there has been a significant change in the environment of the species, a random mutation may happen to produce a variation in the offspring which makes it more adapted to living in the new circumstances than others of the species which lack this new look. Such an individual animal, because better adapted to the new world, may be expected to live longer and have, therefore, more offspring than those of the old model. To them it will, of course, pass on the new modified genes so that eventually this family will outbreed the old-fashioned type. This is called natural selection and, as Darwin saw, it is the way that new species eventually evolve from old.

Two things to notice here: first the parent passes on only the genes it has itself inherited – give or take the occasional random, accidental mutation. It does not pass on to its offspring by way of inheritance anything useful that it may have acquired during its life story. Secondly, the whole account hinges on the random change of a lucky individual's genes which will confer an advantage on its offspring.

(This is perhaps a suitable point to interpolate a protest against those people who think that just because evolution happens by random chance mutations we can somehow stop thinking of God, since his guiding hand has been evicted from nature. I don't know what kind of God these people have been brought up on, but, at least on the traditional Catholic view of God – that of Thomas Aquinas, for example – God the Creator is the source of everything, absolutely everything, that really happens, whether it be random or free or necessitated by other created causes. The whole thing is in the hands of God and that is why God is not mentioned in scientific explanations which are always about why *this* happens instead of *that*. Whereas God is about why anything is happening at all, instead of nothing. End of interpolation.)

For orthodox Darwinianism, then, you might say that communication between one generation and the next is restricted to the passing on of genes and nothing else.

We should now take a look at the linguistic revolution that produced human beings. First I would like to indicate why Professor Anthony Kenny has doubts about whether the capacity for language could have appeared by natural selection as I have roughly described it. And secondly I would like to say why this revolution changed the meaning of what it was to be an animal. And finally I would like to show that all this is because by language we have a capacity not just for meaning but for truth. This is because in language, while remaining individuals, we transcend our material individuality.

Now the rule-governed nature of languages makes it difficult to explain the origin of language by natural selection. The explanation by natural selection of the origin of a feature in a population presupposes the occurrence of that feature in particular individuals of the population. Horses, for instance, may have developed the length of their legs through evolutionary stages. One can very easily understand how natural selection might favour a certain length of leg: if it were advantageous to have long legs, then the long-legged individual in the population might outbreed the others. Clearly, where such explanation of the occurrence of features is most obviously apposite, it is perfectly possible to conceive the occurrence of the feature in single individuals. There is no problem about describing a single individual as having legs n metres long. (There may or may not be a problem about explaining the origin of the single long-legged specimen; but there is no logical difficulty in the very idea of such a favoured specimen.)

Now it does not seem at all plausible to suggest, in a precisely parallel way, that the human race may have begun to use language because the language-using individuals among the population were advantaged and so outbred the non-language-using individuals. This is not because it is difficult to see how spontaneous mutation could produce a language-using individual; it is because it is difficult to see how anyone could be a language-user at all before there was a community of language-users.

If we reflect on the social and conventional nature of language, we see something odd in the idea that language may have evolved because of the advantages possessed by language-users over non-language users. It seems almost as odd as the idea that golf may have evolved because golf-players had an advantage over non-golf-players in the struggle for life, or that banks evolved because those born with a cheque-writing ability were better off than those born without it. (Kenny, 1989, pp. 155f.)

The sensuous interpretation of the environment that I have called 'experience' and which is shared by all animals, including ourselves, is determined by the inherited structure of our nervous system which, thanks to the parents' genes, is passed on more or less undamaged to the offspring. The other level of interpretation, which is the exclusive preserve of the linguistic animal, is not so inherited but made by our ancestors and ourselves. Animal experience is shown in the way that they *behave*; human understanding is shown in humanly devised *symbols*, symbols whose meaning is conventionally decided by us. This is to say we have given them a *function* in a new *structure*. Symbols are, of course, material objects, but they are material objects used not for their natural properties but for the significance that has been given to them by us, their place in the structure, by convention.

That assertion demands a very important qualification. It is not true to say that it is only the conventional and not the natural properties of our symbols that matter in a language. The full, complete and perfectly precise use of language is what we call *poetry*. In listening to or reading poetry we have to pay attention not only to what I might call the 'dictionary meaning' of a word but also its sensual value, how we interpret it through our natural bodily nervous system, its rhythm and how it sounds and feels along the nerves. The reason why we can genuinely enjoy what we think of as 'obscure' poetry is that we often respond to our sensuous experience of the material words spoken before we can give a critical account of the 'meaning'. And this is just as true of the poet who first speaks them as of his readers. The poetic use of language, which I imagine is its primitive use, appeals to the complex interaction of experience and understanding.

What F. R. Leavis at Cambridge and his followers who produced *Scrutiny* used to call 'the seventeenth century dissociation of sensibility' was the splitting apart of sensual experience and dictionary meaning which occurred when the technological and scientific use of language became more respectable than poetry. I am entirely in sympathy with this critique of the culture we have inherited (indeed it is yet another aspect of what I think of as the Cartesian Age), but for the moment I want to concentrate on the 'dictionary meaning' because I want to make clear the *difference* between language and experience.

The most striking thing, it seems to me, about the advent of the linguistic animal as a form of development is that evolution here becomes out of date. Suddenly the passing on of acquired characteristics (which is anathema to strict Darwinian evolution) becomes the most important, you might say the *only* important vehicle of development for the human animal. Because they have language and thus understanding, which is nothing but being able to use language, the parents can discover their own (*shared*, of course) inter-pretation of their environment and express it in shared linguistic symbols. And (because this is language) they can communicate it to share it with their offspring. At a stroke, the whole tedious and cumbersome mechanism of natural selection which has to take many generations to establish a signifi-cant variation in the species becomes irrelevant; it is replaced by *tradition*, the linguistic transmission of information to the next generation; and *history* is born, to replace evolution. In the last few million years that human animals have existed we have not, by natural selection, become significantly different from our remote ancestors; the real differences, for better or worse, have been cultural, to do with language. It has taken a million years for trivial differences in my bodily state to emerge, I suppose by natural selection, but (going back to the television programme about the chim-panzees) in my grandfather's youth nobody at all had any notion of how to make a television set. Because of language, not because of DNA or anything genetic, in my time television has arrived and radically changed the human way of life – and of course the development of cybernetics is very rapidly going to carry this transformation much further. And in all this hardly a gene has quivered. It is all due to language, to tradition and education.

I would like now to look at three very important features of language. (It will be evident, I hope, that I am using 'language' to mean any system of con-ventional signs, not just words but logos and liturgical gestures, and such like.) It is characteristic of such conventional signs that you have to *learn* them. You have to learn your own native language and in the same way you can learn other languages. And this introduces the first of my three features of language.

So far as their dictionary meanings are concerned, all languages are *inter-translatable*. The dictionary meaning is the foundation of what we particularly call language. Poetry is the dictionary meaning approaching sensual experience as music is sensual experience approaching meaning.

We are not, of course, born with a language; we are born with the bodily infrastructure that makes us able to create language. We are born within a particular culture that sustains a language by tradition, by handing it on from one generation to the next. Perhaps I ought to say that tradition is for *taking part in*, not for *believing in*. Someone who says she believes in tradition may rightly be suspected of wanting everything to stay the same as it used to be, to be 'conservative'. But, of course, tradition is almost the opposite of that: it is the wonderful new linguistic way humans have devised of speedy change. To be within a tradition is to be able to alter it in significant ways. To refuse to be traditional is usually to want to stick unchangeably in present ways. To be traditional is to recognize that you are in process; it is the very opposite of being 'conservative'. It is to be critical of the tradition you receive but, since you are within the tradition, to be effectively critical.

Now because we learn our language and are not determined by it, we can also, in principle, learn every other human language. You learn a foreign language essentially by living (really or imaginatively) with those who speak it. This is what I mean by inter-translatability. This, of course, usually only extends to the dictionary meanings of words. You have to live with them a lot longer and more deeply to make poetry in their language. This is part of what Wittgenstein meant by saying that to learn a language is to learn a form of life.

But now the question arises: but what about other animal species? Do some of them perhaps also have language? The answer is not, as I see it, to be found in whether they make regular and predictable noises or gestures. As far as I can see, the dancing of bees which indicates the best direction to go to find the makings of honey, the warning cries of birds, the mysterious creaking of whales, are all just pieces of *behaviour* – behaviour with a definite function in the life pattern of these animals. They are, like other non-linguistic animal behaviour, genetically determined and surely arise by natural selection.

The only acceptable evidence that other species had language would be if we as a matter of course chatted with them from time to time, as we do with

Japanese and Hungarians. It is true that we cannot experience the lifestyle of buffaloes or bees in the way that we can with the Japanese, but we could know about their lifestyle, understand it, quite sufficiently to understand what their lifestyle is, and hence what their language is and how it is used. Wittgenstein, it seems to me, was wrong when he said, 'If a lion could talk we would not understand him.' Our language, although it arises out of the particular form of life we have, is not *determined* by it and is indeed our way of transcending it. As I shall be arguing, the deployment of meanings is itself a transcending of our individuality such as has no place in sensual experience. Moreover if a lion could talk *he* also could transcend his individuality. If we worked at it we could understand the 'dictionary' meanings of a lion's utterances even though we would be lost amongst his poetry. And the lion could do the same with regard to us. If they were much more intelligent and diligent than we are, buffaloes and bees would have learnt English by now, even though they could not speak it and never experience the full awfulness of being English.

I should add that I think people frequently underestimate the capacity of non-linguistic animals to imitate and join in with *play*. Discovering how to play a game with another player does not necessarily involve language or understanding any more than a skilled footballer has to give himself instructions in his head in order to play well. (In his case, of course, he begins with being linguistically instructed, but non-linguistic animals can dispense with this and make do with simple imitation.) What some observers have taken to be an animal learning to speak with us is, I reckon, simply its learning to go through the motions of a new game by watching us and recognizing some moves as rewarding and others as not. And I say all this because of the second feature of language.

Language, at least so far as its dictionary meanings go, is objective and the source of our objectivity. By language we escape from the subjectivity essential to experience – and so would the buffaloes if they had language.

Let us remember David Hume for a moment. He takes it for granted that sensations and ideas are both some kind of picture or image in the head – one being fainter than the other. I have already suggested that this is a mistake about sensations. They are not pictures in the head but the co-ordination of the parts of an organic body. It is the relevance of what happens in the eye to what happens in the teeth and claws and feet that makes the eye an organ of sight. And Hume makes an even greater mistake about ideas. To have an idea or notion of what a horse is, is not at all to have a picture of a horse in mind; it is having a capacity or skill, it is being able to use the word 'horse' (or its equivalent) as part of a language (rather as the eye is used as part of the nervous system). Always the great difference is that sensations and the capacity for sensations are received by genetic inheritance, whereas understanding, the capacity to catch our sensations in the web of words, is something we create or socially ('legally') inherit.

When you have a sensation it is impressed upon your body. For you to have a sensation is a bodily condition and one that is a pre-condition for the use of language, but language itself is not a bodily condition even though it is the use of material things like symbols.

The use of language involves being bodily for these two reasons: it *arises from* (and is) an interpretation of bodily experience, and it is *expressed* in the use of bodily symbols. This is just as true of 'talking' to myself as it is of talking with others: to imagine myself using words is an operation of the brain. Aristotle discovered a long time ago that 'understanding has no corporeal organ' as sensation has. Now just because your sensations are bodily operations your sensations and feelings are your own, uniquely, sub-jectively, your own: they cannot be mine, though, since we belong to the same species, they are not likely to be very different from my own. That is why there can be physical empathy between members of the same non-linguistic species. There can be body-language, there can be ritual courtship displays and communication of fear or of affection amongst non-linguistic animals, but the actual feelings and emotions are private and unique to each individual because they are themselves bodily.

Now it is not so with linguistic communication. When I use a word it is not that I hope you have a *similar* idea to mine in your head. I hope you have the *identical* idea to mine. Of course you may not: we may be at cross-purposes, but this is a minor matter if it is soon obvious enough and we can sort it out. (If I am talking of *amateurs* and you think I am talking of *hamsters*, we soon realize this.)

And this, as Wittgenstein tirelessly said, is because meanings, the proper way to use signs, are not in your head or in mine: they are in the language itself. When I use an intelligible sign like a sentence (e.g., 'The cat is on the mat'), I am not expressing my personal bodily feelings, but simply saying something. It would not make sense to say, 'The cat is on the mat for *me*, but doubtless for *you* it is in the washing machine.' 'For me' and 'for you' simply don't come into it. The cat either is or is not on the mat quite regardless of my or your feelings.

And this brings us to the final feature of linguistic life and its distinction from sensual life. If you love to eat strawberries in moderation, you cannot simultaneously hate to eat strawberries in moderation. Opposing feelings and sensations cannot co-exist. An experience of one sort cannot simultaneously be an experience of an incompatible kind.

However, to understand the meaning of 'The cat sat on the mat' is not only compatible with but *identically the same as* understanding 'The cat did not sit on the mat.' To understand a sentence is also to understand its negation. There is no parallel to this in the world of sense-experience. You can say 'I wouldn't know what it feels like to be hot if I didn't know what it felt like to be cold.' But that is not about *sensation*. It is about *understanding*. What you cannot do is *feel* hot and cold in the same act of sensation. Whereas you *must* always understand a meaning and its negation in the same act of understanding.

Negation is, as I have suggested, the really wonderful thing about language, for it enables us to entertain simultaneously two opposite possibilities. In other words, it enables us to ask questions, and so to seek to answer them. And this is how uniquely, and exclusively, the linguistic animal comes to grasp truth. For we do not grasp truth by having a language but by using it in a particular way: to ask questions and look for answers.

Fourteen

Aquinas on Good Sense

Elizabeth, Anne, and Emma

I am concerned here with the virtue which Aquinas calls *prudentia*. But, as is almost always the case with Aquinas's technical vocabulary, the nearest English word to the Latin one would be a mistranslation: *prudentia* does not mean what we call prudence. Prudence suggests to us a certain caution and canniness, whereas *prudentia* is much nearer to wisdom, practical wisdom.

Fortunately, however, we have a nearly perfect English equivalent in Jane Austen's phrase 'good sense'. I take Jane Austen to be centrally concerned not with presenting the ethos of the new respectable middle class but rather with the failure of the new bourgeoisie to live satisfactory lives because of the inability of the older 'aristocratic' tradition to transmit to them a certain outlook and way of behaving and education that came down to the author via the remains of a Christian morality. The eighteenth-century ideal of civilized living collapsed because it involved the loss of this tradition, a tradition which (as Gilbert Ryle and others have pointed out) is, broadly speaking, Aristotelean.

Of course, no novel is a philosophical treatise, but much of Jane Austen's writing can usefully be seen as an exploration of this tradition and in particular of the notion of *prudentia*. Elizabeth Bennett (in *Pride and Prejudice*) is shown as having and growing in good sense, in contrast both to the silliness of her younger sisters, who think of nothing beyond present pleasure and, on the other hand, to the pedantry of her elder sister Mary, who thinks that book-learning is enough. She also stands in contrast to her witty and perceptive but almost purely voyeuristic father, who uses his intelligence to survey a life in which he refuses to become involved. Finally, there is a contrast with her friend Charlotte, who succumbs to worldly wisdom and marries the dreadful Mr Collins for 'prudential' reasons. All these people are presented as morally inferior (and thus ultimately unhappy) because they lack good sense. Anne Elliot (in *Persuasion*) is, of course, centrally concerned with what Aquinas regards as a major constituent of *prudentia*: making proper use of the counsel of others. And one aspect of the education of Emma (in *Emma*) is even more interesting, because this is not completed until at the end of the book Mr Knightley, who in part represents an alien imposed morality, is integrated into her life – he marries her and goes to live in her house together with the totally undisciplined father. The scuffles between the super-ego and the libido are being resolved in what begins to look more like virtue.

Conscience

Anyway, it is with good sense that we are concerned. A prominent part has been played in post-renaissance moral thinking by the notion of conscience, and people are often shocked to discover that this plays so small a part in Aquinas's moral teaching. Like the notion of the sheer individual in abstraction from social roles and community, and like the idea of 'human rights' attaching to such an abstract individual, it was a notion for which nobody has a word in either classical or post-classical antiquity or in the Middle Ages. Aquinas does use the word *conscientia*, but for him it is not a faculty or power which we exercise, nor a disposition of any power, nor an innate moral code, but simply the judgement we may come to on a piece of our behaviour in the light of various rational considerations. Usually it is a judgement we make on our past behaviour, but it can be extended to judgement on behaviour about which we are deliberating. Plainly such judgements happen, and they are important when they do; but what is meant in modern talk by conscience is normally something quite different. Nowadays we speak of someone 'consulting her conscience', rather as one might consult a cookery book or a railway timetable. Conscience is here seen as a private repository of answers to questions, or perhaps a set of rules of behaviour. Someone who 'has a conscience' about, say, abortion or betting is someone who detects in herself the belief that this activity is wrong or forbidden and who would therefore feel guilty were she to engage in it.

To have a conscience, then, in this way of thinking is to be equipped with a personal set of guidelines to good behaviour, and to stifle your conscience is not to pay attention to these guidelines. Since following the guidelines is often inconvenient or difficult, it is necessary to exert our will-power to do so. So the moral life, for this way of thinking, is an awareness of your rules of behaviour coupled with a strong will which enables you to follow these rules.

For most of those who think in this way, the verdict of conscience is ultimately unarguable. If someone says honestly: 'My conscience tells me this is wrong', she is thought to be giving an infallible report on the delivery of her inner source of principles which must call a halt to argument. It is believed that the reason why violating the consciences of others – i.e., coercing them to do what is contrary to their conscience – is a very grave evil, is that there can be no rational appeal beyond conscience. For this reason there are 'conscience clauses', and for this reason a tribunal for conscientious objectors to war service is essentially concerned to determine whether a person who claims to have a conscientious objection is telling the truth about the delivery of his conscience. Such a tribunal is not expected directly to consider the validity or otherwise of the objector's position: what matters is simply that it is the decision of his conscience. This concern for conscience as such is admirably expressed in Robert Bolt's play about Thomas More, *A Man for All Seasons*; though it is not an attitude that would have been shared by an old-fashioned thinker like St Thomas More himself. For this modern way of thinking there exists a *prima facie* right for individuals to follow their consciences, and hence societies in which, for example, there is no such provision for conscientious objection are seen as necessarily unjust and tyrannous.

In the tradition with which I am concerned, there exists no such right; for rights have a quite different foundation. On the other hand there is a principle of good sense in legal matters that even activities thought to be anti-social are not to be prohibited by the apparatus of the law if this will cause more social harm than tolerating them. A society that legally tolerates any number of devious and peculiar sexual or financial practices is not proclaiming its belief that these are harmless (still less that they are possible options for the good life); it is proclaiming its belief that, whatever harm they do, sending in the police or opening the way for blackmail, would be immensely more disruptive and dangerous to the general good. Similarly, much more harm would be done by imprisoning or forcibly conscripting people who genuinely believe that war (or this war) is unjust than by tolerating them. It is for this reason, and not because of the alleged absolute rights of conscience, that it is a bad thing not to respect conscientious objectors. It is not the strength and sincerity of my conviction that the use of nuclear weapons must always be evil, but rather the grounds for this conviction that make it morally right for me to refuse any co-operation with such use. Obviously, no members of a tribunal could accept these grounds without becoming conscientious objectors themselves; short of this they can only make a sensible, and therefore just, decision to tolerate me.

The truth of this can be seen, I think, if we ask ourselves whether there should be tribunals to judge whether a man really holds as a matter of conscience that he should strangle all Jewish babies at birth or that his children's moral education is best served by starving them or burning them with cigarette ends. It is, I think, a mark of the confusion that has prevailed in moral thinking that intelligent people can find it quite hard to give a reasoned answer to such questions. So let us turn from this to the Aristotelean tradition as developed by Aquinas.

Prudentia

In this view we come to decisions, the 'deliveries of conscience', by practical thinking, and such thinking, like so many human activities, can be done well or badly, 'conscientiously' or sloppily, honestly or with self-deception. The virtue which disposes us to think well about what to do is *prudentia*, good sense.

We should notice that, like most thinking, this would normally be a communal activity. We would ordinarily try to get the thing right by discussing the matter with others, by asking advice or arguing a case; we would have a background of reading books or watching Channel Four, of listening to preachers or parents or children, of criticizing the views and behaviour of others; and all things for which we could appropriately be blamed, and this shows that to be disposed not to behave like that is to have a virtue. We may on particular occasions pity the credulous, foolish or stubbornly unreasonable person, just as we might pity the coward or drug-addict, but ordinarily we would think it also proper to blame such people (and therefore, of course, proper to forgive them).

Unreasonableness, pig-headedness, bigotry and self-deception are all in themselves blameworthy, and they are constitutive of the kind of stupidity that is a vice. That is why no stupid person can be good. In case anyone should think that this gives academics and intellectuals a moral advantage over ignorant peasants, let us remember that what is in question is not theoretical thinking and the handling of concepts and words, but the practical shrewdness and common sense in matters of human behaviour. In this matter I think the 'ignorant' peasant may often have the edge over the professor. One of the hindrances to acquiring the virtue of good sense is living too sheltered a life. There is, of course, a sense of 'education' (rather different from the one in common use) in which the educated person does indeed have a moral advantage over the uneducated; if this were not so, education would not be a serious human activity. It will be clear that in this Aristotelean view, conscience, the moral judgement I have come to, is in no sense infallible. For what I have called the modern position, the delivery of conscience is a base-line: moral questions concern simply whether and to what extent you follow your conscience. For the older point of view you can be praised or blamed for the moral principles you hold. People who have come to the conclusion (who have convinced themselves) that torture can be a good and necessary thing and who thus carry it out cheerfully without a qualm of conscience would, in accordance with the older view, be not less but more to blame than those who recognize that torture is evil, who do not want to do it, but nevertheless do it out of fear of reprisals should they fail in their 'duty'.

Concerning judgements of conscience, Aquinas asks two interesting questions in succession. Is it always wrong, he asks, not to do what you mistakenly think is right? (Is it always wrong to go against your conscience?) He says that it is always wrong to flout your judgement of conscience in this way – he holds, for example, that someone who had come to the conclusion that Christianity was erroneous would be wrong not to leave the Church. But then he asks the following question: Is it always right to do what you mistakenly think is right? (Is it always good to follow your conscience?) This is where he departs from the modern view: he says it is not necessarily right for you to do what you think is right, for you may have come to your decision of conscience carelessly, dishonestly or by self-deception. He holds, in fact, the disturbing view that you can be in the position of being wrong if you do not follow your conscience and also being wrong if you do. But, he argues, you can only have got yourself into this position through your own fault. It is only by continual failure in virtue, by the cultivation of excuses and rationalizations, that you have blinded yourself to reality. It is not at all uncommon for individuals through their own fault to have put themselves in positions in which the only courses left open to them are all bad. Then they simply have to choose the lesser evil, which does not on that account become good.

Suppose, for example, that a government has established in a remote and desolate area a large set of factories for the wicked purpose of manufacturing nuclear weapons. Unemployed people from distant parts of the country get on their bikes and flock to this place to get jobs. Once this has happened the government may continue its genocidal activity or else it may throw these thousands of people out of work with no hope of work. It has put itself in the position where all its options, for which it would rightly be held responsible, are bad.

Thus, for Aquinas, a clear conscience is no guarantee of virtue. We should always, he says, fear that we may be wrong. We should have what he calls *sollicitudo* about this. As Oliver Cromwell (not always an assiduous disciple of St Thomas) said to the General Assembly of the Church of Scotland: 'I beseech you, gentlemen, in the bowels of Christ, to bethink you that you may be mistaken'.

Good sense is the virtue that disposes us to deliberate well, to exercise our practical reasoning well, and it presupposes that we have some good intention, that we intend an end that is in itself reasonable. The *intentio finis*, intending the end, is an *actus voluntatis*, a realization or actualization of the power we call the will, the power to be attracted by what we intellectually apprehend as good. (We should be on our guard against translating *actus voluntatis* as an 'action' or performance of the will: that primrose path leads to the dualistic notion of an interior performance of the will, an intention, accompanying the exterior action. The *actus voluntatis* here is the condition or state of being attracted to some good, which is *actus* in that it fulfils the potentiality of the will as the oak fulfils the potentiality of an acorn, not as the kick fulfils the potentiality of the leg. It must be said that Aquinas's own language is not always as guarded as it might be on this important point.)

It is in and by the will that we are in a state of intending an end; it is by the will, that is, that we find this end attractive as an end. The will is being actualized or exercised because we present the end to ourselves rationally (in language or other symbols). This is to be distinguished from being attracted to some good that presents itself to us simply as sensually apprehended. The latter attractions and appetites we share, more or less, with other non-linguistic animals. Such animals can, of course, in Aquinas's view be moved by an end or purpose in what they do, they can act willingly (*voluntarie*); they cannot be said in his technical language (which I believe he invented) to *intend* that end. In modern English I think we would say that the dog intended to chase the rabbit, but all that we would mean is that the dog's seeing of the rabbit, its sensual apprehension of it as desirable, is the reason why it is chasing. We do not mean that the dog *has* this reason, for this would only be possible if the dog were able to *analyse* its situation in language, to see, as Aquinas puts it, 'the *end as end* to be pursued by these or those means'. So while we may certainly say the dog is willingly (*voluntarie*) chasing (as opposed to unwillingly, involuntary, or without willing, *non-voluntarie*) we cannot say that the dog has the intention, *intentio*, of chasing it. Although it is acting willingly, *voluntarie*, it is not acting in terms of a state or condition of willing.

Synderesis

So, for Aquinas, good sense, good deliberation, does not concern itself with the *intentio finis*, the wanting of the end, but with the adjustment of the means to the end. The intellectual presentation of the end that we find attractive (which we want or intend) is not in the field of practical reasoning but of an intellectual disposition that Aquinas calls *synderesis*. This is a very peculiar word for a very peculiar and interesting concept. It is, for one thing, a piece of fake Greek that seems to have been invented by Latin-speaking medieval philosophers and does not occur in any classical Greek text. The clue to understanding it, I believe, is to see that, for Aquinas, in the sphere of practical action *synderesis* is related to deliberation in the way that, in the theoretical sphere, *intellectus* (understanding) is related to reasoning.

Aquinas thought that in any kind of true knowledge, any *scientia*, there must be certain first principles that are simply taken for granted; they are not part of the subject of the *scientia* itself. Keynesians do not argue with Milton Friedmanites about whether $1 + 1 = 2$; economists take for granted truths that are argued to by philosophers of mathematics. The statistical study of economics is permeated by the truths of arithmetic but it is not about them. Economics is done in terms of arithmetic, it does not seek to establish these truths. The economist needs the arithmetical *habitus* or skill, but what he is engaged in is something different. Now, as I understand him, Aquinas would think of the economist as having *intellectus* with regard to the arithmetical principles he takes for granted but exercising his *ratio*, reasoning, about his own particular topic. We should notice that the arithmetical truths are not premises from which truths of economics are deduced; they are terms within which, in the light of which (to use Aquinas's own metaphor), the argument is conducted. Aquinas frequently says that *intellectus* is the *habitus* of first principles, while reason, *ratio*, is concerned with how to draw conclusions in the light of these principles in some particular field.

'First principles' must be a relative term, for what are the first principles of one science (e.g. economics or chemistry) will be the conclusions of another (e.g. mathematics). Aquinas did not think there could be an infinite regress of sciences, each treating as arguable what the one below it took for granted. We must, he thought, eventually arrive at some first principles that nobody could think of as arguable, as the conclusion of a reasoned argument. He instances the principle of non-contradiction: that the same proposition cannot simultaneously be both true and false. And indeed this cannot be argued since any argument, to be an argument at all, must take this for granted; it must be conducted in terms of, in the light of, this. (This principle must not be confused with the principle called the 'excluded middle', which says that a proposition must be either true or false: this can be rationally denied and all multi-valued logics start from rejecting it.) So the absolutely ultimate first principle in theoretical reasoning, the principle in terms of which any reasoning whatever must take place, is something like the principle of non-contradiction, and *intellectus* in its ultimate sense is the *habitus* or settled disposition to conduct argument in terms of this principle: that is, the disposition simply to conduct argument, to use definite meaningful symbols, at all.

Now Aquinas sees *synderesis* as parallel in practical reasoning to *intellectus* in theoretical reasoning. Practical reasoning begins with something you want; it takes for granted that this is wanted and deliberates about the means of achieving it. The intellectual grasp of the aim as aim (not the attraction to it and intention of it, which is the actualization of will, but the understanding of it) is *synderesis*. The deliberation takes place in terms of this end presented to us as understood by *synderesis* and found attractive as an end, intended by us in virtue of our being able to want rationally (because we have a reason), and it concludes to an action or decision to act.

But, of course, what might be the starting point of one deliberation may be a conclusion come to in a previous one. We do not, says Aristotle, deliberate about aims; but what we aim at, what we have *synderesis* of intellectually and intend as a matter of will, may be the result of a previous deliberation. In each bit of practical reasoning, if we take them separately, it is by *synderesis* that we intellectually grasp what by the will we intend, find attractive (i.e., good); and it is by practical reasoning (preferably disposed by good sense) that we decide what we will do about it.

Now, just as with a hierarchy of sciences in theoretical reasoning we get back to some ultimate first principles that we simply grasp by *intellectus* (principles which cannot be the conclusion of any previous reasoning) like the principle of non-contradiction, so in practical reasoning there is *synderesis* not only of relative first principles but also of some ultimate first principle, such as that the good is what is to be wanted (which could not itself be the conclusion of some previous practical reasoning). Just as all theoretical reasoning is conducted in terms of, in the light of, the practical principle of seeking what is in some respect good (which lies at the root of all meaningful human action – what Aquinas calls an *actus humanus* as distinct from a mere *actus hominis*). Practical reasoning is practical reasoning because it is conducted in this light, just as theoretical reasoning is theoretical reasoning because it is conducted in the light of non-contradiction.

Synderesis, then, in its ultimate sense is the natural dispositional grasp of this ultimate practical principle; and we should remember that in neither the theoretical nor the practical case is the principle a premiss of some syllogism, although it can be stated as a proposition. It is rather the principle in virtue of which there is any syllogism at all.

Practical reasoning

Another way of putting this is to say that just as the *intellectus* of the ultimate first theoretical principle is the natural (and unacquired) disposition to be 'truth-preserving' in reasoning so the *synderesis* of the ultimate first practical principle is the natural (and unacquired) disposition to be 'satisfactoriness-preserving' in deliberation. I owe these terms to Dr Anthony Kenny and what follows draws heavily on his *Will, Freedom and Power* (1975), especially Chapter 5. Kenny notes that theoretical argument has a truth-preserving logic: its concern is that we should not move from a true premiss to a false conclusion. And he suggests that practical thinking is to be governed by a satisfactoriness-preserving logic which will ensure that we do not move from a satisfactory premiss to an unsatisfactory conclusion. Take the thinking: 'I want to get this carpet clean; the Hoover vacuum cleaner will do it; so, to the Hoover!' We should notice that the first clause expresses an intention (the *intentio finis*) and the last, in the optative mood, may be replaced simply by the action of using the Hoover. This action as the conclusion of a piece of practical reasoning (that is, done for a reason) is itself meaningful. It has become an act of cleaning the carpet because of the intention with which it is being done. What, to a less informed observer, might seem to be the same act, might have had other meanings and been a different human action: if, for instance, I used the Hoover because I wanted its noise to irritate my hated neighbour. In that case there would be a different piece of practical reasoning exhibiting the meaning of my action, exhibiting, that is the intention with which it is being done.

The intention with which it is done centrally defines a human act as the sort of human act it is. Thus, if you accidentally drop a five pound note and I pick it up, I may do so with the intention of keeping it for myself or with the intention of giving it back to you. The first intention specifies my action as one of stealing, and the second as one of restitution. My intention or motive in picking up the note is not an occurrence inside my head which causes me to pick up the money in the way that an agent brings about an event (as 'efficient cause'). It is what Aquinas calls a 'final cause' in virtue of which I, the agent, do the action and in virtue of which the action has its 'form', its specification. It is the practical reasoning, exhibiting the intention with which the action is done, that shows what, in human terms, the action counts as or is. Nobody, of course, suggests that whenever you act meaningfully you go through some particular chain of reasoning in your mind. That would be no more true of practical thinking than it is of theoretical thinking. We can act or think quite reasonably without going through syllogisms or other arguments. But in both cases it is possible to spell out the thought in some such way in order to show whether it is really a valid piece of reasoning or a muddle. A muddle in theoretical thinking can lead to your being mistaken. A muddle in practical thinking can lead to your not doing or getting what you want, what you intended.

Some philosophers, Alasdair MacIntyre, for example in *After Virtue* (1981, Ch. 12), hold that the conclusion of a practical syllogism is always a meaningful action (or meaningful inaction) rather than a proposition, but this seems unnecessarily restrictive. It is clear that the conclusion is not a theoretical proposition (in the indicative mood) but it may well be not simply an action but (in the optative mood) a plan of action or, as Aquinas prefers to see it, a command addressed (in the imperative mood) either to others or to oneself.

The logic of practical reasoning differs from that of theoretical reasoning most evidently in being based not on necessity but on sufficiency. Its conclusion is an action or proposal of action which will be sufficient to attain the aim expressed in the major premises, one that will sufficiently preserve the satisfactoriness of the original aim. What will be excluded are practical conclusions which do not thus preserve satisfactoriness. In theoretical reasoning, on the other hand, the conclusion will be what is necessarily entailed by the premises; what will be excluded will be conclusions which are not thus necessarily entailed, which may be false when the premises are true.

Thus one common form of theoretical reasoning goes like this: 'If p then q; but p; therefore q.' 'If he's from Blackburn then he's from the north; but he's from Blackburn; so he's from the north.' One form which would be excluded would be: 'If p then q; but q; therefore p.' 'If he's from Blackburn, he's from the north; but he's from the north; so he's from Blackburn.' Plainly this is not necessary, for he may be from Stockton or Carlisle.

Now contrast this with a piece of practical reasoning: 'If I use the Hoover the carpet will be cleaned; but I want the carpet clean; so I'll use the Hoover.' This provides a practical conclusion sufficient for my purposes. It is not however necessitated. There may be many other practical conclusions which would attain my aim, which would preserve the satisfactoriness of getting the carpet clean. The shape of this valid practical reasoning resembles, however, the shape of invalid theoretical reasoning. We seem to be arguing: 'If p then q; but q; therefore p.' But such a form of reasoning is only invalid if we are seeking a necessitated conclusion. In practical reasoning we are never doing this. We look simply for an action which will be sufficient for our purposes.

One very important contrast between theoretical and practical reasoning is that if we have a valid piece of theoretical reasoning no number of extra premises will render it invalid. Thus I may argue as follows: 'All clergymen are wrong about the meaning of life; but all bishops are clergymen; therefore all bishops are wrong about the meaning of life.' This conclusion remains valid however many other things I may find to say about clergymen or bishops: it makes no difference whether or not they play the piano nicely or have long furry ears and prehensile tails or are (some of them) my best friends or whatever. In this argument, so long as the original premises are true the conclusion is necessarily true. This does not go for practical reasoning. Take the argument: 'If I take this train it will get me to London; but I want to go to London; so I'll take the train.' This conclusion is practically valid so far as it goes but it ceases to be so if we add: 'I am always sick on trains' or 'This train is about to be blown up by crazed fascists.' In such a case the meaning of the action of boarding the train is no longer to be seen simply as going to London but also as becoming sick or being killed, which I may not want at all.

Thus the logic of theoretical reasoning can provide us with formulae which tell us what it is reasonable and what it is unreasonable to think, given certain premises. Practical reasoning, concerned with what it is reasonable to do, is not closed off by any such formulae. If we are to think well practically we must have an eye to all relevant additional premises which may serve to invalidate a conclusion. Actions done for reasons can be done for an indefinite number of reasons. And no single reason necessarily compels you to the action; there could be others dissuading you. It is just this multifacetedness of actions done for reasons that, in St Thomas's view, lies at the root of our freedom. No particular reason, no particular good that is sought, can necessitate our action; only the vision of the ultimate infinite good, God, can thus necessitate us.

Good sense, then, for St Thomas, as the disposition to do our practical reasoning well, involves a sensitive awareness of a multitude of factors which may be relevant to our decision. It involves, he says, bringing into play not merely our purely intellectual (symbol-using) powers but our sensuous apprehension of the concrete individual circumstances of our action. In his view, since our rather limited form of intelligence can only deal in the meanings of words and other symbols (for him our thinking is conceived on the model of our talking), and since no concrete individual can be the meaning of a symbol, we grasp the particular individual not by our intelligence but only by our sense powers. Thus, for him, you cannot identify a particular individual simply by describing it in words (any such words could be referring to another individual); in the end you have to point at it or single it out by some such bodily act. He concludes from this that if we are to be good at practical decision-making, if we are to have good sense, we need to exercise well our sensual, bodily apprehension of the world; so we need to be in good bodily health as well as clear in our ideas. The depression (*tristitia*) which for him comes principally from not getting enough fun out of life is likely to impede the virtue of good sense just as it impedes the sensual virtues of courage or chastity.

Aquinas's treatment of the ancillary dispositions that attend on the virtue of *prudentia* is one of the most interesting and, I think, original parts of his treatment, but I cannot discuss it here. I will conclude with a glance at one important topic: what is the difference between good sense and cunning?

Cunning and good sense

The logic of practical reasoning is neutral as between good and bad ends; the same canons of argument apply to thinking about how to get your uncle his Christmas present and thinking about how to murder him. But, in Aquinas's view, practical reasoning is directed towards good ends. The cunning practised by the one seeking apparently good but actually evil ends is not misdirected prudence but a degenerate form of practical reasoning, a false prudence. There are more ways of being unreasonable than being illogical.

Aquinas gives us a clue to the difference between cunning and good sense in one of his many comparisons between practical and theoretical reasoning. It is like the difference between dialectical argumentation and *scientia*. By true *scientia* we know that something is true and really why it is true. The characteristic cry of the one with *scientia* is: 'Yes, I see, of course, that has to be so.' *Scientia* traces facts back to their first principles by argumentation. Now consider this argument: 'All slow-witted people are subjects of the Queen of England; all the British are slow-witted; so all the British are subjects of the Queen of England.' This is a perfectly valid argument and it comes to a true conclusion although both its premises are manifestly false. It is not true that all slow-witted people are subjects of the Queen; nor is it true that all the British are slow-witted. There is nothing logically odd about deriving a true conclusion from false premises; as we have seen, it is deriving false conclusions from true premises that has to be excluded by a 'truth-preserving' logic. But although the falsity of the premises does not make the argument illogical, it does make the argument unscientific. We would be misled to say: 'Yes, I see, the British must necessarily be subjects of the Queen because they are slow-witted.' We would be using the wrong middle term to connect being British and being subject to the Queen. What the correct middle term would be it is a little hard to say – one would need to know something about how the House of Hanover established its legitimacy in Britain.

It is not merely false premises but also 'improper' or irrelevant premises that render an argument unscientific. Thus if we were to substitute going out in the midday sun for slow-wittedness you might, for all I know, have true premises but nonetheless you will not have truly explained the matter since it is not because of this propensity that the British (or at least Englishmen) are subject to the Queen. If your premises are either untrue or irrelevant or both, but your argument is logically valid and your conclusion true, you have what Aquinas would call a piece of merely dialectical reasoning. *Scientia* is distinguished from dialectical argument by its aim, which is a true comprehension of the order of the world, one the premisses of which are both true and 'proper'. Now, in a similar way, good sense is distinguished from cunning by its aim, which is acting well, pursuing ends which constitute or contribute to what is in fact the good life for a human being.

Thus good sense, for Aquinas, is not mere cleverness but presupposes the moral virtues, the dispositions that govern our appetites and intentions, for it is concerned not merely with what seems good to me but with what is in fact good for me; and it is the lynchpin of humane and reasonable living because without it none of these goods will be attained.

Fifteen

Original Sin

I can remember the time, it seems quite a while ago, when it was definitely not respectable to talk about original sin. The notion of original sin plainly belonged to some depressing and pessimistic version of Christianity, according to which we were all born in sin. And there was some not too explicit connection between being born in sin and the general sinfulness of the processes by which we came to be born. Babies anyway were born damned, and unless you rushed them to the font they were in danger, if not of hellfire, then at least of the chilly awfulness of limbo. Original sin seemed to be the expression of a feeling that the world is an awful place and the best thing to do is to get out of it as quickly as possible. Also it was tied up with the idea that we somehow can't help sinning, that whatever we do we are so twisted and distorted from birth that we are bound to be corrupted. It was all very sombre.

Against this dreary doctrine there was propounded a more enlightened and certainly more cheerful Christianity, emphasizing both the responsibility of the individual and the goodness of God. God is not going to condemn us except for our own personal failings and every individual person is free to make his or her own choice of good or evil. People, it is true, are often selfish and thoughtless. But a bit of healthy moral effort will usually see to that. The world is not an awful place, but a good, though a challenging, place. Christians propounding this view were very often to be found quoting the great sentence from Genesis: 'God looked on all that he had made and found it very good.'

The other thing that made original sin less than respectable was its connection with the whole Adam story. It seemed ludicrous that one man's failure should somehow infect everybody else. And, any way, how many people could still possibly believe in anyone called Adam? The whole story belonged to a pre-Darwinian world. Once we had recognized the garden of Eden story as mythological, there really didn't seem much left of original sin.

As I say, I can remember when that was the sort of chat that was going around, the days of liberal progressive Christianity, a form of religion ideally suited to the liberal democratic way of life in which people were expected to be basically rather nice, and changes, if any, came about by talking round a table and exercising your free choices at elections. It was a time when the highest virtue was tolerance and the finest praise you could give people was to say that they were moderate. It was the good old days: a kind of garden of Eden from which, however, we have all been expelled. This is just as well because it was a place of not very innocent illusions. The most prominent angels guarding the entrance are, I suppose, Freud and Marx; but we were actually expelled from the garden by God himself. And this event has had two major effects. In the first place, we have maybe grown up a little. And in the second place, we have become aware of original sin. It is the young, of course, rather than the old who have grown up. The old were, for the most part, past growing up.

In general it is young people who know that the world is lousy, who know about what is happening in places like South America and Northern Ireland. It is the older people who have to cling to comforting myths about defending democracy somewhere or bringing prosperity to somewhere else or about how their country's troops are doing a marvellous job in the face of vicious and cowardly attacks. There are just a few people left who believe that the problems are all due to misunderstanding and if only people would talk together it would be all cleared up. All of these people are over 35.

The rest of the people are either retreating into despair, drugging themselves with alcohol (or one of the less harmful substances that have become popular), or else recognizing the way out of all this: the thing that Christians have called baptism, or death and resurrection, or conversion or revolution. For some, it is more obviously political. For others it takes forms only remotely connected with the *polis*, the city. But for all of them it involves an act of disbelief. They do not believe in this world.

Perhaps they should start reading the Gospel of John. Its author is a pretty unchristian writer in any modern meaning of the word 'Christian'. He has very little to do with what we have come to think of as Christianity – that rather attractive, idealistic, but ineffective set of attitudes that make up the Christian spirit (a way of responding, a warm friendly way of responding to people, because people are fundamentally nice). He has little to do with the

Christianity that on the east coast of America has been called a belief in the Fatherhood of God and the brotherhood of man and the neighbourhood of Boston. This Christianity has, of course, social responsibilities. Christians, you remember, ought to improve things in the world, they ought to play their part in making this world a better place, they ought to help people live together in unobtrusive friendliness, persuading them not to be violent and so on. But with all this Christianity, John has nothing to do. He doesn't want to improve the world. He wants it destroyed. John thinks violence is inevitable, especially if the gospel is preached. Salvation for him is not making this world a better place. It is salvation from the world. It means smashing and defeating the world. John has no use for the world at all.

And John doesn't have any idea of the brotherhood of man either. He doesn't even ask us explicitly to love all men (could you get more unchristian than that?). Paul does and Matthew does and pretty certainly Jesus himself did, but John doesn't say it. To the good progressive Christian, John has to look narrow and sectarian and exclusive. John believes in love all right, in fact he believes in nothing else – he is the one who says 'God is love.' But he thinks love is rare and difficult and in one sense impossible. He thinks what he calls believers will love each other, but he has no idea at all that the sight of Christians loving each other will be so charming to the world that people will fall over themselves in admiration. On the contrary the world will hate them. When it sees this characteristic solidarity of the Christian movement, the world goes for its gun. It is not having any of this sort of thing.

John's Gospel (and his Epistles) are much in tune with a generation that simply cannot afford the cheerful optimism of the past. There is a harsh realism about John that says something to us. No writer in the New Testament tells us more about love than John does. And none is less lovely. John directs us to the real world. He makes us look at it. It is in John we read 'The truth shall set you free.' But for him, seeing the truth is (like love) rare and difficult. For him, indeed, it depends on love. Not on loving, though; he doesn't say that if you love you will see the truth. For him it depends on being loved. This is love, he says, not that you loved, but that God loved you.

The reason why John might appeal to us is that we have rather recently become aware, as he was vividly aware, of the interlocking complexity of evil. I mean the time has gone when we could think of bad actions in isolation, as random results of the individual free will. We have become aware of the way in which cruel and destructive behaviour in, say, the family is related to the very structure of the family, and the way in which this structure is determined by relationships of exploitation and domination in the whole social order, and how this is linked in its turn with violence and oppression in political affairs. We have become aware, in fact, of a whole system of human exploitation, a balanced and self-adjusting system, almost like an animal organism, a very resilient and flexible system. In the higher animals, just because of the complexity of their structure, damage can be contained or repaired. And it is a bit like that with the system. If you attack it in one place, it adjusts itself. It may appear to give in to your attack, but in fact it has found another way of carrying on its life. Often it will take your weapons and use them for its own purposes. It is in many ways a fascinating system especially in its capacity to disguise itself, to impose systems of value which justify it. It has a hypocritical smiling face. It is loud with high-sounding stuff about freedom and love and fellowship. So much so that some of its enemies in despair think that it has co-opted all language, that every significant word has been twisted to the service of the system and that all we are left with is the cast-off words, the obscenities, the shockwords that the system hasn't yet found a use for.

We have become aware of the system. We now realize that the evil and inhumanity in the world is not for the most part, or hardly at all, due to individuals being especially wicked, being wickeder than we are. On the contrary, there are just hundreds of thousands of people playing the roles assigned to them in the structures. President Nixon was not, I suppose an abnormally corrupt man. The reason why you could trace a direct line from him to the children covered in clinging phosphorous jelly and burning to death in Vietnam or Cambodia is simply that he occupied a key point in the system. It is not as though by changing his mind he could have altered it all. It would have been no good shouting obscenities at him and telling him that he was a criminal. Millions of people spend their days and nights just being parents or teachers or salesmen or soldiers or priests – ordinary decent people. And what they are doing is dominating, exploiting, humiliating, and tormenting other people simply because this is the way their roles fit into the system.

We have become aware of this complex system; we have become aware, in fact, of the World. Because this is exactly what St John means when he talks about the World. The world for him plainly does not mean the earth, the world of nature, creation, the material things around us. It means the way of being together that people have worked out. It means the kind of society we have achieved by our efforts. The World, for John, is, if you like, a political concept. It is most clearly exemplified for him in the Roman colonial society of his own time. The Book of Revelation, the Apocalypse, is not, of course, by the author of John's Gospel; but it plainly belongs to the same school of thought and it is extremely clear about the political and social meaning of the World. It is true, of course, that in the early part of John's Gospel the author says 'God so loved the world that he sent his only begotten son.' But the point of this is that the world rejected this love of God, that it showed itself in fact incapable of it. By a later chapter Jesus is saying 'I do not pray for the world.' The world here is past praying for. It can only be smashed.

The world, it must be re-emphasized, is not just a system of overt social relationships. It can't just be analysed in what we now call political or sociological terms. It is a pervasive system that enters into what we call our private lives, or what we hope are our private lives. My self-indulgence, meanness, dishonesty, and laziness, which I like to think of as secret, are an indivisible part of the same network that we find in political depression and social injustice. In John's view we cannot tinker with this world. We need to be redeemed from it. The attempt to work within it to improve it only means in the end that you are co-opted by it and find yourself working for it. John's viewpoint is what we should nowadays describe as thoroughly revolutionary rather than reformist. In this world, for John, there is no brotherhood of all men, and any attempt to pretend that there is is illusion and deception. For him we shall only have real human brotherhood when this world has been destroyed and a new one has arisen, when the world has gone through a conversion, a radical change, a change that means the ending of an old life, the complete collapse of the old system, and the start of a new one.

It should, I suppose, be clear by now that there is a connection between this notion of the world (what St John calls the Sin of the world) and original sin. Original sin means sin with which we are infected from our origins. The word 'original' refers not to the origin of mankind in Adam but to my origin, my coming into being. It is the sinfulness I have from my beginnings, as distinct from the evil due to particular individual choices. There is no doubt that for the main Christian tradition this original sin is fundamental; personal or actual sins are merely the effects and symptoms of it. This tradition, in fact, does not see sin first of all as the product of my isolated free act of choice. It is first of all a human condition within which I come into being. For medieval writers and for others since then, this could only be seen in terms of biological generation. And original sin was seen as something like an hereditary defect passed on with the genes and chromosomes. Of course they did not see sin itself as a matter of physical structure; sin meant deprivation of divine life. But the manifestation of this (the incarnation of it, if you like) was in a distortion of our human life, a radical malfunctioning of our desires and emotional life.

I think that today we can see this more adequately in terms of my self-creation. I mean by this that in order to become me I need more than simply to be conceived and born. What and who I am is also the product of socialization, of my relationship and communication with my world. I do not mean that the new-born baby, or for that matter the foetus in the womb, is not a person, or that it was something other than me. I mean that there is a process in becoming this person, and a vital part of this process occurs after birth in the human relationships into which I enter. I make myself in terms of the kind of communication I have with my world. It follows from this that if the ways in which I can communicate, the available *media* of communication, are themselves inadequate, twisted, and distorted, there will be a radical distortion in me. We could put the whole thing summarily and hastily by saying that what human beings need for becoming themselves is love. It is not just that having become themselves they then have a great desire to love and be loved, a great need for love if they are to be happy rather than miserable. The fact of the matter is that love is constitutive of the human being. Deprived of love we are deprived of ourselves. Now this of course raises the complex and indeed mysterious question of what we mean by love. I am certainly not referring merely to the warmth and affection shown, say, by the mother to the child, though obviously, in a very visible way, this is of paramount importance in the child's development, in children becoming themselves. I am not referring simply to physical and linguistic contact with particular individuals – love can be exemplified in what look like 'impersonal' social structures. I used earlier the word 'solidarity' in reference to the love which John expected to find among Christians; certainly the solidarity of, say, the members of a revolutionary working class would be quite like the kind of thing he had in mind.

The point is that we are born into a society which in various ways fails us as we stand in need of love. And for this reason we are born crippled (using the word 'born' in a more extended sense). And our society does not fail us simply because of the ill will of individual members but because of the structures it represents, because of the role it assigns these members. You could be born and brought up in a group who were all individually saints and you would still be subject to the deprivation we call the Sin of the World.

We can ask how this condition originated. How does it come about that mankind should be in this sorry state? We can also ask why a loving God tolerates this. The various Fall stories in Genesis (the story of the garden, the story of the tower of Babel), are all mythological investigations of the problem of evil, of evil as a human condition. The authors of these stories were not stupid or simple people. They were wise and profound thinkers. But their methodology was myth. It is we who are stupid or simple if we imagine they were trying to write history or anthropology. But it seems reasonable for us to try in terms of our ways of thinking to answer the question 'How come human society is the way it is?' Once more to be very hasty and to summarize, I would say that the answer that seems to be emerging from ethologists and others is that human beings fell not down but up.

That is to say, humans are maladjusted because they have powers which are greater than they can control. Once linguistic animals emerged with the interdependent powers of communication and of technology, they had a capacity for aggression and destruction which went beyond anything that could be controlled by the old checks built into their biological system. To give a very simple example, most animals that look after their young have a built-in inhibition which prevents them from attacking them. This is obviously the result of natural selection; without it the species would die out. And this undoubtedly survives in the human animal. Only very disturbed people could face killing a child with their bare hands (they can of course be trained to get over this inhibition, but most people would be pretty squeamish). The case is quite different when I kill a child at long range, when technology has separated the action from my immediate experience. Then the natural inhibition is simply not powerful enough. Anyway, the human animal in its short history so far has not found a way of adjusting to its own powers. It is thoroughly maladjusted and you might say it was a freak and failing experiment of nature, doomed to disappear like so many previous species that for one reason or another failed to adjust. In this case the failure would not be through mere weakness (an inability to contend with greater natural forces) but through misdirected strength. The human race would fail through internally directed violence. It would commit collective suicide. It would be evidently an absurdity. Human history would collapse in nonsense.

All that would have been theory until August 1945. By then this monstrous animal species had actually constructed the machinery for destroying not only itself but all animal life on the planet. I mean the actual apparatus is here; it only needs to be switched on. And in case something goes wrong with the nuclear bombs, we have accumulated poisonous substances which could eliminate all human life. But these developments are merely products of the logic of the human system. They are signs of our maladjustment. They are the final authentic signs of the meaning (or rather unmeaning) of human history and life.

Having reversed the direction of the Fall itself from down to up, I would now like to do another reversing act: over the question of original sin being 'committed'. In one strict sense, of course, original sin is not committed, it is the state of sin within which we live. But there is a Pickwickian sense in which you could speak of the sin of Adam as the sin that was committed and resulted in original sin. That, at least, is how medieval theologians saw the matter. That, indeed, seems to have been how St Paul saw the matter – 'through one man's sin death came into the world . . .' where Paul is referring to Adam and contrasting him with Christ, the second Adam, through whom life and resurrection from the dead came into the world. I would like to propose a Pickwickian sense in which the occasion on which original sin was committed was the crucifixion of Jesus – not, of course, in the sense that this caused our original sin (there was a state of original sin for centuries before the crucifixion), but in the sense that this finally gave meaning to this state as Sin. In the crucifixion of Jesus it is finally manifested that the mal-adjustment of man amounts to a rejection of God's love. The sin of the world, if you like, comes to a head in the crucifixion, shows itself fully for what it is. And, of course, in coming to a head it is simultaneously conquered. The Cross is both the manifestation, the sacrament, of the sin of the world, and the manifestation, the sacrament, of the redeeming act of God. It is just as we realize our death that we find life. It is only when it appears as sin that it can be forgiven.

Let me try to get that clear. The best thing is to go back to St John for a minute. For John, the opposite of love is fear; the first characteristic of people deprived of love is that they are afraid, and the first effect of love is to cast out fear. To speak of the world as unloving, to speak of the sin of the world, is to speak of its fear. Take as a picture of this condition children who in an obvious sort of way are deprived of love. They are insecure and defensive. They need to justify themselves all the time. They can't admit to being wrong. They constantly have to preserve their self-esteem by making excuses for themselves, by building up a self-flattering image of themselves.

But all the time they live in fear; fear that really means nothing, that is worth nothing. The louder they tell themselves about their achievements and successes, the deeper they drive the ultimate self-doubt. Those who are deprived of love cannot face the truth about themselves. They spin a web of deceit to hide from themselves. They prefer, as John puts it, darkness to the light.

Now that is a picture. And it is very clearly a picture of our society. It is a picture of what Karl Marx called mystification, the distortion of language and of ideas which are necessary for the smooth running of an exploitative society. It is mystification when workers can be got to believe in 'loyalty' to the firm which is systematically robbing them of half the value of their work; it is mystification when people in a slum called the Shankill can believe that their real enemies and oppressors are the people who live in the adjoining slum called the Falls; it is mystification when young American soldiers can believe they are saving the world from communism or young British soldiers that they are keeping peace or upholding law and order. But it is unnecessary to multiply examples. The important thing is that we are mystified because we dare not believe the truth. For years many people simply couldn't face the idea that all those people had been killed in Vietnam for no good purpose. The burden of guilt would be too much. The Anti-War people soon found out that stressing the number of people killed didn't work as a way of getting people to reject the war. On the contrary, it became ever more important to believe in the war – otherwise, what do we face about ourselves? It is fear that makes us welcome the lies. It is love that casts out fear, and makes us able to face facts. And this, as John says, will make you free.

Situations such as I have referred to will not, as the liberals and moderates (I might call them 'Pelagians') always believe, be cured by exhorting people to be more friendly, to love each other more. This is the kind of thing that Christians have now got a reputation for saying, but it is not Christianity. It is a form of moralism. No, the situation will only be cured or resolved by people seeing the truth, taking notice of the facts instead of clinging to illusions and lies. And this they will be able to do only if they are loved, if they have the security that comes from being loved. And this of course is the gospel, not only for John but for every New Testament writer. The gospel is not a recommendation or command or exhortation to love people more. It is not a recommendation or command or exhortation at all. It is news, good news – the news that we are loved, not simply by this or that person (though that is always reassuring), but fundamentally loved, that the *basic* thing about us is that we are loved. And this news is not simply told to us as a piece of information, a theory about us we might verify; the fact of our being loved is communicated to us. This is what we mean by our having faith. To have faith is just to know that the ultimately true thing about you, the deepest irreducible fact about you is that you are loved. This is what Christians mean by believing in God. 'I believe in God', for a Christian means 'I believe that the life and death of Jesus Christ made sense.' Let me spell that out a little.

Jesus accepted people. That's what made him attractive to them. Of course all your friends accept you. That is what you mean by calling them friends. You can relax, be at ease in their company; no need to defend yourself against them; no need to be always impressing them; you can be liberated by their presence. Now the presence of Jesus clearly worked that way, except much more so. In his presence, in his bodily presence, people felt a depth of liberation, so profound that they called it the forgiveness of sin. They felt freed for the first time from the constriction of the sin of the world. They were liberated and able to see themselves, able to admit to being what they were. This is what we mean by the confession of sin. It is not something we do so that God will forgive us in return. It is something we do because we have forgiven ourselves, accepted ourselves. And we can do this because we know that God loves us. We can risk even the truth about ourselves. Confessing your sins is really just another way of saying you believe in God. Indeed, in the earliest texts the sinner's confession always meant his or her praise and acknowledgement of the love of God.

Now the kind of acceptance Jesus offered created around him a commune of people who were liberated, able to love one another, able to accept one another. There are many things to be said about this little group, but one of the most obvious things is that it posed a threat to the established society – whether the Roman colonial set-up or the established religion. It was bound to pose a threat to any society based on less than love. This is why Jesus had to be destroyed. He was not killed by accident, nor was he murdered by a chance meeting with individually wicked men. The people who killed him, both the chief priests and the Roman colonial authorities, in their different ways had a point. He was subversive, not so much because of a theory he preached (though his preaching was deeply disrespectful especially of the priests), but because of what he had created simply by being around the place. Jesus posed a political threat not by being a politician but by making people secure, by creating a kind of relationship that couldn't be accommodated within a society ultimately based on domination and fear. I personally think there were complicated reasons for the actual arrest and execution of Jesus to do with dissension within his following. I suspect that he was betrayed to the authorities by the extreme nationalist guerilla group who were disappointed in him, who saw him as missing the moment of the national rebellion when he refused to mobilize his mass following against the Roman soldiers. Be that as it may, however, the need to kill Jesus showed up the Palestinian society for what it was. But, more than that, it showed up the human race for what it was. For what was being offered in Jesus was not just a kind of friendship, not just a limited sort of love, but the love which is the meaning of all human existence. To believe that Jesus is of God is to believe that, in rejecting him, people are making the most ultimate kind of rejection, the final contradiction of themselves. The crucifixion is not just one more case of a particular society showing its inhumanity. It is the whole human race showing its rejection of itself. The resurrection is the Father's refusal to accept this self-rejection of man.

Before the crucifixion Jesus is presented with an impossible choice: the situation between himself and the authorities has become so polarized that he can get no further without conflict, without crushing the established powers. If he is to found the kingdom, the society of love, he must take coercive action. But this would be incompatible with his role as meaning of the kingdom. He sees his mission to be making the future present, communicating the kind of love that will be found among us only when the kingdom is finally achieved. And this is incompatible with coercion. I do not think that Jesus refrained from violent conflict because he thought violence was wrong, but because it was incompatible with his mission, which was to be the future in the present. Having chosen to be the meaning of the kingdom rather than its founder, his death was inevitable. He had chosen to be a total failure. His death meant the absolute end of his work. It was not as though his work was a theory, a doctrine that might be carried on in books or by word of mouth. His work was his presence, his communication of love. The authorities were right in calculating that once dead he would do no more harm. His disciples would scatter and that would be the end of him except for legends and memories. In choosing failure out of faithfulness to his mission, Jesus expressed his trust that his mission was not just his own, that he was somehow *sent*, that the sense of absolute security he had was due to the love of the Father sustaining him. In giving himself to the cross he handed over everything to the Father. In raising Jesus from the dead the Father responded. The kingdom which Jesus failed to establish now comes as gift. That is why Christians say that what they mean by God is He who raised Jesus from the dead, He who made sense of the senseless waste of the crucifixion. It is because Jesus is of the Father, wholly of the Father, loved into being by the Father, that His total acceptance of the human condition in death was also the redemption of the human condition by the Father's love. It was in one act that the sin of the world manifested itself and was defeated.

The total elimination of the sin of the world will, of course, be in the establishment of a new human race, of a society in which there is no fear, in which the bonds between people are bonds of love, in which people do not have to seek outside themselves for a meaning to their lives, in which they do not have to believe in the gods or in any ideology. This will be the final overcoming of original sin. But we claim that this world to come, this post-revolutionary world, is already with us; the future intersects with the present. The resurrection of Jesus from the dead means that he is alive and with us, that the love which constitutes the future kingdom is already among us. And Christians are people who proclaim that they belong to the future, that they take their meaning not from this corrupt and exploitative society but from the new world that is to come and that in a mysterious way already is, that although original sin is still all around us, although it attacks us and will finally kill us, it does not enslave us. We do not take our meaning from it. We are free.

In conclusion, I would like to consider the *oddness* of what I have been saying. I have been using such a lot of Christian clichés and enunciating such a lot of platitudes that the reader might be in danger of forgetting what an extraordinary idea has to lie behind them all. Let me explain by talking about friendship.

We have friendly relationships with all kinds of people, and I want to suggest that this sort of relationship is usually not only compatible with a certain kind of hierarchical inequality but even has it built into it. In this kind of friendship, the commonest kind of friendship, we are normally towards one end or the other of the parent-child relationship upon which, I suppose, all our experience of close human relationship is initially based. I think, if you consider the matter, you will recognize this inequality. I don't mean it is a permanent or fixed thing. And in different circumstances the relationship easily reverses itself. But in most friendships there is a dominant person – I don't mean a dominating, still less domineering, person, but one who is characteristically looked up to, a leader. I do not think there is anything at all wrong with this; it seems to belong to our nature, and the complex web of human relationships would be impossible without it. There are of course people we actively dislike, and there are lots of people with whom we hardly have a close enough relationship to call it friendship (the people we meet casually on the bus or at work or whatever). With these last people there is a certain relationship of equality: we don't know them well enough to recognize the polarity I am speaking of. There is a kind of democratic quality here which is, so to say, negative. We recognize these people as our equals because we have no reason to do anything else. But as soon as we become more personally involved, more intimately acquainted then, I think, the hierarchical polarity sets in.

Let me re-emphasize that I think this is a good thing, and anyway something we are born with or at least develop immediately on account of our parent-child relationship. It is a good thing, but not the best thing. When we grow up, if we grow up, we get occasional glimpses of another kind of relationship for which I am going to reserve the word 'love'. This is a notoriously mysterious word, but maybe I could suggest part of what it means by saying that love seeks always to get beyond another's possessions or attributes or whatever, seeking the sheer person himself or herself. What I am trying to draw attention to here is the fact that in ordinary friendship there is a centring on the virtues or qualities of the other person. That is why there is a hierarchical relationship, a relationship of superiority and inferiority (let me stress again I mean something good by these words; I am not talking of domination and submission). But love is a relationship of *equals*. Not with the kind of negative equality we find in our dealings with people we don't really know, but with a positive equality, an equality that seems almost to be created by the love itself, or at any rate is only revealed by the love itself. This is a sense of equality which we only recognize in love.

Now, as I say, this love seems a rather rare thing. For most purposes we get along with friendship and benevolence and affection, all of which are perfectly compatible with inequality. I don't, of course, want to suggest that the two are absolutely distinct or contrasting. There can be an element of love, in the sense of the recognition of an equal, in all sorts of friendship. It is even possible for parents to love their children. But notice that the evidence for this love is not the things they do for them, their benevolence and kindness. The evidence that parents actually love their children is in their willingness to let them go, to be themselves, to be, in this deep sense, equals of the parents. You will see clearly why love is connected with liberation. Friends give each other presents; they do things for each other. So do lovers. But the essential gift that you give to one you love is the gift of space to exist, the gift of liberation.

Space is not something that is simply *there*. We should not imagine that we are atoms floating freely in a void. On the contrary we are hedged and hemmed around with *things*. It is only a person who can *give* us space. And to love another is precisely to do that, to provide them with the free space in which they can be themselves. When you love someone you give them life, you let them be themselves. Love in this way is surprisingly like indifference, though it is at the other end of the spectrum. There is the resemblance of positive and negative equality.

Love, then, is between equals. To love is to give to another not possessions or any such good thing. It is to give yourself, which means providing a space in which the other can be himself or herself. Love is rather rare and comes with maturity when we can get away from the need to be dominant or to find another who is not dominant. It is infinitely more rewarding to find one person in whom you really recognize this fundamental and absolute equality, than to have hundreds of people who look up to you or admire you or obey you.

You will, I know, immediately recognize that this presents a problem about God. God is evidently incapable of loving us simply because there cannot be this relationship of equality between God and his creatures. Of course God can be loving in the sense of *benevolent* and *kindly*. And in this sense he *is* quite frequently said to be loving. But if we take love seriously as the relationship of equals, then it seems clear that he cannot love us. He is our Creator, we depend on him for everything we have and are. How could we be his equal, and how, therefore could he love us?

I think we easily miss this difficulty because we don't take love seriously enough. We cheerfully speak of a loving God but we don't really mean it; we mean a kindly, forgiving, benevolent God. And this of course is reflected or lived out in our institutional way of representing our belief. The Church at its best is usually a structure of kindness and benevolence (it is quite often not even that) but it is not usually a structure of love. (The only definitive structures of love in the Church are the sacraments themselves, which we have a constant tendency to distort and conceal.) We have the feeling that we will settle for benevolence, that, in ecclesiastical matters especially, kindness will do. They can and should both be expressions of friendship, but they are not at its deepest level expressions of love. Cardinal Heenan of Westminster, when asked to sum up in one word what Catholicism meant to him, said

'Authority'. This, to my mind, is the remark of someone who had probably never fully experienced the relationship of love, of love between equals – someone who had ignored, perhaps systematically ignored, the glimpses of love that must have been present to him during his life. Such a man wants to be a kindly benevolent ruler or a willingly obedient subject. He wants life to be conducted in a rational and friendly way. He wants to adjust things so that there shall be no scenes. And, if possible, he wants nothing to happen for the first time. But love is closely connected with things happening for the first time, with creativity and radical newness.

God being Creator, then, and we being his creatures, it seems impossible that there should be love between us in the deep sense I have been talking about. God may be kindly and forgiving and he may reward us if we behave ourselves (he may even reward us when we don't). But, in the end, he is Master and Lord, and we are his slaves, and there cannot be love between master and slave as such. There can be love between human masters and slaves in peculiar circumstances just because the slavery relation is not the only or most fundamental relation between them: they are after all both human. But in our very being we are dependent on God, slaves of God. We may be well-treated slaves or rewarded slaves, but we remain slaves. It was because they clearly recognized this that Nietzsche and Karl Marx rejected God, even the God who, so to say, was on man's side. The God of righteousness who summons mankind to justice remains a slave-master. Belief in such a God is, for them, in the end a belief that people are fundamentally slaves, fundamentally alienated from their own being, receiving their destiny at the hands of another. If there is such a God, freedom is not at the centre of our being.

Now the central thing that Jesus of Nazareth said is that his Father loves him – this at any rate in the Johannine perspective. And we are now in a position to see the appalling implications of this. The announcement is not that God is nicer and kinder than we thought. On the contrary, it is with the Gospels that we get all that talk about hell for example. Quite evidently the Father is not represented as treating Jesus well. Apart from anything else he is tortured to death without the Father intervening in any way. He dies asking God why he has forsaken him. What we are told is something else: that the Father loves him. And to claim this is to claim equality with the Father. To claim this is to claim that Jesus is not fundamentally dependent, that in the depth of his being he is not a creature made by God, that although, of course, he *comes from* God he is *not created* but loved into being as an equal.

In this revelation God is at last able to grow up. Or you can put it by saying that our image of God grows up. The picture of the creator God surrounded by his creatures, all dependent on him, is in the end an infantile picture. It does not allow God to experience the mature relationship of love. The announcement of Jesus is that this picture is out of date. In Jesus the Father has one whom he loves as an equal and the gospel is that we are called to share in the exchange of love between them, to share in the Holy Spirit. The doctrine of the Trinity lies at the foundation of the Christian gospel because it announces the most ultimate liberation of people, their liberation from God, or to put it less dramatically, their liberation from mere creaturehood. The gospel announces that we stand before God not simply as creatures before a benign creator. We stand before him as Jesus does, as equals in an exchange of love.

So if we seek the significance of the life and death of Jesus we have to see it, as indeed classical theology has seen it, not only as liberation from sin but liberation from creaturehood itself: divinization. To take the doctrine of the Trinity seriously is to say that divinity is now found in people, that they create their own destiny in virtue of this divinity. It is to say that the picture of the prearranged plan worked out by God up there, to which we must conform, is only a provisional picture, an inadequate one. There is no heaven waiting for us; it is we who will create heaven, but only because of the divine life we already have within us.

The humanist believes that we can create some kind of heaven by means of what we control, by means of our power and assets. This kind of optimistic humanism is rarer now than it was. The Christian believes that it is indeed men and women that will create heaven, but not through what they possess, not by their power, but through the love that springs within them, the identical love that sprang within Jesus, the Holy Spirit which leads us as often to failure as to success. We help to create heaven by failing to make it. The suggestion is paradoxical. But that is what the crucifixion meant. Jesus failed and that is how the kingdom was established.

Sixteen

Predestination

According to St Paul: 'Those whom God foreknew he also predestined . . . and those whom he predestined he also called and justified and glorified' (Romans 8:28–30). So it looks as though each one of us is born with a destiny. If we are destined to be called and justified and glorified, all well and good; if on the other hand we are not, then not so good. And God has arranged all this beforehand; there is obviously nothing we can do to alter our destinies. Whether we get to heaven or not, it seems, has nothing to do with what we choose to do: it has all been fixed beforehand by God. As the limerick has it:

> There was a young man who said 'Damn,
> It is clear to me now that I am
> A being that moves
> In predestinate grooves:
> Not even a bus, but a tram.'

Now when I was a lad I thought this was what predestination meant and I thought it was a Protestant doctrine, specifically a Calvinist one. The picture we had was of God planning the world deciding that some people would be the elect, the chosen, the predestined and others would be damned – to the greater glory of God. It was particularly the notion of people being predestined to damnation that sent a chill down the spine. God had apparently in this Calvinist view made some people in order to send them to hell. In those days I was very glad to be a Catholic, for I thought we didn't believe in predestination at all. Whether I went to heaven or not was just a matter of how I behaved. If I decided to be good I would go to heaven; if not I would go to hell. It was simply a matter of what I chose to do, like whether I would choose to study Latin or chemistry.

Later on I discovered that I had been wrong about all this. Catholics do, after all, believe in predestination; but predestination is not a gloomy or spine-chilling doctrine. On the contrary it is a delightful and joyful and liberating doctrine, all about the love of God and the glorious freedom of the sons of God. I must add that I do not know for sure whether any Calvinists really *did* believe that God created some people simply for the pleasure of burning them forever in hell. Very likely this is just a Catholic caricature. If you want to *know* what they believed and believe, please ask a Calvinist; don't rely on me. What I can assure you is that Catholics do *not* believe that anybody is predestined by God to sin and be damned. The Catholic doctrine is that there is only predestination to heaven. The notion that anyone can be predestined to hell is totally unscriptural and, therefore, foreign to the Catholic faith.

What then does the Catholic teaching on predestination say? It says exactly what Paul says: that the life, passion, death, and resurrection of Jesus of Nazareth was not just something that Jesus happened to think up one day. He was implementing the plan of God. In Jesus it is God who saves us because of God's great love for us. God was in Christ reconciling us to him, liberating us from sin.

Predestination means first of all the predestination of Christ, and this means that the life of Jesus was a divine drama, God's self-revelation, the enactment of his plan. And Paul is saying that what we mean by our salvation is our being taken up into that same plan of God in Christ. The life of Christ is a huge wave, a great surge of the love of God sweeping us up to him. We are carried by this wave even into the courts of heaven, even into the life of the Trinity itself, the life of eternal love. Our predestination means that our Christian lives are part of the pattern of God's revelation of himself in Christ. We are playing our part in the divine drama. We are 'conformed to the image of his son in order that he might be first born among many brethren'. It is not that there is a judgement like an exam where our answers are marked as good or bad and on the basis of that we pass or fail. It is a question of being part of the divine drama which is the death and resurrection of Christ, of arriving into heaven with Christ and in Christ, taking part in the Ascension. So that in seeing and welcoming us, God is seeing and welcoming his beloved Son.

We are, therefore, swept away on the crest of the wave of God's love, swept into the presence of God. Does that mean that we have lost our freedom, that we cannot choose for ourselves? Well of course is doesn't. The predestined one, remember, is primarily Jesus Christ; he is the one fulfilling the plan of God, enacting the divine drama. Does he strike you as unfree? As obsessive? As incapable of spontaneity, imprisoned by neurotic fears and guilt? Of course not: he is obviously the free human being. Not only because he is human and not a machine, but because he is not hampered by all those anxieties and illusions which are the way that sin seeks to enslave us: the shackles of the kingdom of darkness. In the plan of God, Jesus is precisely predestined to be free, to be uniquely himself, and our predestination is nothing but our sharing in this predestined freedom that Christ has.

Our very existence and the existence of everything we actually do, everything that really exists in the universe, is the creative act of God. Nothing can be except because of God. Nothing at all. And amongst the things that exist are our own free spontaneous choices and actions, free of constraint from outside, springing from our *own* being; and these free acts of ours are also God's creative acts – among the greatest of his creative acts. God's creative act does not constrain his human creatures; how could it? It is by this creative act that we are ourselves, it is by this creative act that our selves flow out into spontaneous love and freedom.

But God's engagement with us has to do with even more than his creative act. God engages with us at the level of his own uncreated life. God (we know because he revealed it) so loves us as not just to create us but to share with us his own life, to live his eternal life, to share in the life of his uncreated Son, to be divine with him. And of course to be divine, to share in God's life, is not to be less free than to be human. The grace that the man Jesus had (his sharing in the divine life) did not constrain him. It made him free, free with a freedom that could liberate his brothers and sisters and bring them also to divine freedom. And to say that we are predestined is just to say that all this story of ours coming to divinity is the plan of God's love for us. But still there are worrying things in all this. Especially two worrying things: firstly, there is still a nagging worry about it all being planned and fixed up beforehand; and secondly, there is the worry about people who go to hell – if God predestined good must he not also predestine evil?

Certainly, a race or a fight that is fixed beforehand is a bogus race or fight; and a human life that has been fixed beforehand is a bogus human life. What has happened here is that we are taking the 'beforehand' too literally. Predestination is not something we have from birth, from way back, 'beforehand'. We do not *have* predestination at all; it is the plan in the mind of God, it is nothing whatever in us. Predestination exists in eternity and only in eternity, in the eternal timeless mind of God. It is not before or after or even simultaneous with anything. When we plan something and then carry out the plan, there is first the plan and then later the execution. But this cannot be so with God. God has no lifetime, no before and after. There are not times or dates to the thoughts and acts of God. His predestining Jesus to ascend into heaven does not come before his bringing Jesus to heaven. Nothing in God comes before anything else, they are all the one thing which is simply the eternal timeless life of God himself. So we must not take the 'pre' in 'predestination' literally. What is predestined happens but it doesn't happen later than its predestination because predestination is only in the timeless mind of God. It is always wrong and a muddle to say 'What I just did must have been predestined thirty years ago' because predestination, like the thought of God, has no date at all. It does not mean that we move in predestinate grooves that are there beforehand, like tram lines.

But what about the other worry, what about those who do not come to heaven? Jesus plainly thought that there were such people, or talked as if he did. Why are these not simply predestined to sin and hell? Well the first thing to be clear about is that we are taken to heaven by the grace of God of our own free choice. We have, through the love of God for us, the grace to choose freely to love him. If we choose instead some lesser good at the expense of loving God, if we sin, we do that too of our own free choice, but there is no such thing as an anti-grace, an inspiration of God, by which we choose evil. When we sin it is entirely our choice of something instead of God's friendship. To come to God's friendship in Christ is to choose a good, the greatest good and the greatest good for us; and the creative and gracious power of God is in us as we freely make this choice. It is both our free work and God's work. To do good is to choose the highest good; but to fail to do this, to sin, is not to choose evil. Nobody chooses evil, it cannot be done. When we sin what we do is choose some trivial good at the expense of choosing God's friendship. Sin is sin not because of the thing we positively choose: the human satisfaction, the pleasure or the power. It is sin because of what we *fail* to choose, what we sacrifice for the sake of a minor good. Sin is sin because we have opted *not* to grow up to our flourishing, our happiness which is life in God's love and friendship. To say that people sin is to report what they have *not* done, what they have freely chosen *not* to do – freely choosing not to be just and kind, because they have opted for a trivial good like wealth or whatever. And what is not done, what is not there, is not the work of God. The fly buzzing on the ceiling is the work of God, but the elephant which is not behind me is not the work of God. The sinner's failure to choose happiness is just that – a failure, a not-doing, and this not-doing is not the work of God. The only thing there is the sinner's own failure. Sin and hell, because they are failures, absences, undoings, are the only things that are uniquely and solely the work of human choice with which God has nothing whatever to do. They are purely and simply the result of private enterprise and initiative.

But we really have to work very hard indeed to achieve such private enterprise. It is a difficult thing to reject the gift of God who is so deeply in love with us. It is difficult to harden our hearts against such love. Again and again God brings us the grace of contrition for our sin; again and again we refuse him as he humbly begs us to come back to him. It is very hard to hold out for a lifetime against such love; and perhaps nobody ever does. It is not hard, though it is always painful, to relax and to let ourselves be led by God's love towards our happiness, to play our part in the predestinate plan of God, to go with Christ and in Christ into divinity itself, into the love which will be our joy and delight in eternity.

Seventeen

Teaching Morals

People engaged in the necessary tasks of the world very frequently find the moralist a nuisance and a bore. It is all very well to sit in your armchair or stand in your pulpit and talk about ideals and all that, but none of this has much relevance to practical affairs. You may succeed in making people feel guilty or complacent, but in the meantime the practical questions have to be decided. All this talk of morality is really very abstract and has little to do with the practical affairs of life. People often suspect that moralizing is just a way that the weak, incompetent and impractical man has found for blackmailing the poor fellow who is up to his neck in the real risks and compromises of decision-making.

If this is true then it seems probable that we had better not teach morals at all: perhaps all we could do is produce prigs and puritans eager to sit in judgement on their fellows without soiling their own hands with the dirty business of real life. Here, then, since I can tell you absolutely nothing about teaching, I thought I might serve some slight purpose by trying to defend morality against this kind of attack. I want to present a view of morality quite different from the one I have mentioned; and if what I describe is not morality as commonly understood, then I reckon it will do instead.

I think morality is concerned with human behaviour, and its concern is of a special kind: what characterizes morality, as distinct from the many other ways of looking at human behaviour, is first that it is the most practical approach and secondly that it is the least abstract approach.

Let me explain those in turn. First morality is practical. When you learn about morals you are learning not some theoretical truths but how to do something. So learning morality is more like learning music or carpentry than it is like learning astronomy or physics. I'll have more to say about this later but just for now let me explain how Thomas Aquinas saw this matter.

He thought that human intelligence is displayed in two broad areas which he called theoretical and practical. It is very important to see that the difference between these is not simply one of subject matter. It is not a matter of whether we are thinking about atoms or about actions. Practical intelligence is displayed not in thinking about actions but in doing them. The sports reporter at the football match is exercising his theoretical reason in describing and analysing the game; the footballer on the pitch is exercising his practical intelligence in playing it. He is playing intelligently, we may hope. Incidentally it is simply because the footballer is playing intelligently (or unintelligently) that the sports reporter can produce the kind of report that he does – basically a critical narrative, or an evaluating story. You cannot report the behaviour of bees or earthquakes in this way. If you are teaching morals your primary aim is to produce someone analogous to an intelligent footballer, not someone analogous to an intelligent reporter. The two have obvious interconnections, but the important thing to see is that the fact that a player is not good as a reporter does not make him an unintelligent player. It is just that if you want to explain how intelligent his play is you have to report it intelligently. You have to use your theoretical intelligence.

The aim of theoretical reason is to understand the world; the aim of morals is to change it. Understanding the world is much more than being well informed about what is the case. We understand something when we know not merely that it is the case but the reason why it is the case. Anyone may know that sugar, unlike marble, dissolves in water; it takes a physical chemist to explain why this has to be so given the molecular structure of the materials involved. If the physical chemist has done his job we are able to say: 'Yes, of course, the sugar dissolves.' Science, theoretical understanding in general, deals not in facts but in explanations. And this is one excellent human activity. But if you want to understand human activity as thoroughly as you can, and especially if you want to teach people how to be active as well as they can, you will get more tips from the football coach than from the physics teacher.

Of course things are not as simple as that, for the physics teacher is not just teaching the truths of physics. He is mainly engaged in teaching people how to be physicists, how to do physics. And that, of course, is a practical matter.

What then is the difference between the football coach's concern with the human activity of playing football and the moralist's concern with human activity? This is where our second characteristic comes in: The moralist is less abstract than the football coach. What I mean by this is that the well-doing of football abstracts from a great deal of the complex business of human living. It is not of any direct relevance to playing football well that you are, say, kind, or a good physicist passionately interested in stamp-collecting. The moralist, on the other hand, is concerned not with an isolated abstract feature of human living like football, but with the activity of human living as a concrete whole. He is concerned not just with what it is to be a good physicist or carpenter or footballer, but with what it is to be a good human being. He is concerned with the good life for a human being taken as a whole.

So first of all I have distinguished between theoretical intelligence, concerned with understanding the reasons why things are as they are, and practical intelligence, concerned with changing the way things are, with human activity. And within this human activity, I have distinguished between acting well in the particular abstract field of endeavour (this is a matter of acquiring skills and techniques) and acting well in the field of endeavouring to be a human being (this, as we shall see, is a matter of acquiring virtues).

It may seem odd to talk of the endeavour to be a human being: are we not simply human by being born as such? Well, yes and no. A human being, unlike, say, a crystal of rock salt, is not a static thing. A human being is a human life which begins and develops. I take it that the whole *raison d'être* of teachers is to enable people to develop their human lives towards flourishing or maturity. They, and a lot of other people, face the task of helping people through the tricky transition from infancy to a fulfilled instead of a thwarted adult life.

All this is because we are not just human beings but human becomings. Like all other animals and unlike rock-crystals, for us to be is to have a lifetime, a development; but for us, and unlike for other animals, our lifetime is a life story. The difference is that the characters in a life-story in part make their own development; they make decisions, sometimes crucial ones which determine how the story will go on. Human animals are to this extent in charge of their lifetimes, their life-stories. That is why the study of human behaviour is ethics, while the study of other animal behaviour is only ethology. When the novel *Watership Down* came out it was reviewed in the *New York Review of Books* and the writer described it as a charming tale about some middle-class English children disguised as rabbits. And so they were. You could not have a story about actual rabbits. Because they do not control their own stories by decisions of the human kind there could be no drama, no comedy, no tragedy. Morality, then, is just the study of human lives considered precisely as life-stories. And what it is concretely to be a human being is to be a character in a life-story.

Whatever extra padding goes into it, the report of a football match is essentially a report on a series of solutions to practical problems, problems that are being solved (or not solved) by the players on the field – not in talking about them to others or to themselves in their heads, but in their intelligent activity. Intelligent activity, whether in the limited and abstract area of a human life, is not a matter, or does not have to be a matter, of first thinking something out in words with your theoretical intelligence and then acting on the conclusion to which you have come. Aristotle compared intelligent activity to a kind of reasoning in which the conclusion you come to is not a proposition but an action.

Of course one big difference between the game of football and the game of life is connected with the abstractness and simplicity of football. It is relatively simple to say what counts as successful activity, well-performed activity in football because the aims and purposes of the players, as players, are easy to understand. They are easy to understand because we invented them. What counts as winning, what counts as good or bad play, and also what counts as inadmissible play, is decided by the Football Authorities.

This does not seem to be the case with the game of life; nor could it be. I should say immediately that there were a whole lot of twentieth-century philosophers, for example the existentialists in France, and people like Richard Hare in Britain, who thought that the point and purpose of human life can be a matter of individual decision, or, as Hare would say, a 'fundamental option'. I think these people have to be wrong because of what decision is. I shall be trying to argue that a decision can only be an incident in the course of a life-story. It is essentially *against the background*, in the context of the story. There cannot be a decision about the story itself. I think these philosophers have been led astray by a mistaken idea called 'free will'. I am not opposing free will to determinism or any mechanistic theory of human behaviour. I am opposing it to what Aquinas calls 'free decision' (*liberum arbitrium*). But more of that in a moment.

So it is quite easy for us to understand that the point and purpose of the game of football is a matter of a decision we make within the game of living; it is not so clear how we come by an idea of the point and purpose of living itself.

To cut a long story relatively short, because I haven't time to argue everything, it seems to me that the point of human living cannot be to amuse the birds, in the way in which the point of machines does lie outside themselves: they are to amuse and be useful to human animals. I think it is true, and very importantly true, that the point of human living lies beyond itself, but not outside itself. This is because I think that in the end the point of human living lies in God, who is beyond us but not outside us. God, unlike the birds or any other creatures, cannot lie outside us because he creates us and sustains us all the time, making us to be and keeping us as ourselves. So to say that the point of our lives is in God is not to point to something outside us but to a greater depth within us.

However, before we come to God I would like to suggest that with human animals, as with all the other animals, *the purpose of life is living with each other*. This means that a good and well-functioning animal, a healthy animal, is one that lives well with the rest of its species. Living well with them involves, for example, mating with them, but also competing for mates and, in the case of at least one species, eating your mate after intercourse. We have all been learning from various zoologists how extraordinarily diverse and peculiar are the various solutions that different species have found to the problem of surviving. But, whatever the oddity of the set up, a healthy well-functioning shark or praying mantis is one that fits into the requirements of the species, one that lives well with its kin, according to its kind.

What distinguishes the human animal is the extraordinary new way it has found of living with its kind. What binds the human species together, and what is thus necessary for its flourishing, is not just kinship, blood-relationship, but what we may call culture – that whole area that arises from our capacity to create symbols, centrally of course, to use language (but we have to include music, painting, the building of cities, the development of communications of all kinds, all the technologies, arts and sciences). It is because of all this that our lifetimes are life-stories, that our lives are in our own hands.

We have a special name for human living with each other. We call it friendship (what Aristotle called *philia*). Friendship is more than people wishing well to other people. It involves what Aquinas calls *communicatio*, sharing, and the New Testament calls *koinonia*, sharing a common life. Friendship is a matter of being *with* others.

Now if the purpose of human living is to live with each other, and if this involves living in friendship, so that the good life for human animals is one in which friendship is fostered and preserved, this is *not* something that we have resolved upon, not a decision or option we have come to, not even a 'fundamental option'. It is something that belongs to us because of the kind of animal we are, the linguistic or rational animal. We are born as players of this game; we do not *decide* what shall be its aim and purpose; we *discover* these things. Of course discovering what kind of animals we are and what this implies takes a very long time and centuries of poetry and drama and critical philosophical thinking, and even then we are likely to make a lot of mistakes. That is why Thomas Aquinas thought it was very decent of God to help us out by giving us an outline of what it is to live in friendship: the Ten Commandments. God thought that, after some reflection, we might come to the conclusion that friends would not kill each other or seduce each other's husbands or wives or get them falsely convicted of crimes or kidnap them and enslave them or seek to defraud them of their possessions; but all the same it would be a good idea to get all this down in black and white, or better still, on tablets of stone. Well, it wasn't quite like that: the Decalogue is part of God's summons to Israel to be his people, to share in his life and his right-eousness. God is telling them that the first step to being God's people is to be human people, and that means living in friendship.

It is, however, important to see that what is provided by such a document as the Decalogue is precisely an *outline* of friendship. That is to say it draws a boundary around friendship to show where it stops: beyond these limits friendship does not exist. This is the characteristic function of *law*. When I was talking about football and saying that it is our invention and that its aims and purposes are decided by the Football Authorities, I said that their decision in the end determined what counts as *good or bad* play, and also what counts as *inadmissible* play. These are two different kinds of stipulation. It is the difference between perhaps not playing football well, and not playing it at all, but perhaps pretending to. Someone who commits a foul is seeking to obtain a result which looks like winning a football match, without playing football. It is with such matters that laws are characteristically concerned, and they are very important. But you cannot learn how to play football well simply by knowing what such laws are. Learning to play football well is a matter of acquiring skill by practice. For this you need the guidance of a teacher who already knows how to play well, though it may also be useful to read a book written by such a teacher. In either case you do not learn by listening to what the teacher says or by reading him. You learn by *practising* in accordance with what he says. If it is a matter of some com-plicated athletic feat or manoeuvre, you will begin by laboriously following the dotted lines in the diagram and going through the process many times, telling yourself what the next bit is. During the early stages of learning you will be listening to yourself or listening to your teacher and following the instructions. As you carry on you will gradually develop a skill; the thing will become, as they say, 'second nature' to you. This is what Aquinas calls a *habitus*, a disposition. *Habitus* does not mean habit. To be able to drive a car is a *habitus* or disposition. It means you can drive without an instructor, without constantly referring to a manual, without having to tell yourself when it is safe to overtake or when you should use your indicator. You just do these things intelligently and effortlessly. To drive skilfully in this way is not to drive out of habit in the sense that you may have a drink habit or a habit of smoking. A disposition or skill or *habitus* makes it *easier* for you to do what you want to do; a habit makes it *harder* for you not to do what you do not want to do.

The dispositions you need to acquire in order to play football well are skills, dispositions towards producing a good *result*, a good solution to a particular footballing problem for example. The dispositions you need to acquire in order to play the game of life well are called virtues. It is because we are not just human beings but human becomings that we need virtues. We need dispositions that will make it easy for us to make good practical decisions in carrying on our life-story. So while a skill or a technique is directed to the excellence of the thing produced, a virtue is directed to the excellence of the producer. The excellence we are concerned with when we look at human behaviour in the totally practical, totally non-abstract way that we adopt in moral judgement is not the excellence of something that *results* from a human action but the very *human action* itself. This is going to mean: Is it directed towards or against the being human (or becoming human) of this human actor? And this is going to mean in the end: Is it or is it not a preservation and fostering of friendship – that kind of friendship upon which human community and thus human existence depends? I say this is what it means in the *end*, because this is what the good life is for a human animal. But this is not what our immediate moral judgements are about. You do not criticize a move by a footballer simply by saying it is bad football; you say in what particular way his actions have failed in skill. And the skills involved in football are many and various; but nothing like as many and various as the virtues required for the good human life.

There is one important connection between technical skills and virtues I'd like to mention because it has to do with learning or acquiring virtues. Besides individual skills like being able to carve the turkey or play the flute, there are skills about skills, like being a good host or playing in an orchestra, which involve co-ordinating many skills and, most importantly, co-operating with others. Even learning an individual skill ordinarily involves a relationship with a teacher; and learning how to work with a team or with an orchestra involves even more complex relationships with people. It is most commonly when learning how to engage in large scale communal projects of this kind that virtues are developed – even though virtues themselves are not simply complex skills.

Virtues are dispositions that have to do with practical behaviour. So they belong to our living, which is a complex interweaving of knowledge and desire. We share with the other animals desires which arise from our sense-interpretation of our world: things are attractive to us (or not) because of how they feel to us. But being linguistic animals we also interpret our world in terms of what can be *said* of it. To speak of the world is not merely to express how it makes us feel but how it is and is not. It is our linguistic capacity that makes us able to grasp truth, to escape from the subjectivity and privacy of feeling into objectivity. And this is because linguistic meanings do not belong to anyone in the way that feelings do. Meanings do not *belong* to anyone in the way that feelings do; meanings are in the language, which is, of its nature, public and common. So nobody could have my sensations, only more or less similar ones; but everyone must be able to have my thoughts. It is most unlikely that you have exactly the same sensations as I have in drinking a pint of *Guinness*, but we all mean exactly the same by the clause 'drinking a pint of *Guinness*'. As Aquinas sees it, understanding a meaning is transcending our privacy, subjectivity, materiality, to share with each other, communicate with each other in terms of truth, in ways which are not simply bodily, by the use of signs and symbols to express meanings. So to have language is to be able to know the truth about the world, and, of course, by the same token, to make mistakes about it. What we feel is just what we feel and there is no way of 'correcting' it; but what we say of the world is open to discussion with others and within ourselves. Using our intelligence, unlike seeing, is a task, a work of investigation, something we have to do. And we may or may not want to do it. For just as our sense-knowledge gives rise to desires (we are attracted or not by what we sense) so does our rational knowledge, our linguistic way of interpreting the world. And the thing about this linguistic interpretation is that it isn't simply there like a sensation. A hungry dog seeing a juicy steak, unless it is sick, cannot but desire it. It can only be aware of the steak under the aspect of its smell and pleasant appearance. But we are aware of things not just in terms of their sensible appearance but also under a description, in fact under an indefinite number of descriptions. We are not only attracted by the smell etc.; we also recognize the steak as, for example, belonging to somebody else, being produced by the slaughter of harmless beasts, high in cholesterol, extremely expensive . . . and so on. All these are thoughts or considerations about the steak, and plainly they could go on indefinitely. How much we will think about the matter is in part a matter of how much we want to. For considering something is a human activity and human activity is done because we want to do it, because we find it attractive, or at least not repulsive to do it.

Suppose that my neighbour's wife and I are extremely attracted to each other and wish to go to bed together. Of course I know quite well that she is my neighbour's wife. But there is a difference between knowing something and considering it, bringing it before my mind: just as you knew five minutes ago who was the President of the United States but you were, I like to think, not paying any especial attention to this piece of knowledge. Now it is quite possible for me to find the thought of my beloved as my neighbour's wife an unpleasant one to contemplate, and so I push it to the back of my mind where it does not provide a motive for action (or inaction). In this way I will be motivated to do what I know quite well to be irrational and wrong and which on later consideration I will acknowledge to be such. It is our linguistic capacity to understand things and situations under an indefinite number of descriptions that, in St Thomas's view, is the root of human freedom, the root of our capacity to make actions really our own, flowing from our own decision, and also of course our capacity to deceive ourselves and behave irrationally.

In the story I have been telling about my alleged sex life what was missing, of course, was a good education. If I had only acquired by education certain elementary virtues, things would have appeared differently. What I needed was, for example, the virtue of temperateness in my emotional life so that I would not be simply overwhelmed by sexual attraction but keep it in its proper place among many other aspects of human living. I would also need the virtue of justice so that I just naturally took account of what was owing both to my beloved and to her husband; I would be reluctant to exploit her affection for me, and reluctant to deceive him and make their marital life even more difficult than most marital lives are. The result of acquiring such virtues would be that I would have had a truer view of the situation, I would be considering the important things about it and not the relatively trivial good to be attained by going to bed with her, or anyway not concentrating exclusively on this trivial good.

But above and beyond such virtues as temperateness and justice, I would need to have acquired the virtue of good sense, or *prudentia*. This is not reckoned by St Thomas among the moral virtues because it has not to do directly with desires but with understanding. He says it is an intellectual virtue, but since it is concerned with the practical intellect it is all tied up with the virtues that govern desires, and without it there can be no true moral virtues. Good sense is the virtue or cluster of virtues that make it easy and second nature to us to make good decisions. Good sense is a kind of clear-sightedness about our problems which enables us to put them in proper perspective, to see what is more important and what is less so. It also, and most importantly, involves a certain clear-sightedness about my self.

Moralists from the late middle ages onwards, and particularly since the sixteenth century, have seen the characteristic human act as one flowing from the free will, viewed as a separate faculty from intelligence. For Aristotle and for Aquinas, the characteristic human act is one done for a reason, the product of practical intelligence. In such practice, desire and understanding interact at all stages: we desire what we consider good and we consider when we want to.

The pattern of moral thinking for the later thinkers consisted of two sharply divided stages: first, the understanding assembled all the facts and worked out what would happen if we did what was in accordance with moral law. At this stage you know what is right and proper to do. Then comes the crucial question. After all the reasoning has been done, we still have to find out whether you will act on these findings or not. This is the sacred province of the free will: you will to go one way rather than the other.

This is the theory of decision-making that is satirized in the BBC comedy show *Yes, Minister*. Humphrey, the civil servant, is supposed to be a pure intellect and fact-gathering machine with no policies of his own; when he has delivered his findings Jim Hackett, the minister, will exercise his will and action will follow. The point of the programme, of course, is to show that it is actually Humphrey who makes the policy decisions, for there is no such thing as pure will. How you act depends on how the facts are presented and this itself comes from an interplay of desire and understanding. Once this is done, Jim Hackett's alleged decision is a foregone conclusion. This is as true of individual personal decisions as it is of politics. There is no practical intelligence standing neutrally above the fray. How you think about a situation, even how you identify a situation, crucially depends on your policies or, as we say in the personal case, your virtues or vices.

The consequence of the sixteenth-century 'voluntarist' view of the moral life was that the work of the intelligence was seen as something that could be detached from the actual moments of decision. You could think of a solution to moral problems in the abstract, in the quiet of your study, and you could write your conclusions in books – thus we got the handbooks of so-called moral theology giving you the solution to each problem. Of course it was recognized that in the concrete no two moral problems are exactly the same, so as time went on more and more complicated qualifications were added, and the science of casuistry was born. In the face of conflicting reasons for thinking an action lawful or not, principles of decision called systems of casuistry were devised – 'It is OK to follow the most probable view', or even 'any probable view', and so on. I will not deter you with these. The important point is that when with the aid of your handbooks and your casuistry you had seen the light. There then remained a decision for Jim Hackett, your free will.

It is, as always, a relief to turn from all this muddle to the sanity of Aristotle and Aquinas. For them, acting in terms of reasons is *of course* free because thinking is free. The way you interpret the world through language and concepts is not determined by your bodily structure, your nervous system and brain, as is the way you and other animals interpret it through the senses. Thinking is creative interpretation. But how you interpret your world will depend on what kind of person you are, what virtues or vices you have developed. In what, in this tradition, is called the 'practical syllogism', an *action* follows from premises in a way parallel to the way a *conclusion* follows from premises in a theoretical syllogism. Practical reasoning is not just thinking about what means are the best way of achieving this end; it is much more crucially thinking what sort of action follows from the kind of person I am.

As Aristotle said, in a remark which has puzzled modern moralists, you have to have a *character* in order to make a decision. To make a decision is to make an action *your own*, one that really flows from you, flows from the dispositions that have made you the person you are. Just plumping for one thing rather than another, as a child might, just being persuaded by the handsome canvasser on the doorstep or threats from the pulpit, is not to make a decision of your own. Of course when it comes to praise and blame, when it comes to deciding whether you are engaged in leading the good life, carrying on your life-story in a human way, not making a decision may be as blameworthy as making a bad decision.

The basic point is that teaching morality (or anything I could recognize as morality) must be a matter of enabling people to make good decisions which will be their *own* decisions. And this is done by helping them to acquire dispositions both of heart and mind. I suppose this might sometimes be done by story-telling – not telling moral tales, but entering imaginatively into the life-stories of interesting people, and also by imaginative dramatic reconstruction of situations of decision and so on. That is just a suggestion I throw out. I am, however, sure that the task is not to be achieved by getting people to read handbooks of moral theology.

But perhaps the most important conclusion of all follows from the recognition that morality is about doing and making and not first of all about explaining. The modern philosopher who has done more than anyone else in recent years to rehabilitate the Aristotelean idea of morality as based in virtue is surely Alasdair MacIntyre. For him all philosophical thinking is a kind of traditional craft that has to be handed from generation to generation, so that if the sequence is broken certain disastrous results follow. Whether or not this is in general true, it seems to me quite obviously true of moral philosophy. Of its practical nature it must be traditional, that is to say deriving from and criticizing and modifying a tradition. If your aim is to teach the craft of making violins, you do not give your student some wood and some tools and tell him to get on with it. You show him how violins have been made – and this is part of showing him what a violin is. He will copy the work and techniques of skilled men of the past, and after several years, or nearly a lifetime of this, he may be ready to add to and modify the tradition into which he has been introduced. And I now I leave it to you to consider whether the craft of making human beings, or human becomings, is likely to be any quicker and easier to acquire than the making of violins. For me, I think to imagine that you can read it all up in a book (*Teach Yourself Human-making* as it might be named) must be crazy; though that is what they sometimes call being traditional. It is just as crazy to imagine that the beginner is somehow automatically competent to decide or even understand or even recognize what human decisions are, off his or her own bat. Learning morality is, it seems to me, learning to be free; and doing that in any depth has to take most of a lifetime, most of a life-story.

Eighteen

The Role of Tradition

The word 'tradition' has a considerable range of meanings. There is, for example, a college in the University of Oxford where on a certain day of the year, at a certain feast, the fellows of the college, having finished an excellent dinner, take their wineglasses out into the quadrangle and fling the dregs of their wine at the wall dividing them from the adjacent college while shouting some ritual words of abuse (which I shall not quote). If you ask why grown people should behave in this way, you will be told that it is a college tradition. Nobody, it seems, knows or cares when or why it originated. I instance this as a case where 'tradition' is a substitute for understanding or argument – the view of tradition taken by the great English conservative Edmund Burke.

There are many gradations of meaning between this and the one that I shall be recommending: the sense in which tradition is a matter of identity, so that to have lost touch with tradition in this sense is to be as crippled as an amnesiac who just doesn't remember who he is. Just as an individual explores her identity by continually, as it were, re-writing her autobiography (not, of course, to change the past but to find new significance in it), so a culture, an institution, a church must continually re-write its history. This is not precisely because the previous autobiography or history was mistaken (though of course it may well have been; self-deception and chauvinism, for example, are constant temptations), but because we find new questions to ask and answer.

There is something extremely odd about the idea of a 'constant and unvarying tradition', which sounds like a constant and unvarying history where nothing would count as happening unless it had already happened before. There is a certain kind of appeal to tradition by some moral theologians that seems to make some such assumption. One of the things I shall be arguing is that a tradition is not there first of all to be *appealed* to, but to be *lived*. And the comparison of sentences uttered in the twentieth century with superficially similar sentences from the sixteenth or thirteenth centuries is not necessarily the best way of living in a continuing tradition.

I suppose no one has done more in recent years to rehabilitate the notion of tradition than Alasdair MacIntyre, especially in what we may think of as the trilogy of books that began in 1981 with *After Virtue* (followed by *Whose Justice? Which Rationality?* [1988, based on his Carlyle Lectures in Oxford 1982] and *Three Rival Versions of Moral Enquiry* [1990, his Gifford Lectures in Edinburgh 1988]). And those who know his work will recognize how deeply I am indebted to him. Speaking of 'the use to which the concept of tradition has been put by conservative political theorists' (he might have added moral theorists) he says:

> Characteristically such theorists have followed Edmund Burke in con-trasting tradition with reason and the stability of tradition with conflict. Both contrasts obfuscate. For all reasoning takes place within the context of some traditional mode of thought, transcending through criticism and invention the limitations of what had hitherto been reasoned in that tradition; this is as true of modern physics as of medieval logic. Moreover when a tradition is in good order it is always partially constituted by an argument about the goods the pursuit of which gives to that tradition its particular point and purpose. So when an institution – a university, say, or a farm, or a hospital – is the bearer of a tradition of practice or practices, its common life will be partly, but in a centrally important way, constituted by a continuous argument as to what a university is and ought to be or what good farming or good medicine is. Traditions, when vital, embody continuities of conflict. Indeed when a tradition becomes Burkean, it is always dying or dead. (*After Virtue*, p. 206)

I would want to add – as MacIntyre himself does here and in his succeeding works – that it is *only* in some such institution that the argument and fruitful disagreement of which he speaks can take place at all.

Consider what it is like to be initiated into a tradition. Let us say you are learning physics or how to play an instrument in an orchestra. There are at least three phases in this process of initiation. Let us suppose you begin at school. Here there are certain items on the syllabus and you begin by working at them because you hope to please your teacher and to pass an exam. The goods you are aiming at are, at this point, external to the tradition you are entering. If your aim is *simply* to receive an appropriately high mark in the examination then, for instance, it will be in your interest to cheat in the exam. It is not an understanding of physics or a skill in music that you are directly aiming at but something only contingently related to this. The situation changes rapidly as you become, as you may, interested in the subject itself and enjoy it for its own sake. Now you may still, of course, hope to pass the exam, but you have now established and are fostering a project and a satisfaction in goods *internal* to that subject, that will, with luck, remain when the whole regime of success and failure in exams is behind you. You are now on your way to not merely knowing *about* physics or music but to being a physicist or a musician. During this second phase your work will essentially be to imitate the great practitioners of the past. You will try to play like Yehudi Menuhin or think the thoughts of Albert Einstein. Such careful attention to and imitation of the past masters is the only way to enter into the tradition. The third and final phase will begin as you yourself become, if you ever do, a master of the practice. You are then ready to enter critically into the tradition, ready fruitfully to depart sometimes from recognized rules in some respect. You might even, like Einstein himself or Thomas Aquinas, be responsible for a revolution in the tradition. You will be engaged in what MacIntyre calls 'an argument about the goods the pursuit of which gives to that tradition its particular point and purpose'.

In this *final* phase it is not just that, say, physics is playing an important part in the biography of *you*. You are playing a part in the history of *physics*. I would hope that in our teaching of the theology of human behaviour, beyond making our students aware of the great (and often conflicting) voices of the past tradition, we are also expecting at least some of them later to be contributing critically and creatively in the present to the tradition itself. This cannot be done by simply reciting some suitably tidied-up version of 'what the Church has always taught'; it is important to discuss the disagreements as well as agreements between honest and intelligent Christians in the history of Christian moral thinking, and to convey that neither agreement nor disagreement is valuable for its own sake but only in so far as it is part of arriving a little nearer to the truth.

I have illustrated the process of initiation into a tradition by looking at the acquisition of skills (in science or music) but, of course, skills are not virtues. I should like to remind you of the difference between skills and virtues first of all, and then to talk a little about the overlap between them. And that should take us into a look at that most interesting and important of the virtues that can be acquired by education: *Prudentia* or Practical Wisdom (or what one of the greatest of the English moralists, the novelist Jane Austen, calls 'Good Sense').

You call someone skilful when she *makes* things or performances well; you call her virtuous when she acts well, or does things well. A skill is measured by the good of the product; a virtue, by the good of the producer, or agent (*agens*). Both skills and virtues are dispositions (*habitus*). I shall not go into the logic of dispositions which has been a topic of increasing interest to philosophers in what we might call the anglophone tradition since Wittgenstein and especially since the work of Gilbert Ryle, whose *The Concept of Mind* (1949) was one of those books with which every reader found fault but none was uninfluenced by. Of course, the whole of the *Secunda Pars*, the largest section of Aquinas's *Summa Theologiae*, deals throughout with the dispositions, good or bad, that govern human behaviour. It is true that the *Secunda Pars* also offers a short, fascinating, and highly intelligent treatment of Law, which includes a few pages on the 'Natural Law'; but all this is firmly in the context of virtues and vices.

Let us, for a moment, compare human living to playing a game such as football. Virtues are like the skills or dispositions to play the game well; we are gradually educated in such dispositions with the help of advice, practice, and training. Laws, on the other hand, are mostly concerned with defining the game itself, stating what counts as playing it and what counts as bogus or foul play. To commit a foul is not to play football badly; it is not to play football at all, but to pretend to. To know the laws of football is not to know how to play football; spectators can be just as expert here as players. Moral laws define the kind of actions which would count as sacrificing the aim and purpose of human living for the sake of some lesser external good. Virtues, on the other hand, are dispositions to attain that aim and purpose more readily, to *enjoy* attaining it.

These behavioural dispositions have their origin in the *meanings* we perceive in our world. All perception is the *discovery* of meaning around us; all action is the imposition of meaning around us. We perceive meaning at two levels. In the first place there is meaning in terms of our *sensual experience* of the world, a meaning determined by our bodily *structure*, in particular the nervous system including the brain. Secondly there is the meaning of the sensual experience in terms of our *understanding* of the world, a meaning determined by the *structure* of the language we were not born with but have created.

Perhaps I should expand these enigmatic utterances. As I see it, *meaning* is always the role or function of a *part* within some organized structure. An animal *is* an animal (has a 'soul') because what happens to, or is done by, a *part* of the animal has meaning because at another level it happens to or is done by the *animal as a whole*. When light hits the retina of the eye, this is a *photo-chemical occurrence* at the level simply of the eye, in abstraction from its role in the whole body; it is called *seeing* because this photo-chemical reaction is also relevant to all the rest of the body, the whole animal, determining its behaviour. It is the whole structure that *behaves* and not the bits in isolation – as it is the whole structure that sees and not the eye or the brain or any other part. To have a soul, to be animate, just is to be an organic structural unity in which the parts are relevant to, have *meaning* for, the whole. We can construct machines which in some respect are imitation animals. But, of course, animals are not machines any more than people are imitation statues. To make machines we assemble parts together to fashion a structure: the structure is secondary to the parts. Animals are not made in this way; here the first thing that exists is the structure, the coded instructions in the genes of the animal, and the parts are developed in terms of this structure. The structure of the whole is physically there prior to the parts.

It is because the organs of perception (eyes, skin, ears and so on) each have meaning within the bodily structure that (through the operation of these organs) the world has meaning for the animal and its behaviour. Things in the world are perceived as good to eat or dangerous or sexually attractive or whatever. And these perceptions express themselves in tendencies to action. Humans share this way of interpreting the world with their fellow animals in varying degrees. What makes the difference between us and the other animals is that, besides the meaning-bearing *inherited* structure of the nervous system, we have another meaning-bearing structure which we make ourselves and call language. Besides the relatively *passive* interpretations of sense-experience, we interpret the world *actively* by what we say about it to others or to ourselves. How we interpret our world linguistically depends in the first place on our vocabulary, what meanings we have created (not, of course, individually, but as a culture, a tradition). I am told that in one of the Polynesian languages there is a quite short word which means 'for two people to look at each other, each hoping the other will do something that both want done but neither wishes to do'. I have always thought this would be a word of great power in any religious community. But what meanings you have available in your language is a matter of your tradition, your history (and not, of course, of your genes). In the second place, how we interpret our world as individuals depends on what questions we ask with our language and seek to answer. There is no equivalent to questions and answers at the level of sense-experience. Non-linguistic animals may be bewildered and uneasy and may seek ways of alleviating their difficulty, but not by questioning, not by language. With language comes the power to express not only what is so but what-is-not-so-but-might-have-been.

The non-linguistic animal interprets the world by, so to say, catching it in the web of its individual, material nervous system. Animals of the same species interpret the world subjectively but in predictably similar ways because their bodily structures are much the same. But the interpretation remains individual and incommunicable. No animal can have another's sensations any more than it can kick with the other's foot. But, besides all this, the *linguistic* animal also interprets the world by catching the sensual experience in the web of language and, since there can be no such thing as a *private* language (no meanings are just *my* meanings, or *yours*, in the way that sensations are just *my* or *your* sensations) this *linguistic* interpretation transcends our material individuality. Understanding, as Aquinas insists, however much it may demand concomitant bodily processes such as *imaginatio*, cannot be itself a bodily process; it is a trans-individual immaterial act. Wittgenstein says the same when he shows in the *Philosophical Investigations*, for example, that the notion of *private* language is senseless. We *share* our linguistic interpretation of the world. *Because* others can have, not just a *similar*, but the *identical* idea or meaning that I have through language, we can achieve *objectivity*. We no longer just react to our own sensations; we can begin to ask identical questions and agree or disagree about the answers. No other animals can disagree; they can merely react differently.

It is with the successful resolution of disagreements that we come closer to formulating an account of what is the case; and so we arrive at (in MacIntyre's phrase) 'the best that can be said so far'. This, in its simplest form, is the fruit of any human tradition of exploring the truth. That is why human animals can disagree in friendship and, indeed, as part of friendship. Confronted by a juicy steak, a healthy, hungry dog which has not suffered any human training will interpret it quite simply and absolutely as desirably *edible* and will seek to eat it. In the same circumstances I might have similar reactions but my interpretation and my behaviour would also be governed by what I could say to myself about the steak – that it belongs to someone else, that it is full of cholesterol, that it came from the slaughter of harmless beasts . . . and so on, indefinitely. It is just in the indefinitely and indeterminately ranging meanings, which can supply reasons for action or inaction, that Aquinas locates human freedom. The dog cannot *but* seek out the steak, unless he is trained not to, in which case he cannot but *refrain* (however unwillingly) from seeking it out.

Non-linguistic animals act for reasons. We can truly say the dog is running *because* he has seen the rabbit and wants it. And animals can obviously act willingly or unwillingly. But we cannot say that animals *have their own reasons* for acting. Their range of desirable objects is circumscribed by their genes and the structure of their nervous systems or their training. We cannot say they have *will* (*voluntas*), which is the appetite that springs from what we *say* about things, how we *understand* them.

For Aquinas, humans are free because they act for their *own reasons*. He sedulously avoids speaking of the 'free will'. His phrase is always '*liberum arbitrium*' and this free *decision* is a complex psychological act involving, first of all, our *sensual* interpretation of the world (which is to take it up into our nervous system), and the appetites and emotions that arise from this; and then our conceptualization of the world (which is to take it up into language) and the appetites (volitions) that arise from that.

The appetites arising from our *sensual interpretation* of the world are the field of the many moral virtues covered by *temperateness* (for the appetites of sensual desire) and *courage* (for the sensual aggressive appetites). The appetites arising from what we *tell* ourselves of our world are the field of the cluster of moral virtues we call justice. The whole process by which all these are brought together in practical reasoning to produce an action which is decisively mine is, or should be, governed by practical wisdom, *prudentia*.

Practical wisdom is a somewhat ambiguous virtue. St Thomas sees it as primarily not a moral but an intellectual virtue, governing not our appetites but our understanding. But it is an intellectual virtue that can only be exercised in the context of moral virtues. Unlike the recent so-called 'Catechism of the Catholic Church', he does not see *prudentia* as concerned with the *aims* at which we direct ourselves – these, for him, are a matter for the *moral* virtues. Following Aristotle he sees *prudentia* as concerned with the *means* by which we seek to achieve these ends. And for it to be *genuine* practical wisdom (and not its caricature, *astutia* or cunning), the ends in question must be in fact good for us, the outcome of virtue and not vice. So an account of *prudentia* takes in both intellectual and moral considerations.

I mention this because of the light it may shed on our teaching of what is nowadays called 'moral theology', and this in its turn may make clear the real importance of a living tradition in which this teaching takes place. In such teaching we are seeking to inculcate an intellectual *skill*. We are concerned that our students become better, more reasonable, more intellectually honest in their *thinking* about human behaviour in the light of the gospel. We are not directly and immediately inculcating moral virtue: we are not seeking to make them humanly better people (saints) but only better in respect of this fundamental skill in growing up. And yet the very intelligibility of our teaching does depend on a certain moral development as well. Coming to understand the theology of human behaviour does demand a certain moral maturity (which comes only from living within a tradition) in the same sort of way that *prudentia* demands a context of moral virtue. I am trying to explain what I meant by saying that tradition is not just something to appeal to but something to live. We do not just have to know what people *said* in the past, we have to be in continuity with their wrestling with their problems (as W. B. Yeats clearly saw). And this is a continuity that depends on more than neutral historical scholarship (if there be such a thing). It demands something more like the mutual loyalty of fellow citizens in an Aristotelian *polis*. It is, of course, a continuity of argument and debate and critical appreciation, but essential to it is a moral unity, a *philia*, an *amicitia*, a friendship.

Now, as Alasdair MacIntyre would insist, this has to be true of *any* genuine intellectual tradition. But it seems to me of central importance in the teaching of moral theology because (I hope to show) of the nature of practical reasoning itself. It seems to me that, in this field in particular, teaching ineluctably involves an element of preaching – and this, of course, makes it a highly dangerous academic operation, to be conducted with the utmost delicacy (and without anaesthetics).

First, though, a brief word about the involvement of moral virtues in *any* serious teaching whatsoever. Students embarking on any study, whether it be mathematics or music or biochemistry, need a certain humility and patience and self-critical capacity. Or, at least, they must act *as though* they possessed these moral virtues. It is, of course, possible genuinely to act humbly or patiently, as it is possible to act justly or bravely, without having yet acquired the *habitus*, the disposition which would make such acts 'second nature' to us. Indeed the performance of such good acts, which are not yet acts of virtue, is the only way in which such virtues can be humanly acquired. A number of authors have suggested that the field in which virtues ordinarily grow is in the acquisition of skill, especially complex skills that require consideration of (and consideration for) colleagues engaged in the same task. On the whole, self-obsessed or vain or arrogant or lazy people do not learn very much.

Nevertheless I think the teaching and leaning of moral theology or moral philosophy is *especially* unsuited to an abstractly academic approach. Before I can make my argument for this it will be necessary to look at two rival versions of what moral deliberation and decision amount to, which I shall call respectively the 'free will' and 'free decision' versions. In the space available here, I shall have to make do with a sketch (not to say a caricature) of each – and especially of the one I am rejecting.

The first version which I am rejecting, the 'free will' version, is rooted in a view of the primacy of moral rules or laws, sometimes called 'natural law'. In this view it is possible by the exercise of *theoretical* reason to work out principles or rules of morality. Manuals of moral theology can be rationally and scientifically composed by scholars examining laws, scholars who are in no way themselves involved in making the moral decisions they write about. Their product is a code of conduct which informs the reader about what is right or wrong action. The manual made famous by Graham Greene's novel *Monsignor Quixote* can tell us that to use an electric washing machine for more than two and a half hours on a Sunday would be only venially sinful. But, of course, simply knowing what would be the correct action is by no means enough for leading a good life: one also has to decide whether or not to act accordingly. And this, according to the view I am caricaturing, is where the free will comes in. This is a mysterious and unpredictable power within us which determines whether or not we will act on the delivery of reason (such as can be read in a handbook of moral theology). On this view there is a work of pure reason (comparable to, say, Euclidean geometry) which results in the code of rules. And that exhausts the task of reason. We move *then* to an option of the will which determines our action.

Turning now to the alternative view: free decision. St Thomas, while he has a place for law, and even for laws specifying absolute prohibitions of certain actions, does not base his evaluation of human behaviour on laws. For him the basis is a notion of the good life for human beings and the need to cultivate, or be educated in, the dispositions which lead to and are partially constitutive of the good life. These dispositions, I have mentioned, are of the bodily *emotions* as well as of the *will* and of *practical intelligence*. For him there are no acts of practical intelligence or of will that take place in isolation from each other: always they are woven together and mutually interact. The intelligence moves the will by bringing out the rational meaning of what we first experience as sensual meanings and which then attract the will (or not). Conversely, the will moves the intelligence because we arrive at judgement by answering asked questions. And *what* questions we ask depends on what we *want* to know and think about.

Thus Aquinas's solution to the ancient Socratic problem: 'How *can* we decide to do what we know is bad for us?' turns on our ability not to ask the awkward question which would bring before our minds *as a motive* the moral understanding which we possess *habitualiter* (rather as you knew your address when you were asleep or three minutes ago [or both] but, since nobody asked you, it was not actively before your mind). If you have not asked yourself the relevant questions concerning the reasonableness of what you might do, the major premiss of your practical syllogism, expressing your aim or intention, what you want, could be left to be determined by unregulated emotion cut loose from the linguistic interpretation which provides an approach to an objective account of the whole picture – the 'veritas' of Pope John Paul II's *Veritatis Splendor*. For St Thomas the act of decision is not a pure act of 'free will' but a whole piece of practical reasoning (a sort of syllogism which ends not with a proposition but with a meaningful action), an argument involving not only the intellectual appetite of the will but the sensual appetites, the emotions, and of course the practical operation of intelligence itself.

Practical reasoning is about means and it has two sides to it: on the one hand it relates means to the *end*; on the other it relates them to the *agent*, the self that I have developed by acquiring virtue or vice or neither. Scholars have been puzzled as to why Aristotle in his rather enigmatic discussion of the practical syllogism sometimes gives the major premiss in the form 'I *want* . . .' and sometimes in the form 'I *am* . . .' So far as I can see, this is simply because these represent the two sides of practical reasoning. The first, relating means to the end, is brilliantly discussed by Anthony Kenny (1975, Ch. 5) who makes clear the difference between theoretical and practical logic. The former is 'truth preserving' and the latter 'satisfactoriness preserving'. The former says 'If these propositions are *true*, then, necessarily, this conclusion is true'. The latter says 'If this is what I *want*, then these means would be *sufficient* for me.' Kenny does not, however, discuss what, from the moralist's point of view, is the more interesting side of the practical syllogism: the relation of this sufficient means to my own established dispositions, to *who* I *am*. More interesting because it is here that decision takes place; it is here that thought becomes action. The root of action is not a bare act of 'free will'; it is the recognition that I am, have made myself or been made by grace, or both, one who is by 'second nature' disposed to take these means. What is on offer is a true expression of who I am, a real continuation of the life-story which is myself. That, I think, is why Aristotle says that you cannot make a true decision (as distinct from a mere whimsical option such as a child might make) without having formed a character, good or bad.

I have talked at such tedious length about decision and hence *prudentia*, not only because for St Thomas this disposition to good practical reasoning is what he has instead of the mysterious 'voice of conscience' hidden in the depths of your soul, but primarily because I think it sheds some light on what the teaching of moral theology should be about. If you take what I have called the 'free will' line, then teaching will be at best the inculcation of an intellectual skill and at worst simply a passing on of information about what rules have been made. If, however, you take the 'prudential *decision*' line, then you are seeking to inculcate what is indeed an intellectual skill but only in the curious sense in which *prudentia* is an intellectual *skill* but also an intellectual *virtue*. It is a skill in making decisive actions that express your self (and, of course, it presupposes that you have already formed a self – Aristotle thought that not only children but adolescents as well could not profitably study ethics). All such decisions are, as both Aristotle and Aquinas insist, concrete and individual. Since by intelligence we grasp only meanings and natures, and not the material individual, we need more than intelligence to take in the concrete circumstances of our decisive action. We need a sophistication of the emotions and feelings if we are sensually to experience the here and now as it actually is. For this, we need to be, as we say in English, 'experienced' or mature.

On the other hand, for those who see human behaviour in terms of law and conscience and free-will, the art and science of *casuistry* has to be brought into play to refine law in such a way that its rational concepts can fit more and more closely to the intransigent individual circumstances. This is all to the good in that it *does* recognize the inevitable oversimplifying implied in any moral code. But it is not, in my view, a substitute for the exercise of *prudentia*, a virtue which arises in us by living in (and not merely reading about) a moral tradition so that the whole of our cognitive and appetitive capability gets closer to a grasp of reality. For the view of morality that starts not with law but with virtues, a decision, and especially a good decision, demands not exactly more refined *thinking* but more refined and sensitive *people*. The real reason why nobody else can make my decisions for me is *not* that I have (when all else is said and done) a mysterious *free will* all of my own, but that *nobody else is my body*, and it is only by my bodily presence that the concrete particularity of my action can be grasped and judged.

Now the teaching of moral theology must involve getting people to recognize what sort of person we are talking of here: a 'mature' person. For this recognition, what the student needs is to discover her identity as a character in a moral tradition, formed by that tradition and, in turn, perhaps in particular ways re-forming that tradition. Such a moral tradition is, as MacIntyre has pointed out, best entered into by narrative, by listening to stories, which are the nearest thing the mind can do to grasping the individual. To discover your identity is to be able to tell yourself the story which forms your life, and the larger stories within which your life exists and has meaning. This history is more than a succession of *teachings*, it is a living succession of *people* who are not *logically* connected but biologically and psychologically and sociologically associated and in *conflict* in a huge diversity of ways. By the exercise of special historiographical skills, such as I do not possess, it seems possible to understand something of *other* traditions outside my own; but the obvious way of understanding a tradition is to be part of it, to live in it as part of it.

The traditional inheritance is no single strand of *teaching* but a whole complex *life* in which some parts come to throw *unexpected* light on other parts. It is a rope woven of a thousand different strands and you never know what unexpected strand may turn out to be relevant to another. Consider, for example, why and how the teaching of Vatican II on, say, sex is radically different from that of St Jerome and St Augustine and even differs markedly in emphasis from the cool sanity of St Thomas, and yet, while in disagreement with (and even flat contradiction to) these Fathers of the Church, we do not doubt that what is taught by the Church belongs to traditional Catholic teaching. Of course what has changed our views about sex is not simply a development of doctrines about sex but changes in our practice and understanding of justice, authority, temperateness, of physiology and psychology; changes also in economic expectations and needs and means of production and, of course, a vast change in the perception of women and their complex roles in society and church. Such changes (for better or for worse as we may now see them) have presented new challenges, new questions to be answered, and these new questions have inevitably placed the earlier answers in a new context.

Again, the Pope is plainly right to think of his condemnation of torture as traditional even though he knows as well as any of us that such has not been the only or even the commonest view expressed in the Church. There has always been a strand of tradition deeply suspicious of torture (the Spanish Inquisition seems to have been a shining light of rationality, gentleness, and sanity in this respect in the Europe of its time) just as there were strands of pacifist and of 'just war' traditions. But none of these could have much claim to be the tradition of the Church. Perhaps, in any case, it is only by hindsight, perhaps only at the Last Judgement, that we can *identify* the 'central' trends of tradition.

But, as I have said, the important thing, and the thing that will make tradition effective, is not to identify it but to live in it in all its complexity and incoherence and conflicts and arguments. The one sure way of killing off a tradition is to identify it with what seems to you plainly true and then to unchurch those who see things differently, to see these people as unclean and to be put outside the camp. There is no camp. Even with electronic communications media, a thousand million people just couldn't manage to be a sect. The Catholic Church is nothing if it is not the sacramental visibility of the *whole* human race being brought, and occasionally dragged kicking and screaming (but also sometimes laughing and singing and joking), towards eternal life under the kingship of God.

Part Four

———

Sermons

Nineteen

Praying as we Ought

'Likewise the Spirit helps us in our weakness; for we do not know how to pray as we ought, but the Spirit himself intercedes for us with sighs too deep for words. And he who searches the hearts of men knows what is the mind of Spirit, because the Spirit intercedes for the saints according to the will of God' (Rom. 8:26–7).

St Paul says 'We do not know how to pray as we ought.' Now that seems to me an enormously encouraging remark. '*We* do not know . . .' – that is, St Paul and the rest of us. It is encouraging because it is quite common for someone to feel that she or he personally is the only one who doesn't seem to know how to pray. Well at least we have one of the greatest saints in history with us. Paul too did not know how to pray. But notice that he didn't expect to, and he certainly didn't try to show us how to. Some people think there are special techniques to be learnt which will make us able to pray better. Well, I expect there are techniques for feeling more at ease when we pray. And the best techniques will be those that show us how not to bother or worry about it anyway. But when we have learnt all this we still do not know how to pray as we ought.

The reason is a very simple one: we do not know how to talk *to* God because we do not know how to talk *about* God. The mystery which is the answer to the most profound problem of all, the problem of why there is anything at all instead of nothing, this mystery which we label 'God', lies far beyond anything we can conceive or put into words. Nobody who talks about God knows what she is talking about; the greatest theologian knows no more of what God is than the smallest child. We are all stretching out to a mystery far beyond our reach, far beyond anything that can be put into our words or our thoughts. That is why often the simplest things are the best things to say of God, the plainest words and the crudest images which no one could be deceived into regarding as adequate. Theology is a difficult and very rewarding occupation but for the most part it is not concerned with trying to say what God is but in trying to stop us talking nonsense, trying to stop people making God in their own images, to stop us from mistaking our concepts and images and words for the mystery towards which they point.

The difficulties of talking *about* God are only compounded when we try to talk *to* God. Who is it that we are addressing? The Bible, especially the psalms, contains an immense variety of ways of talking to God ranging from pleading to gratitude and from cajolery to resentful complaint. The one we address seems sometimes a lover or a friend, sometimes a boss, sometimes forgetful, sometimes cruel and insensitive, sometimes overflowing with generosity. Which of these, if any, is praying as we ought?

The answer is that none of them is, but any will do. We never can pray as we ought, so let's just pray as we can. This is Paul's great liberating teaching: it doesn't matter. There is no special way of talking that will catch God's attention. There is no etiquette, no good manners about how we are to address God. All ways are equally inappropriate and equally good. Let me hasten to add that there is a great deal of etiquette and a great deal of good manners about how we are to pray with other people. It seems to me that the Roman liturgy is a wonderful and sensitive code of good manners for praying with others who belong to this particular culture of Western Europe, so that we do not become an embarrassment or a bore to each other; we can share together in this most intimate activity as civilized grown-ups.

But while that excellent book *The Catholic Directory* begins with a useful list of correct forms of ecclesiastical address for everyone from deacons to cardinals, it rightly has no prior ecclesiastical mode of address for God. When we talk *to* God, as when we talk *about* God, it is usually the plainest and crudest forms that are best – so that nobody could mistake them for something correct. Of course there *are* ways of talking to God which would just be plainly wrong or blasphemous, just as there are statements we cannot make about God. We could not address God as Supreme Creator of Cruise Missiles or Father of Lies any more than we could say that he is unjust or stupid. But these things apart, we should not mind if our prayers sound childish or even superstitious.

The reason for all this is that just as no one knows God except God, so no one speaks to God except God. God understands himself in his own eternal concept of himself, his eternal Word that was made flesh and dwells among us as Son of God. We shall never come to understand him in his Word. One day in heaven we shall understand God with his own understanding, in his Word, but meanwhile we share in that understanding only in the darkness and puzzlement of faith.

And it is the same with prayer. Prayer is God's communion with God, prayer is the Holy Spirit breathed forth by the Father, and by the Son because of the Father. One day in heaven we will communicate with God in *his* way, in Spirit (the Holy Spirit), and in truth. But meanwhile we share in that Spirit in the inarticulacy of our prayer. 'We do not know how to pray but the Spirit himself intercedes for us with sighs too deep for words.'

When we pray it doesn't matter that our words are inadequate because in its real depths it is the Spirit that prays within us. When we pray we are prayed *in*, we become the *locus* of the exchange between Father and Son, the Trinity has its home within us. And for that we do not need the right words. We need an emptying of ourselves to make a room for the Spirit; we need even a slight self-mockery as we see how foolish and childish our words are, and yet we are not ashamed of them. This is not self-abasement, for are we not temples of the Holy Spirit who dwells within us? But there is a kind of irony that the temples should be like *this*. It is because our prayers are the work of the Spirit in us that it is perfectly sensible to ask God for the things we want in prayer. We are not trying to put pressure on God or persuade him, even if our words sometimes should sound as though we are. When we ask God for anything we want, whether we are praying that we will pass an exam or begging for mercy and forgiveness, it is God who makes the prayer as well as the answer to it. The life of the Trinity is living itself out in this particular phase of our development, in the context of these particular needs and desires which will be satisfied (or transformed) as the Father leads us to himself.

All our prayer is a sharing in the eternal exchange between Father and Son, and this means that all prayer is our sharing in the passion and death and resurrection and ascension of Christ. For the death and resurrection of Jesus, his casting himself upon the Father in obedience to his will, and the Father's response in raising him up to sit at his right hand, this is just the enactment in history of the eternal life of the Father and Son, the eternal Spirit of Father and Son. It is a painful and tragic enactment in history because our history is a history of sin. Because of that, Christ's obedience to his Father meant that he was murdered. But in all that blood and horror is the eternal life, the eternal Spirit, of the Godhead.

That, of course, is why the Eucharist is our central prayer. For the Eucharist is the Church's sacrament of the death and resurrection of Christ. In this sense all our prayer is eucharistic, all our prayer is being at Mass whether we are in the Church spatially with the community or not; for all our prayer is the life of the Spirit in us, and the Eucharist is the visibility of the Spirit, the sacramental sign of the communication between Father and Son which was Christ's sacrifice and the Father's acceptance of it.

So all our prayer is an abandonment of ourselves, even when it is that excellent prayer when we are most concerned about what we desperately need and want. It is an abandonment of ourselves because it is a sharing in Christ's abandonment of himself in death. In prayer we stop believing in ourselves, relying on ourselves, and we believe and trust in God. It is all a sharing in Christ's death. And it is this whether we are with all the Church in baptism, the Eucharist or the other sacraments, or whether it is the prayer of a particular community, a group or an individual. It is a sharing in Christ's death looking forward to that ultimate sharing in his death which is our own death in him, through which we rise in him to understand the Father in the Son, to pray the prayer which is the Spirit, to communicate with our Father in joy and love for eternity.

Twenty

A Sermon for the
Feast of the Epiphany

When the pagan Romans constructed their calendar they said that Midwinter's day was 25 December; and they had a feast that day to celebrate the sun beginning to fight back against the lengthening winter nights. The light had been shining in the increasing dark, but the darkness had not overcome it. It was a feast of light, of the Unconquered Sun. Because, however, the year (the time it takes for the earth to circle the sun, giving us the seasons) is not an absolutely exact number of days (the time it takes for the earth to spin on its own axis, giving us night and day), midwinter will not keep still; so, it shifts slowly back through any calendar of days as the year goes on. In fact, the pagan Egyptians, who had got on to the job of making calendars much earlier, had already fixed midwinter on the date the Romans came to call 6 January, and the Egyptians had their feast of light on that date. All this was long before the celebration of the coming of Christ: you had two popular pagan midwinter feasts of light overcoming darkness, one for the people of the East, one for the people of the West. When the Catholic Church became respectable and powerful in Rome, it very sensibly decided not to suppress the popular midwinter festivity but to baptize it, to make it a Christian feast instead – a feast of Christ the true light of the world. And so in Rome they had Christmas, the feast of Christ's birth on 25 December. Christians in the East similarly transformed their pagan midwinter feast into the Epiphany on 6 January – the manifestation of God's love. These were the same feast of the Son of God showing himself among us as a human being.

Very soon the Church in Rome decided to have the Eastern Epiphany as well as their own Christmas, on the excellent principle that the more feasts the better. Christmas was for the rejoicing in the revelation of the Word made flesh amongst the Jews, and Epiphany for celebrating the manifestation to the Gentiles, the Magi. At Christmas, Jesus is worshipped by Jewish shepherds in the tradition of David the shepherd boy: and he is born of the virgin Mary, representing the virgin Israel spoken of by the Jewish prophets. At Epiphany, Jesus is worshiped by pagan visionaries from the East in the tradition of Balaam, the pagan prophet from the East who foretold that a star would arise out of Israel and that a new king would come forth.

Today, then, is feast of the manifestation, the visibility of the Word of God amongst humankind. I think we might spend a minute or two thinking about this manifestation for it is not as simple as we might expect. It is, in fact, a manifestation that is quite easy to miss.

In one of the very earliest Christian writings, before any of the Gospels, Paul speaks of the manifestation of the divinity of Jesus (in his Epistle to the Romans). He says that Jesus Christ 'according to the human nature he took, a descendant of David . . . was proclaimed Son of God in all his power through his resurrection from the dead.' With the resurrection, first the women then the apostles and other disciples began to glimpse the true mystery of Jesus, and as soon as they began to understand they began to announce it. First Mary Magdalene preached it to the apostles and then they all proclaimed: 'The Lord is risen.'

But notice that even Mary, when she encounters the risen Christ, does not at first recognize him. She thinks he is a gardener – though this is, I suppose, a kind of recognition, for he is indeed the new Gardener, the new Adam (who tended our Garden of Eden) come through his resurrection to re-create humankind in grace. But Mary does not fully recognize him until he speaks to her and calls her by her name. In the same way the disciples on the way to Emmaus, although they talk to him all day, do not recognize him until 'they knew him in the breaking of the bread.'

So to recognize the risen Christ is to begin the Good News, the announcement of the gospel. But that recognition needs more than simple human seeing. Quite apart from the fact that the Lord as risen is seen only when he shows himself (we cannot imagine him being caught unawares), even when he does show himself he is identified as the Lord only by faith. It is in the calling by name, in the eucharistic celebration (in the invitation to Thomas to touch him), that faith is given and we see him, as believing Thomas does, as 'My Lord and my God.'

That is why the historical fact of the resurrection cannot as such bring anyone to faith in the gospel. Historical facts are in principle available to believers and unbelievers alike but only the former see what is really there, the meaning within the fact. To meet the risen Christ, whether at Emmaus or at Mass or in his brethren in need, is a proof for believers but not for unbe-lievers. The most we can do for our unbelieving friends is to show them that what we preach is not an absurdity or an impossibility.

So in an epiphany we are offered both a vision and the faith to interpret the vision, and this always means a potential division between those who do and those who do not accept the faith. An epiphany is a crisis, a division, a judgement, a separation between believers and others. When the earliest Christian preachers reflected on the story of Jesus they told it in these terms, in terms of the crisis produced by an epiphany, the conflict that the presence of Jesus brings about. There is the little group who responds to his love and accepts the devastating critique of all self-deception and self-righteousness; and there are those, especially those with power, the priests and political authorities, who cannot. We must not look in the Gospels for a simple neutral account of the life and times of Jesus of Nazareth; we must not suppose that the priests and the colonial power and, especially, the pharisees have not also a case to put. The Gospel writers had a much more important task in hand: to explore what it means for God to be with us, for God to be one of us. God is with us because Jesus is Son of God, but this we realize only in faith; and if we have this faith the world (the powers that be) will hate us and seek to destroy us as Jesus was destroyed.

The story of the Magi is just such a story of the encounter with Jesus. They are first moved to come to him by the mysterious behaviour of a star (not yet by faith, not by hearing the word of God in Scripture but by reading the night sky). This takes them as far as Jerusalem but not yet to Jesus. To find him they need to be confronted by and accept the prophecies, the word of God that is in the keeping of the Jews. They are Gentiles but, as John says, 'salvation is from the Jews'. The Magi hear the word, believe and find Jesus. Herod hears the word, does not believe, and does not find Jesus. They worship him; the king seeks to kill him. Once the word is proclaimed, once the epiphany has occurred, there is no other choice: we either worship or destroy.

This story is to tell us that the encounter with Jesus cannot leave us unchanged; for good or ill we cannot carry on as before. We either live as those who share his life of forgiveness and friendship, which is the life of the Spirit, or we resist him and seek to reject him. How, then, do we meet him?

This same Gospel of Matthew that tells us of the Magi also answers that question. 'Whatever you do to one of these little ones you do to me.' Whenever we encounter someone in need of our help and our friendship we are experiencing an epiphany and asked to make what is literally an *act* of faith.

Like the pagan Magi moved by the star but not yet confronted by the word, we may set out sincerely by seeking the true way to live. And as 'good pagans' may come to realize that a life without friendship and justice and mercy is not a life fit for human beings. It is only when we are confronted in practice by the risen Christ (especially says Matthew, in his poor, his homeless, his refugees and dispossessed) that we discover that we have to choose between either something more than human kindness and justice or something less, between that human love that goes even beyond the human, that divine friendship that is charity which is a sharing in God's own love, between Father and Son, the Holy Spirit – between this and what is less than human, that failure in rejection of what we were made for that we call sin.

That is why what we have come to call the 'option for the poor' is not simply one expression of the Christian life, but the very heart of it. To make this option is to live dangerously, if only in the danger of disrupting a comfortable and familiar pattern of life; but sometimes in more immediate danger, as the Magi were from king Herod. But if we make this option we will, like the Magi, be saved: we will be saved not only from being destroyed by Herod, but also from the much worse fate of destroying ourselves *with* him. And we will 'go safely home by another way': to the home that belongs to the poor ('for theirs is the kingdom of heaven'), to that life of friendship, joy and peace which is the life of God for eternity.

Twenty-One

A Sermon for
Ash Wednesday

I think we are all accustomed to the teaching that the Catholic Church is not meant to be a community of great saints, a collection of the righteous and holy as distinct from the sinners. We know it is also meant for sinners, for people who haven't yet made it to great sanctity and maybe don't show much sign of doing so.

Today I would like to put in a word for the doctrine that the Church is also not meant to be a community just of *great* sinners either; it is for *mediocre* sinners as well. I think we should realize that mediocre sinners have a definite intelligible place in the Church, and if we don't grasp this we shall never really take seriously the penitential season of Lent that we are just starting.

The trouble I see is that we tend to use such inflated language about sin that we simply can't take it seriously. It becomes unreal; it doesn't say anything clear and concrete to the mediocre sinner.

Let us be clear, of course, that people who are really welcome to the Catholic Church are the murderers, rapists, torturers, sadistic child molesters and even those who evict old people from their homes. It is for loving, welcoming, and forgiving such people that the Church exists. But I would guess that many of you, perhaps even a majority of you, do not come into any of these categories. A lot of you are mediocre sinners, and the season and liturgy of Lent, the season of penance, ought to say something directly to you.

The difficulty is that much of the liturgy derives from the ceremonies for the reconciliation and forgiveness of those torturers and rapists (like the sackcloth and ashes that we remember in our Ash Wednesday ceremonies). It is all a bit like the good people who come to confession and admit that they have sometimes neglected their morning prayers and then recite a terrifying act of contrition all about 'thy dreadful punishments' and 'offending thy infinite majesty'. This is really to use language badly, even to use bad language about God.

The fact is that there is mediocre sin and it has its own rightful place and is to be treated for what it is and not as though it were a total abandonment of God and his love.

Like all very wise men, Cardinal Newman said a number of foolish things in his time, and I think the most foolish of them was his remark that it would be better to see the whole universe consumed in flames than to commit one venial sin. We all know that cannot be true; we can't say it seriously, and the result is that we can't take venial sin seriously at all. Now I think we should see it for what it is in its own right, not just as a poor relation of mortal sin.

When I was a child we used to play cards for peculiar little white things called cowrie shells the way grown-ups played poker for money. I have never seen cowrie shells in any other context or used for any other purpose, but for us they had the same sort of purpose as grown-up money. Now to call venial sins 'sins' is a little like calling these cowrie shells money. I mean they are not very small units of money, like farthings, they are not money at all; but they have just the same function as money in their own context. Venial sin, mediocre sin, is related to real sin, mortal sin, rape and murder and torture, much the way that cowrie shells are related to money. Venial sins are not very small mortal sins, they are not sins at all in that sense; but they are structurally similar. As we say in the schools: the word 'sin' is used 'analogically' of them.

At one time when I was living in the United States some friends of mine belonged to a clandestine organization which helped young men who didn't want to be conscripted into what they rightly saw as an unjust war in Vietnam to escape to Canada and Sweden and such places of refuge. In this organization some people worked very hard and others were less energetic or frankly careless and lazy and unreliable. But they were all devoted to the cause. There was one especially charming and energetic young man who, as it transpired, was engaged in charmingly and energetically betraying the whole set-up to the police with the result that it was broken up and several people went to prison.

Now there is all the difference in the world between being lazy or a nuisance to your comrades and betraying the whole project; that is the difference between venial and mortal sin. As St Thomas says: one is about how you do the job; the other is about not doing it at all, but something else. The job, of course, is loving God.

There is a lovely passage, one of my favourites, in which St Thomas also says that your love for God can never gradually cool, or be chipped away slowly or diminished. It can only be totally lost by mortal sin; venial sin is *not* a matter of cooling and loving God less. So what's wrong with it then? It is a matter of loving the things in this world too much, perhaps dangerously too much, and failing to express your love of God and growing.

Venial sins all carry an ecclesial health warning: sinning can seriously damage your health (your spiritual health).

Every sin, in any meaning of the word, has two sides to it. On the one hand it is some kind of neglect of God's love, whether a total rejection (an option for something else) as in mortal sin, or simply not expressing your gratitude enough in your daily life, as in venial sin. On the other hand, all sin involves an attachment to, even an addiction to, other lesser good things, the things of this world. Forgiveness of sins deals with the first part – whether it is the miraculous grace of conversion and contrition by which we are turned back to God from mortal sin, or the grace of increasing charity by which we pull ourselves together after venial sins.

Forgiveness is what matters most of all; to be forgiven, to be contrite for mortal sin is the most tremendous thing that could happen to you in your life. So of course it is very easy. You do not have to work at being forgiven; you only have to accept it, to believe in the forgiveness of God in Christ, in his eternal unconditional love for you.

But sin, any sin, even venial sin, has given you a kind of addiction to lesser things, the things of this world. So besides being forgiven we need to break out of this addiction. For the only way to God is in Christ, and Christ's way to God was through crucifixion and death to the resurrection. There is no other way. The only way to God is through death. Christ did not die for us instead of us. He died to make it *possible* for us to die and rise again in him. And this is hard.

We have to go through the crucifixion, too. We *can* do it because God's love for us makes it possible to die in Christ; but we have to do it. We have to go through the painful process of curing the addiction, kicking our habit, 'drying out' or 'cold turkey', or whatever.

And this is what Lent is for. It reminds us that we come through death to life, through denial of self to our true selves, and it helps us to start the process – so that we may be ready for the final Easter when we rise in glory and freedom to live for eternity in the love of God.

Twenty-Two

A Sermon for Easter

We do not gather at Easter to celebrate a doctrine, the doctrine of the Resurrection. We come here to rejoice in the presence of one we love, in Jesus who was lost to us and has been found. Jesus went into the ultimate absence which is death. Human love and friendship is a bodily affair; every separation is being out of *touch*, when someone we love is away we cannot touch her or him. We can make some kind of second-hand bodily contact by telephone calls or letters or even the Internet, and this is better than nothing; but it is a lot less than being in the bodily presence of your friend. Every separation is a being out of touch and that is why we rightly say that separation is a kind of little death. Being dead is being ultimately out of touch. We can remember the dead, we can keep mementos and photographs and relics, but that is a substitute for being with them; it is to ease the pain of total separation.

Jesus really died. The living human body which had been Jesus became no longer a human body but a corpse hanging from the cross and the cadaver was put away in a tomb. There was no longer a man, Jesus of Nazareth: he had lived his short life and was no more. True, his soul was, no doubt, immortal, but a soul is not a human being. We only have an individual human being when that soul is the life of its individual human body. We are animals not ghosts; not even ghosts inside animals. What you are is this living flesh and blood, and when your flesh and blood ceases to live, when your life departs, you cease to be. You are totally absent, utterly not with your fellow men and women.

That is what happened to Jesus. He was lost to us. True, Jesus was eternal Son of God and as God he could not die, could not leave us (if he did we would vanish into nothing for he is our creator who keeps us in being for every moment as a singer keeps her song in being). As God, Jesus could not die. But neither could he be born, neither could he be with us to share our sufferings and joys. Of course we can always rejoice in the presence to us of God our creator; but the gospel, the good news, is that God's Son was made flesh and dwelt among us and died among us. It is Jesus as man, as son of Mary, that was our human friend, Jesus, this Jewish prophet, this living, breathing, human source of astounding acceptance and love. It is this man who was killed, this individual who was loved and who was taken from us.

And today we celebrate: we rejoice because he is alive and with us. 'I am risen and with you.' God has risen him up. What had been a corpse, a cadaver, is now a living human body again, and much more, unimaginably more, humanly alive. His body is closer to us now than he ever could have been to his disciples in Galilee, and he is closer to the whole world. In the sacraments of the Church his bodily presence and contact reaches out to all humankind. Especially in the Eucharist we are united to and in his body. And this is not a metaphor, a poetic image; we are united in a bodily contact of which our familiar bodily touching is just a pale shadow.

The gospel we preach is not about memories or ideals or profound thoughts. It contains all these things, but what it is about is the human person, Jesus, alive and present to us and loving us from his human heart. Our Easter faith is that we really do encounter Jesus himself: not a message from him, or a doctrine inspired by him, or an ethics of love, or a new idea of human destiny, or a picture of him, but Jesus himself. It is in this that we rejoice.

If I met you one day, I mean really met *you*, not a picture of you or a televised three-dimensional hologram, or a truth about you, or a dream about you, but really met you, and you said to me, 'By the way, it's a rather interesting thing, my bones are in a cave in Palestine,' I would be astounded. I would not know what to think, but I would be inclined to say that you or somebody had done a remarkable 'conjuring trick with bones'. This would be the really tricky and puzzling thing: that I should meet you (you, and not a ghost or dream but the actual you) without meeting your body.

There is nothing in the least tricky or puzzling or quaint about God giving back life to the dead Jesus – and not just a resuscitation but a new and greater transfigured life in glory. There is deep mystery here, of course, as there is deep mystery in God's giving us life in the first place, in God's creation of the universe. To believe that God creates the whole universe and holds it in being over against absolute nothing, but to find it tricky and unworthy of belief that he should raise a man from the dead to a human life of glory seems eccentric. What we might find tricky, though, would be God raising Jesus to glory by doing something for something quite other than Jesus; producing, by sleight of hand, a substitute risen Christ while the body of Jesus is left buried in the grave.

Of course, if you are not a Christian and do not believe that we really meet the man Jesus himself, if you think that Christianity is about being inspired by his memory, then there is no problem. The resurrection is a metaphor; Jesus is literally dead and his body rotted in the grave.

Again, if you do not think that Jesus was (and is) a real human being of flesh and blood who without his body would be dead (at best a mere soul), if you think he was a god or a spirit disguised in human form, you will not have a problem: Jesus is alive because human beings don't really die; Jesus is alive or 'immortal' just as all those buried in the cemeteries are alive, having shed their mortal bodies. For people who hold any or all of these views, Jesus could be said to live on. But there would be nothing very special or surprising about it, nothing to make a fuss about at Easter, no special cause for wonder or rejoicing.

But if, like all Catholics, you are a materialist in the sense that you think that to be you is to be a living body, and if you believe (as Catholics do) that Jesus was one of us who was born and died as we do, who left us desolate in his death as all our friends do or will do; if you believe (as Catholics do) that God has mysteriously and wonderfully changed that, that by a miracle of new creation Jesus, our human friend, is with us bodily again, and much more with us, and if you also believe (as Catholics do) that because of the new human life of Jesus all our friends too will rise from the dead to a human life of glory, that grieving for the dead, that separation from the dead will come to an end, then, indeed you have something to rejoice about at Easter, a miracle of God's goodness to his creatures. We can celebrate an astounding conquest of human death.

And so on this Easter day we sing with special enthusiasm that great hymn of joy, the Creed: a hymn of joy in life, in the new human life brought back from the grave to share in the life of God himself, brought back from the dead to live as real bodily human beings in the Holy Spirit before the Father through Christ, our risen Lord.

Twenty-Three

A Sermon for Pentecost

When God breathes on you, you come alive. The thing started with Adam: God breathed into clay and it became a living breathing feeling body. In fact, if you look at the other creation story, it began even earlier; for the darkness of chaos was awakened into life and creation by God breathing onto the waters. From then on the breath of God always means vitality, animation, energy, and, above all, prophecy. Every now and then the Old Testament says of people: 'the breath, the Spirit, of God came upon them and they prophesied'. There was nothing hidden or 'interior' or invisible about the effects of the Spirit. The Spirit itself was as invisible as the wind, but its effects were as obvious as those of a storm. Men and women were shaken into singing and shouting and dancing. That is the kind of thing the breath of the Spirit of the Lord does, and this is what happened at Pentecost. The disciples staggered about mouthing strange words, but words that were strangely intelligible. Understandably, people said they were drunk. Peter said: 'Nonsense, its only nine o'clock in the morning'.

It was out of such a scene of exhilaration, even hysteria, of people possessed by strange forces from the unconscious, that St Luke in the Acts of the Apostles says that the Church began. It wasn't a case of people sitting down soberly to consider the merits of the teaching of Jesus or to ponder on the meaning of his death. Not at all. People were just carried away in a kind of ecstasy out of which came prophecy, and that prophecy, that preaching, has gone on ever since.

It is true that there had been a little organization first. (Peter, for example, had arranged an election to fill the vacancy left by Judas.) But it was not the organization that led to the preaching; it was something more like a breakdown of organization, an outbreak of folly, of enthusiasm, and a kind of irrationality.

But the prophecy was not in the experience or the exhilaration. It was in how it was proclaimed: the prophecy was in the preaching, in what Peter starts to say and to explain. It was through this prophetic preaching that the excitement became infectious – so that we are told that about 3000 people received the Spirit. The message of this preaching was that: 'This man Jesus . . . is exalted at the right hand of God; and having received from the Father the promise of the Spirit, has poured out this which you now see and hear.' And what did they see and hear? They saw the signs of the last days, the signs of the coming of the Lord, the signs of the transformation of the world by the mighty power of God.

Now it is interesting that the message is that this man Jesus ('attested to you by God with mighty works and wonders and signs') is important because he is the source of this Spirit by which 'we and you' are possessed. The first thing is the coming of the Spirit. And this is not the only coming of the Spirit – this is the Pentecost of the Jews. There is another outpouring of the Spirit, another Pentecost, for the Gentiles in Acts 19. What first of all matters to these earliest disciples is being taken over by the divine Spirit, being full of the divine breath, the divine life.

Quite a long time before this, Pentecost had become for the Jews, the feast of the Torah, the divine way of life given to God's people through Moses, the law by which these people were to live with the righteousness of God himself; the Torah has this day blossomed into the very living breath of the Lord. Thomas Aquinas was biblically accurate when he said that the New Law is nothing but the gift of the Holy Spirit.

It seems that the first expression of Christian faith was the recognition of the divinity of the Spirit. At Pentecost, Mary and the other women and the apostles believed that the new life within them was the life of God, the vitality and joy and excitement of God. I think it was in meditating and preaching on the fact that it was through this man Jesus, through his death and resurrection, that God has sent his divine Spirit – it was in meditating and preaching on this that the earliest churches came to recognize that we must say that Jesus himself is divine. And in one church in particular (the one we have come to call 'The Community of the Beloved Disciple'), this understanding burst forth lyrically in the Gospel and the Epistles of John.

I think it was not that people first thought Jesus was divine and so thought his Spirit was divine, but the other way round. The divinity of Jesus was attested by the fact that he could breathe the breath of God.

The Spirit of God is not, in any ordinary modern sense of the word, a 'person' (I am not talking of theological jargon at the moment, but just ordinary English). In common English, a person is one with a separate and distinct understanding and will. It would, of course, be quite alien to Catholic tradition to hold that the Holy Spirit has a separate and distinct mind from that of the Father or the Word – as though all three might think different thoughts, or want to enjoy different things. To hold that would be to hold that there are three Gods. It would be to desert and betray our whole Jewish inheritance and the hard-won tradition that 'The Lord our God is one God.'

It is not, then, in that sense that the theologians speak of the Holy Spirit as a distinct person from the Father and the Word. The Word made *flesh* is in one way a separate person in our ordinary modern sense in that he does have a separate human understanding and will which is not his divine understanding and will. So he can say to the Father 'Not my will, but thine be done.'

But the Spirit is not such a person: the Spirit is the life, the vitality, the joy of God. Let me explain how one great Christian tradition has seen this, a tradition going back, ultimately, to the preaching of St John.

God understands, contemplates, his divine life. We can think of God as forming a concept of himself (we don't have to, but we can); we can think of God's understanding as God's conceiving what it is to be God – having an idea of the meaning of being God; God naming himself 'I am.' We can think, as John may have done, of the concept or Word of God that was in the beginning with God, and was God; 'was God' because it was the perfect, utterly adequate thought of God, no different from God. So the revelation of the Word made flesh is God's own idea of himself dwelling amongst us, God's word to himself becoming his word to us.

And then we can think (we don't have to but we can) of the joy that God takes in contemplating his life, his divinity, in the Word – that profound acquiescence in being divine: the immense joy of the eternal God, not now in what he has created or done, but in what he is just in living, in being God. God knows his life and, in knowing it, loves it. Or: in eternity, the Father, contemplating his divine life, brings forth the Word, and through the Word gives forth Joy, the Spirit. So, as a reflection of this eternal life, in history, the father sends to *us* the Word made flesh, Jesus, and through the Word made flesh, gives forth to *us* the Joy of the Spirit, to make the Church. What happens in the story of Jesus is the image, the sign, the sacrament of the divine life in eternity. This is the tremendous mystery that the first disciples experienced (seemed almost to experience in their bodies) at Pentecost, the expression of the immense joy of God.

What the disciples experienced was not just a change in themselves, a change in mood from fear and depression to happiness. It was not just a change in something about them, as though they had come to have or possess a new emotion or feeling or attitude or faith. The gift was not of something they came to possess, but something that came to possess them. It was not that they were given a new religious attitude, but that they were taken over, possessed by, the Holy Spirit. The joy of God became, indeed, *their* joy; but it was first the joy of *God*.

And the joy of God *is* God, as the Word of God *is* God. For with God it cannot be, as it is with us, that there are some things that we are and other things we simply have – so that *our* joy is not what we are but something we have that comes and goes. There could be nothing in God that comes and goes. The Joy of the Father is eternally God. But the Father's Joy is distinct from the Father, for the Word comes from the Father as he understands his divinity, and the Joy is given forth from the Father through the Word as he takes delight in what he understands.

The delight of God in being God is the Holy Spirit. So when the Spirit comes upon the man Jesus at his baptism, the voice of the Father says: 'This is my beloved *son* in whom I have *delight*.' This single sentence contains the whole doctrine of the Trinity. This delight is not some psychological feeling in God; it is his Spirit that the Father has in his Son, and in his Son incarnate, the man Jesus. And it is just this delight that the Father has (and has in just this way) in the disciples at Pentecost. It is just this delight that he has in us in our personal Pentecost of baptism and confirmation, by which we belong to the disciples. This delight that God has in us is his Spirit that he has in us; it is our sharing in the enjoyment that he has just in being. The New Testament has many names for the Spirit of God: it is Joy, it is Peace, it is Unity, it is the *Koinonia*, the community of the disciples. But above all it is Love. When we receive the Spirit we are delighted that God is God, we share in his loving that he is God, and we love and delight in all that comes from God. And above all we love each other for the Spirit of God that is in us or can be in us. This, St Luke is telling us in Acts, is what the Church is supposed to be about: it is the proclamation in the world of the presence of the Spirit of delight and love, the Spirit of the joy of God, and the peace of God which will transform this world and take it beyond itself to the kingdom of the risen Christ, our brother, in whom is the interplay in love between God the eternal Parent, God the eternal Child, the God of eternal Joy and Delight, the interplay of Father, Son, and Holy Spirit for eternity.

Twenty-Four

A Sermon for
Trinity Sunday

Today is the feast of the Trinity, and, of course, it is bizarre, to have a feast of the Trinity alongside the feasts of Catherine de Ricci and John Bosco and Eusebius of Vercelli, as though the Trinity were an item of Christian belief and devotion. Belief in the Trinity is the heart of the Christian faith and every feast and every Sunday is a celebration of the Trinity. Still, I suppose it is a good thing to have one day set aside for reflecting on the fact that it *is* the centre; one day, at least, when you can be sure of hearing a sermon about God.

For the Trinity is what makes the gospel what it is, the kind of good news that it is. It would be good news to hear that we are forgiven, that our sins are blotted out; it would be good news to hear that we are redeemed through no merit of our own, that we are saved from sin by the sheer gracious action of God. That, in itself, would be good news. But our good news goes far beyond that. Our gospel is not just that we are saved from sin but that we are taken up into the life of God himself, that we are raised beyond simple humanity, even beyond sinless humanity, beyond even creaturehood to have a share in divinity itself. This, indeed, is what our doctrine of the Trinity tells us.

Christianity begins with our father Abraham and with Moses and the rejection of the gods. In begins in that crucial period in the history of humankind when some men and women in the Middle East were called to reject the religion and worship of the gods and to listen, instead, to the Voice commanding them to justice and mercy and righteousness among people. This Voice they called the Lord, and he is not a god, or else he is the God to end all gods. He proclaims himself, you might say, as the God of atheism: 'I am the Lord . . . I brought you out of slavery . . .you shall have no gods.' The Lord, if he is God, is the God of human liberation from the slavery and idolatry of injustice.

The Lord is not the local god of this nation or this class or this social system. He does not belong to this or that part of the world. He is Lord of the whole world. He is Righteousness and Justice anywhere and everywhere.

Now this isn't the kind of teaching you could swallow in one gulp. It took centuries for the children of Israel to absorb it, and it took a devastating military defeat and long years of exile before it really took hold. In the writings of the prophets we can see these early Christians of the Old Testament coming to recognize the Lord not as a god among the gods of the world, not as any kind of inhabitant of the world, but as the one creator of the universe. This God is not one sort of being alongside other inferior sorts of beings, he is the source of all being. It is because of this divinity that anything at all is, instead of there not being anything. Everything that is and everything that happens, every thought that crosses my mind, every decision I make, exists because of God who says 'You must have no gods.' This is God who sustains us and all the stars as a singer keeps his song in being. It is quite a thought that if you choose to break the law of God by cruelty or indifference to suffering, it is the Lord who is keeping you in existence while you are doing this, from second to second. To think that you are defying the Lord is the ultimate in absurdity and contradiction, for you only exist, you only are you because of God. This self-delusion, the delusion that you can stand over against God, that you are not a creature – this is what sin is.

And yet sin is itself a strange and distorted caricature of the gift of God. Sin is to grab for yourself autonomy, to deny your creaturehood, to make yourself a god; but the gift of God is to *receive* divinity, to be *taken* beyond creaturehood. Strangely, it is by accepting our creaturehood, by obeying the law of the Lord (which is just the law of our created being, the law of our humanity), it is in obeying this law that we are miraculously carried beyond it into the friendship of God. When we acknowledge our existence, our selfhood, our meaning, as a gift from God we find that his gift is even greater than that, that we are given more than good creaturehood. 'You shall be as gods,' said the serpent to Eve, and he was right. But the question is 'How?' – in the delusory way of claiming a separate, independent divinity for ourselves, or by receiving the only authentic divinity as a gift from God himself in Christ?

God the Creator, then the God of Abraham, Isaac and Jacob, the God of the Old Testament, the God of the Law, the Torah, is the first firm foundation of the good news which is the gospel. The doctrine of the Trinity would be empty without this sure foundation of the one Creator God, who is not a god, not a divine kind of being, but who is beyond all beings and the source of all that is.

'Hear, O Israel' (and that includes us all, Jews and Christians), 'Hear O Israel, the Lord your God is one God. There are no gods.' This is where we start.

The teaching of Jesus is that God, the Creator of the universe, is more than Creator. He is the father who loves him, Jesus. And this is surely an extraordinary and blasphemous teaching, because the love here is not just the providential care and consideration of creator for his creatures, not just the love that the Lord is said to have for Israel, which seemed at the time just to mean that he would be the God of Israel, to be on her side, to be protective and indulgent to her, to forget her offences and reward her faithfulness. That was the love of a kind and forgiving Master for his servant, and it is surely the only relationship there could be between a good and kindly creator and his creatures.

Surely there could not be between the creator and his creatures the kind of love which we sometimes find between grown-up human beings for each other, for that love demands and involves equality. It would be a mutual self-giving which it would be absurd to picture between God and his creatures. But this is the love that, Jesus says, the Father bears *him*. He is not a servant, a slave of God, not even a well-treated servant; he is one of the family of God, related to him by love.

In this claim to be loved by his Father there is already implicit (as the leaders of the Jews of the time saw) the claim to divine life, to making himself equal to the Father, for only equals can give themselves to each other in love – just the claim that looks like the foundation of all sin, and indeed it would be the ultimate sin if Jesus were simply a creature. Jesus must be either ultimately blasphemous or else a mystery of divinity. If he is not totally self-deluded, then at the centre of his being he belongs to divinity. He has the same life as the Father. He is an equal to whom the Father can give himself in love. He is the perfect image of the Father: 'He who has seen me has seen the Father.'

Jesus, then, is not created, not a creature. He owes his being, indeed, to his Father, but he is not like the creatures suspended over non-existence by the creative will of God as we are. The Father did not, so to say, decide that there should be the Son as he decided that there should be America or decided that the Son should take on human nature in Christ. God could no more decide that there should not be the Son than he could decide not to exist. We speak of God 'making' the world, even though it is a unique and quite mysterious kind of making, a making that is not a making out of anything, a making we cannot pretend to understand, but 'making' or 'creating' is the word we have to hand. We cannot in this way speak of the Father making the Son. What we are trying to express is that the Son owes his being to the Father, 'proceeds from the Father', not as a being made by him, not as a creature: he is an equal whom the Father can love.

With Jesus we come to a new vision of God, of the same God who was the God of Moses. Now, though, God is not seen primarily as making, acting, doing, not primarily as holding the universe in being, but primarily as eternal lover of Jesus. The life of God is not primarily the life of sustaining the existence of all creatures: the life of God within the Godhead is ultimately the life of love between Father and Son, and this life of love and delight we call the Holy Spirit. We could put it by saying that with Jesus we come to see that God the Creator is first of all, and before that, God the lover; that, as John finally puts it, God *is* love. Even beyond creating there is loving.

The Christian gospel, the astounding good news, is that God's love is not confined to the eternal love between Father and Son, between these divine equals, but that God extends this same love – not just his kindly creative power but his love to us human creatures. All so that in the Son become man he loves us too as equals. Because of the Son become man we are taken up to share into the love between Father and Son, we are taken up into the uncreated Holy Spirit: our life becomes divine. As St Thomas Aquinas put it succinctly 'God became man so that man might become God.'

If we think of God as he first revealed himself to Israel, as maker and doer, as performing great deeds in Israel and in human history, as creator of the universe, if we see him thus far, there is just the mystery of Divinity. There is no place here for distinguishing Father, Son, and Spirit. There is just God, source and sustainer of all that is (and this universe does not contain any gods). It is only when we come to the relationship of love within the Godhead itself that we distinguish Father and Son loving each other with the love that is the Spirit. And this interior life of the Godhead, which would not matter simply to creatures, matters supremely to us, because by an astonishing gift of God, giving himself to us in his love, we are not just creatures, we are taken up into the divine Trinitarian life. We meet the Father not just as creatures confront their maker, but as God the Son confronts his Father. Our life of grace is not simply something God has made. It is uncreated as Jesus is uncreated, it is a sharing into the interior life of God.

When we call God our Father we are making a fantastic claim. We are not just using a metaphor for our maker; we are speaking in the same tone of voice as God the Son has, who from eternity has spoken with his Father. When we pray we are not just creatures calling upon our creator. We are joining in the eternal dialogue of Son and Father which is the Holy Spirit. We are, as we say, in the Spirit: our worship is 'in Spirit and in truth'.

What we call the sending of the Holy Spirit to humankind is just our being taken up beyond the world of creatures into the life of God himself. This is the core and centre of our faith, and it is to preserve that core and centre of the gospel that the formula of the Trinity was hammered out in the language of 'nature' and 'persons': three persons in one nature. It is a formulation to preserve the truth of the astonishing dignity of the Christian life, the life of divine grace. It must defend the truth that Jesus is truly one of us, a real human being, and just as truly Son of God, not some sort of sub-god but divine with the divinity that is the source of the being of all that is. Without this he could not be loved by the Father, loved with an adult love, not just as a creature but as an equal. Without this it would not be God who became human, it would not be God who died for us on the cross, and so we could not become God. Our doctrine must defend the truth that Jesus, Son of God, is distinct from the Father, that there may be love between them. And it must defend the truth that the spirit of God that we have been given to live by is not simply some great created gift, some extraordinary embellishment of our humanity, but is the very life of God himself. In giving us the Spirit, God gives us himself: the source of the being of all that is, the uncreated life of love that subsists eternally between Father and Son. This same love, moreover, subsists between believers and those they love.

It is because of the doctrine of the Trinity, or the truth that this doctrine expresses, that we can point to the love between people and say quite literally: 'There is God.' '*Ubi caritas et amor, Deus ibi est.*' 'Wherever there is charity and love, there is God.'

It is because of this truth, and the truth of the Incarnation of God the Son, that we can speak not just to our maker, our creator on whom all our being depends, but we can take part in, and make our own, the eternal dialogue of love which is the ultimate meaning of all that is. We can speak with our eternal Father because we are in Christ his Son by the gift of the Holy Spirit of love.

'For you have received the Holy Spirit of sonship. When we cry "Abba Father" it is the Spirit himself bearing witness with our spirit that we are children of God.'

Twenty-Five

The Prodigal Son
Luke 15:11–32

I think we might begin by asking: *Why* did the younger son leave home? Luke has already given us one story about a boy who runs away from home at an early age. We know why *he* did it. When they found young Jesus in the temple he said it was because his parents didn't understand him. But today's story suggests that this rather older lad found home life a bit restrictive. He wanted to be out living his own life, spending his own money. According to the rules of inheritance given in Deuteronomy (21:17) his elder brother was entitled to two-thirds of the estate and he to only one third (and that even if he were the son of a favourite wife). But the family is evidently wealthy, so when he 'gathered together the portion that was his' his third would be a substantial sum. This property in a sense already belonged to him but would normally come to him only when his father died. A father *could* give his son his inheritance earlier – though that canny and street-wise man Ben Sira, who wrote Ecclesiasticus, strongly advises him to do no such thing (33:20–6).

Anyway, the young man is impatient to have his share *now* and take it away to 'a far country'. This, Jesus presents as a parable of the roots of sin. The younger son is valuing the things he gets from his father more than the company, friendship, and affection of his father. He values the gift more than the giver; and it is just here that sin comes in. He is quite *right* to value the gift, his inheritance, but the sin lies in *how* he does so. He is so impatient for it that he treats his father as though he were already dead. Like some theologian of the nineteen sixties he feels that man has already come of age: so God is (kind of) dead.

Sin does not consist in wanting bad things: there *are* no bad things; all things are created by God. Sin consists in how you want *small* things. It is loving, for example, material possessions, which are good and created by

God, at the expense of loving *God* who created a world in which what we do-not-and-cannot possess is greater than the things we can possess – greater and more satisfying and more to be loved.

Yet in spite of this, the father lets his son go with his inheritance, feeling, we might imagine, like God in George Herbert's splendid poem. Let me remind you of some bits of it:

> When God first made man,
> Having a glass of blessings standing by,
> 'Let us' said he 'pour on him all we can . . .'
> [but then] . . . When almost all was out, God made a stay,
> Perceiving that, alone of all his treasure,
> *Rest* in the bottom lay.
> 'For if I should' said he,
> 'Bestow *this* jewel also on my creature
> He would adore my *gifts* instead of me . . .'
> [and he ends] . . . 'Let him be rich and *weary*, that at least,
> If goodness *lead* him not, yet weariness
> May *toss* him to my breast.'

But Jesus' parable is interestingly different from Herbert's. In Luke's story the weariness and self-disgust are all the consequences, the spelling out, of the son's first decision to abandon his father's house for the sake of his father's riches. (By hindsight, at the end, we see the 'squandering of his property' as itself no more than the first phase of the poverty and weariness that he finally recognizes).

His decision is to move from one kind of community to another. The father's house is a community in which the first and fundamental bond is friendship. This is what holds the members of the household together: a willingness to let go of personal possessions, to sacrifice self-interest for the sake of those you love. Of course there can be love in all sorts of communities, but this is a community actually *founded* on the father's love. And it is this that the younger son opts out of. He chooses instead his own self-interest, his own possessions. He will make his *own* way as a free man, *free* from the constrictions of considering others. And because of this he finds himself in a *far* country where this is the norm: a community bound together not by friendship but by *contracts* and the convergence of *self-interests*; a community where either everything is *owed* to you or *forbidden* to you.

The first thing we notice is that this 'coming of age' turns out to be not, of itself, enough. The prodigal son turns out to be unable to manage his wealth for his own happiness; he is without practical wisdom, good sense. He squanders his inheritance in childish pleasures. The Greek text, by the way, says nothing at this point about 'riotous living' or even 'loose living'; English translators have been conned by the vindictive slanders of the elder brother, later in the story. Here we are just told that he spent his money *asōtōs*, 'without hanging on to it' – as though there were no tomorrow. His sin does *not* lie in sensuality and harlots. His *sin* is much more serious. It is in the abandonment of *his father's house*. His extravagance and unwisdom is only the symptom of this.

Anyway, having no money left he has to enter into a contract with an *employer* who *uses* him to feed swine. Naturally enough, in *that* kind of society, the employer finds his product much more important than his employee. Good *husks* are meant to fatten the swine; not to be wasted on a hungry swineherd. We are familiar with all this. A century or so ago Pope Leo XIII infuriated Europe by claiming that the first charge of industry should be the welfare of its workers, when every sensible businessman knew that his first duty was to his shareholders. And things have not changed much since the time of Leo XIII. He also said that raw materials coming from the factory were ennobled by human skills, but the humans themselves came from it degraded. The swine were fat and sleek but the swineherd was wretched and in despair.

And all this, the young man begins to realize, is what is really meant by his imagined independence. He has escaped from the bonds of friendship to find himself in the terrible bonds created by ruthless avarice and self-seeking. He bitterly contrasts his new world with the world he has abandoned. In his father's house there was not only the community of family affection between parents and children, but this human warmth spilled over into a human solidarity with the rest of the household, the hired workers. 'How many of my father's hired servants have bread enough to spare, but I perish here with hunger.'

He decides that, while of *course* he cannot retrieve the sonship he has thrown away, he could at least be better off and happier as a hired servant in *that* kind of community, under his father's jurisdiction – under the Law that comes from his father.

Jesus is saying, of course, that when we reject the offer of divine sonship, which is what in its deepest meaning the Torah, the Law was really all about, when we begin to think that we ourselves are 'as gods, knowing good and evil', trying to run our own lives outside our Father's house, we find, in practice, not freedom and responsibility but enslavement. And our liberation from this enslavement will not come from simply trying to be a hired servant of the Law, not even the magnificently humane law given on Sinai. It is not enough to be a *servant* even in the society of the people of Israel. If we are really to live in accordance with the Law we have to live in the *household* of the Father as his *children*, not as servants.

So when the son comes back home, his father will have nothing of this idea of his coming back as a hired servant. Jesus is saying that in practice, in history, there is no way to build a human society that is really human unless it is *more* than human. Surprisingly enough, it is *not* enough to be a good servant, to be obedient to what is reasonable in terms of the laws of human friendship and justice. The father brushes all that aside. He does not wait for the son to plead for forgiveness; he runs to meet him and embraces him and kisses him. When the young man goes through his set speech of repentance, the father simply ignores it and says impatiently: 'Bring quickly the best robe and put it on him . . .' Forgiveness means not just the curing of our human weakness and selfishness and viciousness. It means being welcomed back into the household of God, not just as good servants, *creatures* restored to humanity, but as *children* of God in his *Eternal Child*, joining in the eternal sonship of Christ.

But, of course, this would not be *Luke's* story if there were not another character to consider. Luke's Gospel is about celebration: and it is about the celebration of those who, by the Holy Spirit, are in solidarity with the *poor* and with the sinners, the outcasts. The *targets* at which this Gospel is aimed are the rich (who do not know that they are poor) and the righteous (who do not know that they are forgiven sinners). *And*, of course, Luke is writing to and for and about his own church. The poor and the rich and the sinners and the self-righteous in question are, without exception, Christians. Do not be misled by this talk of 'scribes and pharisees'.

At one time in the United States, people used to use the word 'Commie'; not to talk about communists, of whom they knew nothing, but about their domestic liberal political opponents. In much the same way Luke speaks of 'pharisees' not to refer to Jews, about whom he was almost equally ill-informed, but to pillory a certain kind of fellow Christian: the kind who felt quite secure in his or her respectability and virtue and drew apart from the black sheep in the Church. It is these who are, in effect, criticizing Christ, saying: 'This man receives sinners and eats with them.' And in this story, of course, they appear in the character of the begrudger, the elder brother. The elder brother finds that there is a celebration going on. And when he finds out why, he is shocked and angry. If there is to be *feasting* surely it must be in reward for good service. It must be earned. And if anybody has earned it, it is surely *him*, and certainly not his wastrel of a brother. 'These many years I have served you, and I never disobeyed your command.' Luke is trying to explain to these self-righteous Christians that this is *not* what the true celebration, which just is life in the Spirit, is all about. The elder brother, in his way, just as much as the younger, in his way, has begun to value the gift above the giving; and this we must not do; even when the gift is real virtue. These Christians are in danger of losing sight of the immense generosity of God, which is the source both of the *virtue* of the good and the *forgiveness* of the wicked. They have begun to value and admire themselves by despising others. But Luke is saying to them: we 'make merry and are glad' in the Holy Spirit, not because of our virtue, important though that is, but because, more deeply than that, we are all sinners who are *forgiven*, who have been embraced by the exuberant, impatient love of God, because 'we have been dead and are alive, because we were lost and have been found'.

Bibliography

Brown, Raymond. 1994. *The Death of the Messiah*. London: Geoffrey Chapman.

Clements, S. and Lawlor, M. 1967. *The McCabe Affair*. London: Sheed and Ward.

Ernst, Cornelius (ed.). 1972. 'The Gospel of Grace' in *Summa Theologiae*, vol. 30. London and New York: Blackfriars.

Geach, Peter. 1957. *Mental Acts*. London: Routledge.

Haughton, Rosemary. 1970. *Love*. London: C. A. Watts.

Hume, David. 1978. *A Treatise of Human Nature*, ed. P. H. N. Nidditch. Oxford: Oxford University Press.

Kenny, Anthony. 1975. *Will, Freedom and Power*. Oxford: Basil Blackwell.

—— 1989. *The Metaphysics of Mind*. Oxford: Basil Blackwell.

Kerr, Fergus. 1987. 'Charity and Friendship' in *Language, Meaning and God*, ed. Brian Davies. London: Geoffrey Chapman.

MacIntyre, Alasdair. 1981. *After Virtue*. London: Duckworth.

—— 1988. *Whose Justice? Which Rationality?* London: Duckworth.

—— 1990. *Three Rival Versions of Moral Enquiry*. London: Duckworth.

Mackey, James. 1983. *The Christian Experience of God as Trinity*. London: SCM Press.

McCabe, Herbert (ed. and trans.). 1964. *Summa Theologiae*, vol. 3. London and New York: Blackfriars.

—— 1968. *Law, Love and Language*. London: Sheed and Ward.

—— 1985. *The Teaching of the Catholic Church*. London: Catholic Truth Society.

—— 1987. *God Matters*. London: Geoffrey Chapman.

Ryle, Gilbert. 1949. *The Concept of Mind*. London: Hutchinson.

Sanders, E. P. 1985. *Jesus and Judaism*. London: SCM Press.

Wittgenstein, Ludwig. 1968. *Philosophical Investigations*, trans. G. E. M. Anscombe. Oxford: Basil Blackwell.

Index